THE BUSINESS TRAVELER GUIDE TO
ORLANDO

Additional Books Written by Jason R. Rich and Published by Entrepreneur Press

The following books are now or will soon be available wherever books are sold, or can be ordered from the EntrepreneurPress.com web site. For more information about these and other books written by bestselling author Jason R. Rich, visit his web site at www.JasonRich.com.

202 High-Paying Jobs You Can Land Without a College Degree

Smart Debt

Entrepreneur Magazine's Personal Finance Pocket Guides

Buying or Leasing a Car: Without Being Taken for a Ride

Dirty Little Secrets: What The Credit Bureaus Won't Tell You

Get That Raise!

Mortgages & Refinancing: Get The Best Rates

Mutual Funds: A Quick Start Guide

Why Rent? Own Your Dream Home

Entrepreneur Magazine's Business Traveler Series

Entrepreneur Magazine's Business Traveler Guide to Chicago

Entrepreneur Magazine's Business Traveler Guide to Las Vegas

Entrepreneur Magazine's Business Traveler Guide to Los Angeles

Entrepreneur Magazine's Business Traveler Guide to New York City

Entrepreneur Magazine's Business Traveler Guide to Washington, DC

Entrepreneur MAGAZINE'S

THE BUSINESS TRAVELER GUIDE TO
ORLANDO

Jason R. Rich

Entrepreneur Press

Jere L. Calmes, Publisher
Cover Design: Brand Architects Inc. and Desktop Miracles, Inc.
Production and Composition: Eliot House Productions

© 2008 by Entrepreneur Media Inc.
All rights reserved.
Reproduction or translation of any part of this work beyond that permitted by Section 107 or 108 of the 1976 United States Copyright Act without permission of the copyright owner is unlawful. Requests for permission or further information should be addressed to the Business Products Division, Entrepreneur Media Inc.

This publication is designed to provide accurate and authoritative information in regard to the subject matter covered. It is sold with the understanding that the publisher is not engaged in rendering legal, accounting or other professional services. If legal advice or other expert assistance is required, the services of a competent professional person should be sought.

City Factoid icon: © Ilkka Kukko
Money saver icon: © Miguel Angel Salinas Salinas
Time saver icon: © Miguel Angel Salinas Salinas
Tip icon: © Carston Reisinger
Warning icon: © Miguel Angel Salinas Salinas

Library of Congress Cataloging-in-Publication Data
　Rich, Jason R.
　　Business traveler guide to Orlando/by Jason R. Rich.
　　　p.　cm.
　　ISBN 978-1-59918-158-5 (alk. paper)
　　1. Orlando (Fla.)—Guidebooks. 2. Business travel—Florida—Orlando—Guidebooks. I. Title.
　F319.O7R53 2008
　917.59'24—dc22　　　　　　　　　　　　　　　　　　　　　　　　2007050560

Printed in Canada
12 11 10 09 08　　　　　　　　　　　　　　　　　　　10 9 8 7 6 5 4 3 2 1

CONTENTS

Acknowledgments xi
Preface xiii

SECTION I
Welcome to Orlando 1
Getting to Orlando 2
Making Your Travel Reservations 2
Contacting the Airlines Directly 3
Online Travel Services 7
Airport Security Considerations and Tips 10
Curbside Check-In at the Airport 15
Navigating Your Way through
   Orlando International Airport (MCO) 15
Ground Transportation Options 25
Frequent Flier Miles—A Business
   Traveler's Best Friend 30

SECTION II
Packing for Your Business Trip 35
Shopping for the Perfect Luggage 36
Packing Tips for Business Travelers 39
Orlando Weather 40
Packing for Your Trip 41
Before-Leaving-Home Checklist 46

SECTION III
Where to Stay While in Orlando 47

Choose Your Accommodations Based
  on Amenities and Services Offered 50
The Business Traveler Top 15
  Business-Friendly Hotels in Orlando. 52
Major Hotel Chains in the Orlando Area 83
Need Additional Help Finding a Hotel? 85
Take Advantage of Concierge Services
  Offered at Your Hotel 86

SECTION IV
Getting Around Town 87

Taxis 88
Rental Cars. 90
Chauffeured Limousines and Town Cars 94
Public Transportation. 96
Shuttle and Charter Buses 98
Driving Around Orlando 98

SECTION V
Where to Dine in Orlando 103

Ordering Room Service 104
Theme and Specialty Restaurants 105
The Business Traveler Top 20
  Fine-Dining Restaurants in Orlando 113

SECTION VI
Entertainment in Orlando 137

Top 15 Activities and Attractions
  for Business Travelers 138
Professional Sporting Events 163
How to See Sold-Out Shows,
  Concerts, and Sporting Events 165
Golf Courses 166
Shopping Opportunities for Busy
  Business Travelers 170
Media Listings for Orlando 173

SECTION VII
Visiting the Walt Disney World Resort **177**
Plenty of Perks for WDW Resort Hotel Guests . . . 181
Disney Theme Parks. 183
Downtown Disney and Pleasure Island 204
Disney's BoardWalk 206
Relaxing at a Disney Day Spa. 206
Hosting Private Corporate
   Events at the WDW Resort. 207

SECTION VIII
Attending a Business Meeting or Convention **209**
The Orange County
   Convention Center (OCCC). 210

SECTION IX
Business Services **225**
Audiovisual Equipment Rentals,
   Photography, and Production Companies 226
Balloons 227
Banking and Financial Services. 228
Boxes and Shipping Supplies. 229
Bus Charters 229
Car and Truck Rentals 230
Caterers 230
Cell Phone Services and Accessories. 230
Computer Rentals, Repairs, Sales,
   Data Recovery, and Technical Support 232
Credit Card Companies 233
FedEx Kinko's Locations. 234
Florists 235
Foreign Currency Exchange Services 236
Golf Courses 236
Jet Charters 236
Lawyers. 237
Limousine and Town Car Services 237
Locksmiths 237

Malls and Shopping 238
Meeting and Banquet Room Rentals 238
Messenger Services 238
Office Supply Superstores 239
Secretarial and Temporary Employment Services . 240
Shipping and Freight Services 240
Ticket Brokers 240
Trade Show Exhibit Sales, Installation,
   Repair, and Dismantling 241
Trade Show and Private Security Services 241
Translators and Interpreters. 242
Traveler's Checks. 242
UPS Shipping Locations. 243
U.S. Post Office Locations 243
Western Union Electronic
   Money-Transfer Services (Worldwide) 244

SECTION X
Personal Services 245

Airline Directory. 246
Alcoholics Anonymous. 246
Chiropractors 246
Dentists 246
Department Stores 247
Doctors. 248
Dry Cleaners 248
Eyewear Stores and Optometrists 249
Fitness Centers and Gyms 250
Florists and Balloon Delivery. 251
Hairstylists, Hair Salons, and Barbers. 251
Hospitals and Walk-In Medical Centers 251
Limousines and Town Cars 252
Jewelry Stores. 252
Massage Therapists and Day Spas. 252
Nail Salons. 255
Pharmacies 256
Rental Cars. 258
Shoe and Luggage Repair and Luggage Sales 259
Tailors and Clothing Alterations 259
Theme Parks 260

Tuxedo Rentals 260
Wheelchair and Scooter (ECV) Rentals 261

SECTION XI
Help for Travel-Related Problems and Emergencies............. 263

Making Last-Minute Changes to
  Your Travel Itinerary 264
Dealing with Travel and Weather Delays 265
Lost Luggage 266
Lost or Stolen Credit Card, Driver's
  License, and/or Passport 269
Lost, Stolen, or Damaged Laptop Computer 270
Buying a New Outfit Fast or Removing a Stain... 271
Prescription Refills 272
Replacing Prescription Eyewear................ 272
Medical or Dental Emergencies................ 272
Cellular Phone-Related Problems 274
Lost Items................................... 274

APPENDIX
Travel Charts and Worksheets 277

Tipping Recommendations 278
Tip Calculation Chart........................ 279
Travel Itinerary Worksheet.................... 280
Expense Tracker Worksheet 282
Trade Show Meeting Planner.................. 283
Frequent Traveler Program Worksheet.......... 284

Index 285

ACKNOWLEDGMENTS

Thanks to Jere Calmes, Karen Thomas, Stephanie Singer, and Ronald Young at Entrepreneur Press for inviting me to work on this project, as well as to Karen Schopp at McGraw-Hill for her help marketing this travel guide series. This series is also possible because of the fine editing and design work of Karen Billipp and everyone at Eliot House Productions.

My never-ending love and gratitude go out to my lifelong friends Mark, Ellen (as well as Ellen's family), and Ferras, who are all extremely important people in my life, as well as to my other close friends Garrick Procter, Christopher Henry, and Chris Coates.

My gratitude also goes out to all of the public relations and marketing people who work for the various Orlando-area hotels, restaurants, shows, and attractions. These people were extremely helpful as I gathered information for this guide. Special thanks go out to Amy Voss and the folks at the

Orlando/Orange County Convention and Visitors Bureau, as well as to Kate Sullivan at Sullivan Communications Group and everyone at Viator.com for their support on this project.

I'd also like to thank my family for all of their support and give a shout-out to my Yorkshire terrier "Rusty" (www.MyPalRusty.com). Yes, he has his own web site, so please check it out! To visit my web site, point your web browser to www.JasonRich.com.

PREFACE

Finally, an Orlando travel guide exclusively for business travelers! Whether you're a frequent business traveler who spends several weeks every month on the road and considers an airplane seat to be as familiar as your own bed, or you have the occasional need to travel for business, you have very different needs than vacationers and people who travel for pleasure. *Entrepreneur Magazine's Business Traveler* series consists of city-specific travel guides designed to meet your needs head-on and provide you with a comprehensive, convenient, and single source of important travel-related information.

From booking your travel reservations to packing, navigating your way around the city, attending conventions or meetings, entertaining important clients, choosing the best restaurants, relaxing after a long day, and dealing with travel-related problems or emergencies, this guide offers you resources, phone numbers, web sites, addresses, and information that will help to make your trip a total success.

The best way for a business traveler or convention-goer to utilize the information within this guide is to read (or skim) it in its entirety. This will give you an overview of Orlando (and the surrounding areas) and what you can expect from your trip. Then, as you plan or experience each phase of your trip, refer to the appropriate section of this guide for more detailed information. Throughout the guide, you'll find helpful Tip, Warning, Money Saver, and City Factoid icons that are accompanied by tidbits of information you'll find particularly useful.

The trick to experiencing the most enjoyable, stress-free, and successful business-related trip is to plan ahead. Not only will this save you (or your business) money, but it'll save you time later and help you avoid the many hassles associated with making last-minute travel plans.

In addition to being one of the country's top tourist and vacation destinations, thanks in large part to the Walt Disney World Resort, Universal Orlando, and SeaWorld, Orlando has also become a top destination among business travelers and convention and trade show attendees. As you're about to discover, the Orlando area offers something for everyone when it comes to fine dining, entertainment, shopping, world-class day spas, plus luxury hotel and resort accommodations.

For business travelers in particular, the city offers thousands of available meeting rooms equipped for any need; full-service

The Orange County Convention Center is ranked second in the United States in terms of exhibit and trade show space. McCormick Place in Chicago is ranked number one.

business centers within virtually every upscale hotel and resort; high-speed internet access (often wireless) at most hotels, resorts, and meeting spaces; the Orange County Convention Center (a state-of-the-art trade show, banquet, and convention facility) and several smaller convention centers; plus countless ways to entertain important clients, customers, or business associates—day or night.

In 2006, 48.3 million visitors traveled to Orlando. This included more than 10.5 million business travelers (about 60 percent of whom attended a convention or group meeting). While the Orlando area has many hotels and resorts with small- to mid-size convention centers, the Orange Country Convention Center, with more than two million square feet of meeting space, is the largest convention center in the state.

The Orange County Convention Center comprises three main buildings—the North Concourse (9400 Universal Boulevard), the South Concourse (9899 International Drive), and the West Concourse (9800 International Drive). Directly across the street from this massive complex, you'll find the Peabody Hotel (9801 International Drive) and the Rosen Centre Hotel and Convention Center, which offer plenty of additional convention, trade show, banquet, and meeting space, plus luxurious and convenient accommodations for business travelers.

Additional information about the Orange County Convention Center can be found in Section VIII, "Attending a Business Meeting or Convention." You'll find details about many of the business-friendly hotels and resorts that also offer convention, meeting, and banquet space within Section III, "Where to Stay While in Orlando."

Because more than 38 percent of businesspeople visiting Orlando bring their families along, in addition to providing business travelers with everything they need to plan their travels, Section VI, "Entertainment in Orlando," along with Section VII, "Visiting the Walt Disney World Resort," will help you plan and enjoy every aspect of your Orlando trip.

CITY FACTOID

In 2005, an estimated 16.2 million people visited the Magic Kingdom, the most popular of the theme parks at the Walt Disney World Resort in Orlando.

As you're making your travel, meeting or convention plans, the Orlando/Orange County Convention and Visitors Bureau (800-

972-3304, www.orlandocvb.com) and the Kissimmee Convention and Visitors Bureau (800-831-1844, www.floridakiss.com) can be excellent resources. These organizations can help you select the ideal location for a function, trade show, banquet, conference, meeting of any size, or any other event and then assist you with every aspect of the event or meeting planning process.

TIP
To track down almost any type of business-oriented service associated with trade shows, banquets, meetings, or conventions in the Orlando area, refer to Section IX, "Business Services."

A BIT OF ORLANDO HISTORY

In the early 1500s, when Spanish explorer Juan Ponce de Leon visited Florida for the first time, what he encountered was primarily swamp land that was inhabited by the Seminole Indians. Later in the 1800s, the Seminoles were forced to fight two wars in an effort to retain their native land. It was in 1842, at the end of the second war, that settlers followed the soldiers into the region now known as Orlando.

A settlement in Orlando formed around an army post called Fort Gatlin. At the time, the region was called Jerigan (named after an early settler). In 1857, the name of the region was officially changed to Orlando, in honor of Orlando Reeves, a brave soldier who managed to warn his fellow soldiers about an Indian raid in 1835.

As time went on, commerce began to thrive in Orlando, thanks to an abundance of cattle, cotton, and citrus. In 1900, Orlando acquired electricity, followed by telephone service and then motorcars. By 1928, the Orlando Municipal Airport (which today is the Orlando International Airport) opened.

It wasn't until 1971 that Orlando was transformed into a vacation and tourism hotspot, thanks entirely to Walt Disney, who chose to open Walt Disney's Magic Kingdom theme park there. By 1973, thousands of tourists were flocking to Orlando each year to visit Mickey Mouse. This was also when SeaWorld opened its doors to the public. In 1990, Universal Studios opened in Orlando and became the next massive theme park and resort destination to attraction vacationers, honeymooners, tourists, and business travelers alike.

Today, the Orlando area is home to more than 90 tourist attractions, 3,800 restaurants, and 450 hotels and resorts. The city also now annually hosts thousands of events, trade shows, conferences, meetings, and other business-oriented gatherings.

ORLANDO GEOGRAPHY 101

Located near the geographic center of Florida, the Orlando area spans three counties and encompasses 2,856 square miles. One reason the Orlando area has become such a popular tourist, vacation, and business travel destination is the year-round mild weather. The average temperature is 72.4 degrees Fahrenheit.

CITY FACTOID
Orlando is located 236 miles from Miami, 200 miles from Fort Lauderdale, 85 miles from Tampa, and 60 miles from Daytona Beach.

As you'll discover, the Orlando area is divided into several distinct areas, all located within a relatively short driving distance from each other. Much of this guide focuses on the International Drive area, where more than 100 hotels, countless restaurants, and the convention center are located. There's also the downtown Orlando area (the city's business district), the Lake Buena Vista area (where the Walt Disney World Resort and many independent hotels and resorts are located), and the nearby Kissimmee area (offering hundreds of additional hotels, restaurants, and attractions). Interactive, full-color maps of these areas can be found online by visiting www.orlandocvb.com/maps.

CITY FACTOID
As of February 2007, the Orlando area was home to more than 450 hotels offering well over 112,000 guestrooms and suites.

One thing that sets Orlando apart from other popular business travel destinations is the vast selection of accommodations available. In addition to literally hundreds of traditional business-friendly hotels, Orlando offers many nicely equipped resorts featuring fully furnished, multibedroom suites. You'll also find an abundance of stand-alone short-term rental properties and time-share resorts in the area, many of which offer world-class golf courses, tennis courts, swimming pools, day spas, and other amenities suitable for business travelers and vacationers alike. You'll learn more about your accommodation options within Section III, "Where to Stay While in Orlando."

LET'S GET STARTED PLANNING YOUR TRIP

As you'll discover, this guide is divided into 11 sections to help you plan and experience your trip. Section I, for example, will help you book your airfare and then navigate your way around Orlando International Airport upon your arrival.

Section II will help you pack for your trip. In Section III, you'll read about Orlando-area hotels, resorts, timeshare properties, and other accommodation options, plus discover which hotels and resorts made it onto the *Entrepreneur Magazine's Business Traveler* Top 15 Business-Friendly Hotels list. In Section IV, you'll discover all of the different ways of getting around Orlando, while Section V focuses on some of your many dining options in the Orlando area. Section VI offers all of the information you'll need to entertain yourself and your most important clients during your trip. Since many meetings, business gatherings, and other events are held at the Walt Disney World Resort, Section VII focuses on this popular resort and theme park destination. In Section VIII, you'll read all about attending a trade show or event at the Orange County Convention Center.

TIP
At the end of this guide, you'll discover four full-color maps that'll assist you in navigating in and around Orlando.

Sections IX and X will help you track down any business-related and personal services you might need during your visit to the Orlando area. Finally, Section XI will help you efficiently deal with any travel-related problems or emergencies that might arise. At the very end of this guide, you'll find a collection of travel worksheets and charts, which are excellent tools to help make your travel more organized and efficient.

If you find this book useful, additional city-specific travel guides covering popular business travel destinations, such as Las Vegas, New York City, Los Angeles, Chicago, and Washington, DC, will also be available in 2008. For details, point your web browser to www.jasonrich.com or www.entrepreneurpress.com.

TIP
If you utilize a wireless Palm-OS or Pocket PC Smartphone device, for a low monthly fee, you can use the Pocket Express service (http://express.handmark.com/index.php) to access up-to-the-minute news, weather, 4-1-1 Directory Assistance, maps, and other information of interest to business travelers. You can also use your cell phone to obtain referrals to restaurants, shops, health services, and travel news by accessing Infospace (www.mobile.infospacefindit.com). For Palm OS PDAs and Treo Smartphones, the SplashTravel software ($19.95, www.splashdata.com/splashtravel/index.htm) offers a handful of useful applications of interest to business travelers, including an expense tracker, a packing list manager, and an enhanced scheduler application. All of these applications can be used while on-the-go to help better organize your trip and make your travels more efficient.

MAP OF ORLANDO AREA

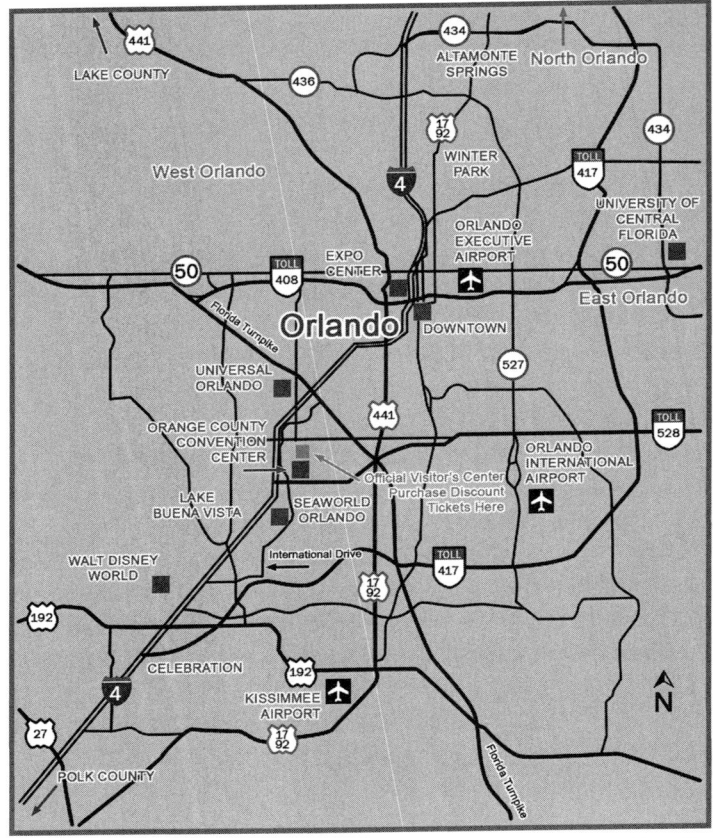

Created by Daniel L. White.

SECTION 1

Lake Eola, Orlando, Florida © Tom Hirtreiter

WELCOME TO
ORLANDO

The easiest and best way to ensure a stress-free journey to Orlando is to invest the time to plan your trip in advance. This will help ensure you're able to book the most convenient flights and obtain reservations at your first-choice hotel. This section provides the information you need to make your travel reservations, find the lowest airfares, and navigate your way through the airport upon your arrival in Orlando.

GETTING TO ORLANDO

While plenty of people drive, take a bus, or ride a train from nearby cities in order to reach Orlando, more than 54 percent of business travelers and convention-goers fly to this favorite destination. Another popular option is Amtrak, especially if you're traveling from a nearby city located along the East Coast. Information about Amtrak is included later in this section.

TIP
For private and/or some charter flights, Orlando Executive Airport, a much smaller but conveniently located facility, is typically utilized.

MAKING YOUR TRAVEL RESERVATIONS

When it comes to making your travel arrangements and then booking your reservations (airline, hotel, and rental car), you have four primary options:

1. You can shop for the best airline, hotel, and rental car rates by calling each company or service provider directly or visiting its web site.

Orlando International Airport (MCO) is the Orlando area's busiest airport, handling arriving and departing flights to and from cities across the country and around the world. The airport is located less than 30 minutes from the International Drive, Kissimmee, and Walt Disney World Resort areas.

2. You can use one of the popular travel-related web sites (described in this section) and book all of your travel arrangements online simultaneously.
3. You can utilize the services of a local travel agent. A travel agent will do a lot of the busywork associated with making travel reservations for you.
4. You can schedule your travel through your company's corporate travel department (if applicable). Or, for those attending a convention or trade show in Orlando, the convention coordinator typically offers travel services with special discounts. In many cases, this option allows you to make changeable travel arrangements and choose accommodations at or close to the convention or meeting you'll be attending.

CONTACTING THE AIRLINES DIRECTLY

As you'll discover, not every major airline services every city or flies into Orlando International Airport. The following chart lists the major airlines that serviced this airport as of mid-2007. Based on this list, you'll need to choose an airline that also services your home city and offers convenient flights to and from the Orlando area. Keep in mind, direct flights might not always be available.

TIME SAVER
Co-workers, friends, and relatives can easily track the progress of your flight online. Visit the Flight Arrivals web site (www.flightarrivals.com) and enter the airline, flight number, and date. This information is also available by calling the airline directly or by visiting the airline's web site. If you have a Palm OS wireless PDA, you can download a free program, called FlightStatus, from www.free warepalm.com/travel/flightstatus.shtml that offers the same real-time flight tracking functionality, but from the palm of your hand.

MAJOR AIRLINES SERVICING ORLANDO INTERNATIONAL AIRPORT (MCO)

(All airlines with a * offer domestic service. This list is subject to change.)

Aer Lingus	(800) 474-7424
www.aerlingus.com	Gates 1-29

MAJOR AIRLINES SERVICING ORLANDO INTERNATIONAL AIRPORT (MCO)

Aeromexico www.aeromexico.com	(800) 237-6639	Gates 60–99
Air Canada www.aircanada.ca	(888) 247-2262	Gates 30–59
Air France www.airfrance.com	(800) 237-2747	Gates 70–99
Air Jamaica www.airjamaica.com	(800) 523-5585	Gates 1–29
Air Transat www.airtransat.com	(877) 872-6728	Gates 1–29
AirTran* www.airtran.com	(800) 247-8726	Gates 100–129
Alaska Airlines* www.alaskaair.com	(877) 872-6728	Gates 1–29
Alitalia www.alitalia.com	(800) 223-5730	Gates 60–99
America West Airlines (part of U.S. Airways)* www.usairways.com/awa	(800) 235-9292	Gates 1–29
American Airlines* www.aa.com	(800) 433-7300	Gates 1–29
American Eagle* www.aa.com	(800) 433-7300	Gates 1–29
ANA (All Nippon Airways) www.ana.co.jp/eng	(800) 235-9262	Gates 30–59
ATA www.ata.com	(800) 225-2996	Gates 1–29
Austrian www.aua.com/us/eng	(800) 843-0002	Gates 30–59
Bahamasair www.bahamasair.com	(800) 222-4262	Gates 1–29
BMI www.flybmi.com	(800) 788-0555	Gates 30–59
British Airways www.britishairways.com	(800) 247-9297	Gates 60–99
CanJet www.canjet.com	(800) 809-7777	Gates 1–29
Cayman Airways www.caymanairways.com	(800) 422-9626	Gates 80–89
Champion Air* www.championair.com	(800) 922-2602	Gates 1–29
China Airlines www.china-airlines.com	(800) 227-5118	Gates 70–99

MAJOR AIRLINES SERVICING ORLANDO INTERNATIONAL AIRPORT (MCO)

Condor*	(800) 524-6975
www.condor.com	Gates 60-99
Continental*	(800) 525-0280
www.continental.com	Gates 1-29
Continental Connections*	(800) 525-0280
www.continental.com	Gates 1-29
Copa Air	(800) 359-2672
www.copaair.com	Gates 1-29
Delta Airlines*	(800) 221-1212
www.delta.com	Gates 60-99
Delta Connection*	(800) 325-5205
www.delta.com	Gates 60-99
Delta Song*	(800) 359-7664
www.flysong.com	Gates 60-99
El Al	(800) 223-6700
www.elal.com	Gates 70-99
Frontier Airlines*	(800) 432-1359
www.frontierairlines.com	Gates 60-99
Hawaiian Airlines*	(614) 414-0717
www.hawaiianairlines.com	Gates 1-29
Iberia	(800) 722-4642
www.iberia.com	Gates 1-29
Icelandair	(800) 223-5500
www.icelandair.com	Gates 60-99
JAL	(800) 585-3663
www.jal.co.jp/en/	Gates 1-29
JetBlue*	(800) 538-2583
www.jetblue.com	Gates 100-129
KLM	(800) 438-5000
www.klm.com	Gates 30-59
Korean Air	(800) 438-5000
www.koreanair.com	Gates 60-99
LTU	(866) 266-5588
www.ltu.com	Gates 1-29
Lufthansa	(800) 645-3880
www.lufthansa.com	Gates 30-59
Martinair	(800) 627-8462
www.martinair.com	Gates 1-29
Mexicana	(800) 531-7921
www.mexicana.com	Gates 1-29
Miami Air*	(305) 871-3300
www.miamiair.com	Gates 60-99

MAJOR AIRLINES SERVICING ORLANDO INTERNATIONAL AIRPORT (MCO)

Airline	Contact
Midwest Air* www.midwestairlines.com	(800) 452-2022 Gates 60–99
Northwest Airlines (NWA)* www.nwa.com	(800) 225-2525 Gates 30–59
Singapore Airlines www.singaporeair.com	(800) 742-3333 Gates 60–99
Southwest Airlines* www.southwest.com	(800) 435-9792 Gates 100–129
Spirit* www.spiritair.com	(800) 772-7117 Gates 30–59
Sun Country* www.suncountry.com	(800) FLY-N-SUN Gates 60–99
TAM www.tamairlines.com	(407) 816-3555 Gates 1–29
Ted (Delta) www.flyted.com	(800) 225-5833 Gates 30–59
Turkish Airlines www.thy.com	(800) 874-8875 Gates 1–29
United Airlines www.united.com	(800) 241-6522 Gates 30–59
U.S. Airways* www.usairways.com	(800) 428-4322 Gates 30–59
U.S. Airways Express* www.usairways.com	(800) 428-4322 Gates 30–59
USA 3000 Airlines* www.usa3000.com	(800) 895-3000 Gates 1–29
Virgin Atlantic www.virgin-atlantic.com	(800) 862-8621 Gates 60–99
WestJet www.westjet.com	(800) 538-5696 Gates 1–29
Zoom www.flyzoom.com	(866) 359-9666 Gates 1–29

TIP

If you're looking to fly to or from Orlando via an airline's business class or first class, contact the airline directly, as opposed to booking through one of the travel-related web sites.

TIP
If you book through certain travel web sites, such as Travelocity, flights and other travel arrangements can sometimes be changed, but for a fee.

ONLINE TRAVEL SERVICES

There are dozens of popular travel-related web sites that can save you a fortune on your airline tickets, rental cars, and hotels. When booking your airfare online through any of these travel sites, however, keep in mind that your flights are typically *not* changeable or refundable. All sales are final, and you typically will not receive airline frequent flier miles for your trips. The benefit is that you can usually save up to 60 percent off published airfares or rates simply by shopping online using one of these services.

Here are a few tips for finding the best airfares to and from Orlando online:

- Book your travel between 7 and 21 days in advance. (This rule does not apply to all the travel-related web sites. Some offer low fares with only 24 hours' advance booking.)
- Plan to leave and return on a Tuesday, Wednesday, Thursday, or Saturday. (Because of the extensive tourist traffic, Monday, Friday, and Sunday are the busiest days to travel to and from the Orlando area.)
- Consider accepting a red-eye flight when traveling from the West Coast to the East Coast.
- Reserve your airfare, hotel, and/or rental car at the same time as a package deal.
- Be willing to accept nondirect flights with one, possibly two stops.
- Before making a purchase (which will often be nonrefundable and nonchangeable), check two or three travel and/or airline web sites to ensure you're getting the best rates. Shop around for the best deals, even if you're traveling on a last-minute basis.

WARNING
If there's a chance you'll need to change your travel itinerary at the last minute, you're better off booking your airfare directly through your desired airline. You'll often pay a bit more, but typically you'll have the option to

change your flight(s). When changing a flight, you'll often be charged a flat change fee of between $50 and $150 (depending on the airline), plus you'll have to pay the difference in airfare between your original flight and the new flight (if applicable). Many airlines will allow you to fly standby to avoid paying these fees, but be sure to check with the airline directly to understand the travel limitations. Optional travel insurance allows you to change your flight, but only if there's a medical emergency, not a change in your work itinerary. JetBlue offers one of the most flexible policies of all airlines for changing flights without incurring high fees.

The following is information about several popular travel-related web sites:

- **Hotwire.com** *(www.hotwire.com)*. An easy-to-use web site for finding and booking airfares, hotels, rental cars, or complete travel packages. This service tends to offer the lowest fares and rates you'll find online. For flights, simply enter your departure and return dates, departure and destination cities, and the number of people traveling to see a variety of low-airfare options. This web site displays the specific airline, flight numbers, travel times, and price for your travel request. The site will also suggest alternate travel times and dates if you're shopping for a lower fare.
- **Kayak.com** *(www.kayak.com)*. This web site does not offer the flashy bells and whistles found on many travel-related web sites; however, it quickly accesses hundreds of other travel-related and airline web sites in order to find the very best deals. Kayak.com is easy to use and often finds extremely competitive airfares, hotel rates, and rental car rates. Once you select an airfare, for example, Kayak.com forwards you directly to the web site offering it. This site is totally unbiased in terms of what deals are offered. No preferential treatment is given to particular airlines or service providers.
- **Nextag.com** *(www.nextag.com)*. This is a comprehensive price-comparison web site that's designed to help consumers find the lowest prices for virtually anything. The travel section of Nextag.com allows you to shop for discounted airfares, hotels, rental cars and travel packages. The site is advertiser based, meaning that in addition to searching other travel-related sites for the best deals,

Nextag.com will also feature offers from companies that have paid to be included and compete for your business.

- ***Orbitz.com*** *(www.orbitz.com).* Find and book airfares, hotels, rental cars, and complete travel packages with ease by entering your departure and return dates, departure and destination cities, and the number of people traveling. This web site displays a variety of specific airlines, flight numbers, travel times, and prices for your travel request. The site is affiliated with LastMinute.com (www.lastminute.com), which offers last-minute travel deals and discounts. Once you book travel through Orbitz, you can take advantage of Orbitz TLC Mobile, which can be accessed using your wireless PDA or Smartphone. This service allows you to obtain travel itineraries, check the status of flights, be alerted of delays, and reserve same-day hotel rooms while on the go.
- ***SideStep.com*** *(www.sidestep.com).* Using this service, you can quickly search for the lowest available airfares from more than 100 airline web sites and travel-related online services simultaneously. Unlike some of the other online travel services, this one also researches several of the lower-priced airlines, including JetBlue.
- ***Travelocity.com*** *(www.travelocity.com).* Find and book airfares, hotels, rental cars, and complete travel packages with ease using this service. Simply enter your departure and return dates, departure and destination cities, and the number of people traveling. This web site displays a variety of specific airlines, flight numbers, travel times, and prices for your travel request. Detailed information about hotels and various destinations is also provided in the form of online travel guides and reviews.
- ***Yahoo! Travel*** *(http://travel.yahoo.com).* Find and book airfares, hotels, rental cars, and complete travel packages with ease using this service. Simply enter your departure and return dates, departure and destination cities, and the number of people traveling. This web site displays a variety of specific airlines, flight numbers, travel times, and prices for your travel request.

WARNING
Check-in mistakes sometimes occur when the ticketing agent attaches the wrong destination tags to your luggage, sending your bags to the wrong city. As you check

your luggage with your airline, double-check that the bags have the appropriate tags indicating what city you're flying to. In addition to your flight number, the airport code that should appear on your departure flight's tags is "MCO" for Orlando International Airport. Manually confirm that the tags are correct. Don't just assume the ticket agent has done this properly. You will receive claim checks for each piece of luggage checked with the airline. In some cases, claim check ID numbers will simply be printed on your boarding pass. Do not throw away your boarding passes or luggage claim tags until you arrive at your final destination. Before leaving the airport and prior to your return home, remove all old tags from your luggage.

AIRPORT SECURITY CONSIDERATIONS AND TIPS

Since the terrorist attacks of 9/11, the security at airports has understandably become extremely tight. While this security is necessary for the most part, having to endure the hassle of long lines and the Transportation Security Administration's (TSA) regulations has become an ongoing frustration for many frequent business travelers.

Refer to Section II, "Packing for Your Business Trip," for more details about packing your carry-on and checked luggage. Additional information about the latest rules and regulations for passengers can also be found at www.tsa.gov. If you're a regular business traveler, refer to this web site monthly to learn about the latest changes in airport and airline security procedures. Being familiar with these procedures will speed up your trip through the airport and help you get through security faster and with less hassle.

WARNING
Never be rude to or disobey the TSA officers. Doing so may cause you serious delays or keep you from boarding your flight. Cooperating with their requests allows TSA officers to conduct their security-related jobs in a timely and responsible manner. To report specific violations and concerns about security, call the TSA Contact Center at (866) 289-9673 or the Office of Civil Rights at (877) 336-4872.

The following strategies will help you pass through security with the least delay and hassle possible.

SECTION I / WELCOME TO ORLANDO ·· 11

MCO is almost always crowded. When you're ready to leave Orlando, allow between 30 and 60 minutes just to get through security. Ideally, you should arrive at the airport between 90 minutes and two hours prior to your flight. This should leave ample time to return your rental car, check in with the airline, check your luggage, go through security, and make your way to the gate. You must be at your designated gate at least 30 minutes before departure for boarding, or you could lose your seat aboard the aircraft and miss your flight.

- While in the airport, carry your photo ID and boarding pass with you at all times and be prepared to present them to security and airline personnel multiple times. According to the TSA, a valid photo ID consists of a driver's license, passport, or military ID.
- Avoid wearing excessive metal when traveling. All metal objects will need to be removed as you pass through airport security. Belt buckles, metal barrettes, large metal body piercings, and shoes containing metal should all be removed or they'll set off the metal detectors and cause delays. Small plastic bins are available to contain your personal items as they pass through security. However, to avoid the possibility of theft, it's better to place these items within your carry-on.

TIP

Once you arrive at the airport and pass through security, keep your boarding pass handy at all times. It likely will be checked multiple times between the time you check in with your airline and when you actually board the aircraft. After passing through the security checkpoint, you should no longer need your photo ID, unless the airport is at a heightened level of security.

- Have a credit card, debit card, or your frequent flier program membership card for the airline with you, along with your photo ID, when you check in using an automatic kiosk at your airline's ticket counter. Most airlines now require this.
- Personal electronics (cell phones and PDAs), your wallet, pens, loose change, keys, metal belt buckles, and all other personal belongings should all be removed from your pockets, placed in your carry-on, and put through the airport's X-ray machine at the security checkpoint.
- As you approach the security checkpoint, remove your laptop from its case and send it through the X-ray machine separately. This is a TSA requirement. Failing to do so may cause you to undergo a more intense and time-consuming security screening procedure.
- Remove your shoes, jacket, and/or coat and send these items through the X-ray machine separately.
- Pay attention to the latest list of items and objects that cannot be carried onto an airplane. Either place these items within your checked-in luggage (if appropriate and allowable) or ship them separately to your destination. Items that can't be carried onto airplanes include knives, sharp objects, weapons, lighters, nail clippers, and hazardous chemicals (including common cleaning products). For a complete and up-to-date list of prohibited items, point your web browser to www.tsa.gov/travelers/airtravel/assistant/index.shtm or call (866) 289-9673.

TIME SAVER
Do not wrap any gifts you are carrying aboard the airplane. You need to make them available for inspection as you proceed through airport security.

- Dispose of all beverages and full-size containers of liquid (or gel) items before reaching the airport security checkpoint. You are allowed up to three ounces of liquid or gels, such as small containers of shampoo or toothpaste, in your

SECTION I / WELCOME TO ORLANDO • 13

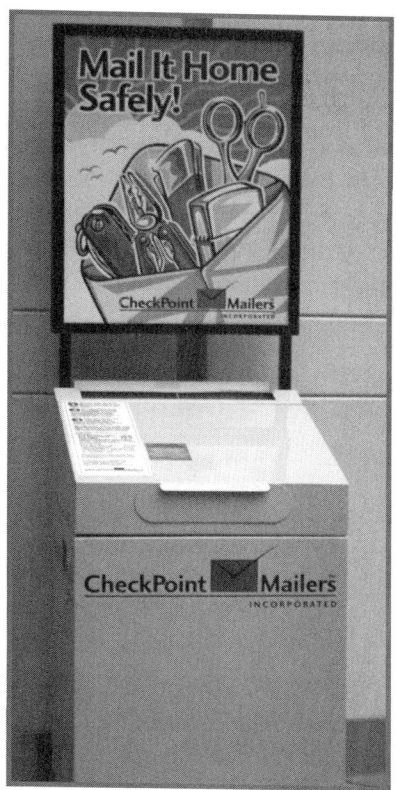

If you are carrying an item that the TSA doesn't allow, instead of throwing it away or turning it over to the authorities, you can mail it back to your home or office. Prohibited items may include pocketknives, lighters, nail clippers, and any other small and/or sharp objects. Self-serve CheckPoint Mailer stations are located near the security checkpoints. Simply place the item(s) in a supplied envelope, complete the label and required form, and your items will be mailed to you for a flat fee of $8 for all domestic packages and $12 for international packages.

If you find yourself lost, confused, or in need of assistance, locate the nearest Travelers Aid or information counter at the airport (they're typically found near baggage claim or in the main terminal areas prior to passing through security). Here, you can get help if you have lost your tickets or ID, get separated from your travel companions, or require information and/or directions. These services are offered free of charge.

"CLEAR" THROUGH SECURITY WITH EASE

Orlando International Airport is one of the first in the nation to test the new Clear program, a premium service that allows frequent business travelers to quickly pass through airport security without having to wait in long lines. The TSA refers to the Clear program as a "fast lane" at the airport.

There is an annual fee of $99.95 to participate in the Clear program. Participants must preregister for the program by completing an online application found at www.flyclear.com. After completing the application, during your next visit to the Orlando airport, stop at the Clear enrollment station, where your photograph and biometric images will be taken and two forms of government-issued identification will be verified. Once this process is complete, the entire enrollment package will be submitted to the TSA for review and approval, at which time you'll receive your Clear card.

After registering for and being accepted into the Clear program, when you arrive at the TSA airport security checkpoint, simply proceed to the special Clear lane, present your ID card, and allow for the biometric images to be matched. The process takes just seconds. There will be no long security lines to wait in, which will greatly reduce the time you spend at the Orlando airport.

For more information about the TSA's Clear program, call (866) 848-2415 or visit www.flyclear.com. Corporate discounts are available, and the number of airports participating in this program is growing rapidly. For business travelers who frequently visit Orlando or other participating cities, Clear is a considerable time saver and reduces some of the frustration often associated with airline travel.

The TSA's new Clear program offers a way for frequent business travelers to circumvent long airport security lines.

carry-on. However, they must be enclosed in a clear plastic bag and declared when you pass through security.

CURBSIDE CHECK-IN AT THE AIRPORT

Many airports and airlines offer curbside check-in as a convenience. While this service used to be free, most airlines now charge between $2 and $3 per bag, plus you're expected to tip the attendant. Instead of proceeding to the airline's ticketing counter within the airport, you can check your luggage and receive your boarding pass just outside the terminal's entrance, then go directly to security and ultimately to your departure gate.

Some of the airlines that offer curbside check-in at MCO include Air Canada, AirTran, American Airlines, American Eagle, Continental Airlines, Delta, Delta Connection, JetBlue, Midwest, Northwest Airlines, Southwest Airlines, Spirit, Ted, United, and U.S. Airways.

Depending on crowds, using curbside check-in can save you time. When using curbside check-in, you should check your bags at least one hour before your scheduled departure time. If the national security threat rises to Code Orange or higher, however, curbside check-in may not be available.

NAVIGATING YOUR WAY THROUGH ORLANDO INTERNATIONAL AIRPORT (MCO)

Address: One Airport Boulevard, Orlando, FL 32827-4399

Airport code: MCO

Web site: www.orlandoairports.net

General information: (407) 825-2001

Flight tracking information: www.flightview.com

Parking information: (407) 825-PARK

Travelers aid: (407) 825-2142 or (407) 825-2353

Airport lost and found: (407) 825-2111

Paging: (407) 825-2000

The Orlando International Airport is the busiest in Florida and the 12th busiest in the United States, with more than 80,000 passengers flying in or out of the facility every day. The airport is serviced by approximately 80 domestic and international airlines (including charters) and is located about 6.5 miles from downtown Orlando. Covering almost 15,000 acres, the airport has four parallel runways, two of which are 12,000 feet long, one which is 10,000 feet long, and one which is 9,000 feet long. The airport can operate three runways simultaneously to handle increased airplane traffic.

In 2007, more than 35.7 million passengers used Orlando International Airport, which offers more than 50 shops, 50 restaurants and bars, a Hyatt Regency hotel, plus a wide range of services for travelers right on the premises.

CITY FACTOID
MCO is designated as a space shuttle emergency landing site. Contrary to popular belief, "MCO" does not stand for Mickey's Corporate Office. The airport designation is based on the airport's former name, which was McCoy Air Force Base.

Terminal Layout and Available Services

Virtually all of the important airport services offered at MCO, from the airline ticket counters and baggage claim areas to the food court, shops, and even a Hyatt Regency Hotel (located in the center of the airport), can be found within the main terminal building. Branching off from this building are two main terminal areas—Terminal A and Terminal B, which are divided into four gate areas, each of which contains at least 30 individual gates (which are numbered). The terminal and gate you arrive to or depart from will be determined by which airline you're flying with.

TICKET COUNTERS (DEPARTURES) AND BAGGAGE CLAIM (ARRIVALS)

When you arrive to Orlando International Airport by plane, upon exiting your aircraft, follow signs to the baggage claim area, located

MAP OF ORLANDO INTERNATIONAL AIRPORT

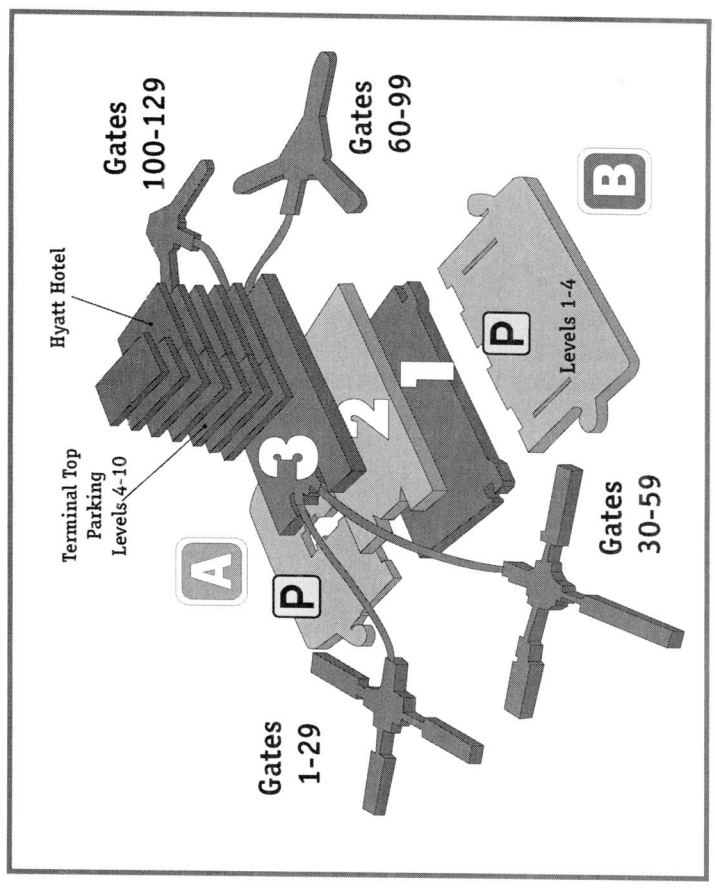

Map courtesy of Greater Orlando Aviation Authority.

in the main terminal building on level 2. Elevators, stairs, and escalators can be used from level 2 (baggage claim) to level 1 (ground transportation). If you arrive in Terminal A, proceed to Baggage Claim Area A to retrieve your luggage. If you arrive in Terminal B, proceed to Baggage Claim Area B to retrieve your luggage. Above the individual baggage claim conveyor belts are signs indicating specific flight numbers.

The ticketing and check-in counters for departing passengers are also located within the main terminal building, on level 3. Follow the appropriate signs for your airline. Once you check in at your airline's ticket counter, you will need to reach your airplane's gate, which will be located in one of the airport's other terminals. After proceeding through security, you'll take a short automated tram ride to your gate. The tram departs every three minutes. Follow the signs to your designated terminal letter and gate number.

TIP
While passing through airport security could take up to one hour, getting from the main terminal building to your airplane's gate via the tram will typically take five to ten minutes and will require some walking.

The main terminal building at MCO has three main floors. Elevators, stairs, and escalators allow visitors to travel easily between floors. The following table lists what you'll find on each floor.

STORE OR SERVICE LOCATION IN ORLANDO INTERNATIONAL AIRPORT	
All airline gates	Level 3
Baggage claim (all airlines)	Level 2
Bank and ATMs	Level 3
Currency exchange	Level 3
Ground transportation	Level 1
Hyatt Regency Hotel	Level 3
Limo pickup	Level 1
Rental car counters	Level 1
Restaurants	Level 3
Shops	Level 3
Shuttle bus stop	Level 1
Taxi stand	Level 1
Ticketing (airline ticket counters)	Level 3

RETAIL SHOPS AND SERVICES

Orlando International Airport is a large and well equipped airport. In addition to dozens of fast-food and sit-down dining options, the airport offers several mall-like shopping areas, featuring everything from last-minute souvenir shopping opportunities from the Magic of Disney World, Universal Studios, SeaWorld, and the Kennedy Space Center, to shops and boutiques you'd find at your favorite mall or shopping center.

Following are some of the shops and services you'll find in the main terminal building.

- *Airline ticket counters*—located on level 3 of the main terminal building.
- *Automated Teller Machines (ATMs)*—located throughout the airport, including all terminals.
- *Baggage claim area*—level 2 of the main terminal building
- *Banking*—there's a full-service SunTrust Bank located on level 3 of the main terminal building.
- *Business center*—within the Hyatt Hotel (located in the center of the main terminal building) is a full-service business center.
- *Car rental counters*—level 1 of the main terminal building. Some rental cars can be picked up in the garage just outside of the main terminal building, while other cars can be picked up at remote lots, accessible via a free shuttle bus. See "Rental Cars" later in this section.
- *Coffee*—located in the main terminal building and near several of the gates, you'll find Starbucks Coffee and/or Seattle's Best Coffee locations.
- *Food court*—located in the center of Level 3 in the main terminal building is a large food court offering more than a dozen fast-food options, with plenty of nearby seating. McDonald's, Nathan's Famous Hot Dogs, Carvel Ice Cream, and Sbarro are among your options. Additional fast-food restaurants are located near the various gates.
- *Foreign currency exchange*—several Travelex foreign currency exchange kiosks are available throughout the main terminal building.
- *Ground transportation*—outside the main terminal building, at level 1.
- *Information*—free information and assistance is available from the information kiosks located throughout the main terminal building.
- *Lost and found*—there is a lost-and-found office located in the main terminal building, adjacent to the food court on level 3.
- *Passenger pickup*—outside the main terminal building, at level 1
- *Postal services*—a full-service U.S. Post Office is available (during business hours) near the food court in the main

terminal building (Level 3). Several UPS and FedEx drop boxes are available within the airport.
- *Shoeshine service*—located in the main terminal building (near the food court on level 3).
- *Shopping*—some of the retail stores you'll find on level 3 of the main terminal building include Airport Wireless, Crocs, Brookstone, Borders Books, L'Occitane, Harley Davidson Gift Shop, the Magic of Disney, Universal Studios Gift Shop, SeaWorld Gift Shop, Westwin Bookmark, Lush, Lids, Perfumania, Ron Jon Surf Shop, Swatch, Sunglass Hut International, Oakley, In-Motion Entertainment, and two duty-free shops (for international travelers). A variety of newsstands are located throughout the airport.
- *Spa and salon*—d_parture spa and salon is a full-service day spa located in the main terminal building, near the food court.
- *Taxi stand*—a taxi stand is located just outside of the main terminal building on level 1.

FAST-FOOD DINING OPTIONS

The following are the fast-food restaurants available within the airport. In the food court area, plenty of nearby seating is available.

RESTAURANT	LOCATION
Au Bon Pain	Gates 100–129 area
Burger King	Gates 1–29 area and Gates 60–99 area
Café Azalea	Gates 1–29 area and Gates 30–59 area
Carvel Ice Cream	Main terminal food court and Gates 60–99 area
Chick-Fil-A	Main terminal food court
Cinnabon	Gates 1–29 area
Fresh Attractions	Main terminal food court and Gates 60–99 area
Freshens Yogurt	Gates 30–59 area and Gates 100–129 area
Johnny Rivers Smokehouse Express	Gates 100–129 area
Krispy Kreme	Main terminal food court
Manatee Lounge	Gates 30–59 area

RESTAURANT	LOCATION
McDonald's	Main terminal food court and Gates 100–129 area
Miami Subs	Gates 30–59 area
Nathan's Famous Hot Dogs	Main terminal food court and Gates 60–99 area
P.S. Lounge	Gates 1–29 area
Pepito's Cuban Café	Gates 1–29 area and Gates 30–59 area
Sbarro	Main terminal food court and Gates 100–129 area
Seattle's Best	Main terminal and Gates 100–129 area
Snacks on the Fly	Gates 60–99 area
Starbucks Coffee	Main terminal, Gates 1–29 area, and Gates 60–66 area
TCBY	Gates 1–29 area
Villa Pizza	Gates 30–59 area
Zyngs	Main terminal food court

SIT-DOWN DINING OPTIONS AND BARS

The following restaurants offer full-service, sit-down dining within the airport.

RESTAURANT	LOCATION
Chili's Too	Main terminal (level 4)
Fox Sports Bar	Main terminal (level 3)
Hemisphere	Hyatt Regency Hotel, level 9 (main terminal building)
Kafe Kalik Bar & Grill	Gates 100–129 area
Macaroni Grill	Main terminal (level 3)
McCoy's	Hyatt Regency Hotel, Level 4 (main terminal building)
Outback Steakhouse Outpost	Gates 60–99 area

AIRLINE CLUBS AND LOUNGES

Two airline clubs are located within Orlando International Airport. For a per-visit fee or by paying an annual membership fee, you can relax in these quiet, comfortable, and convenient lounges.

Operated by the individual airlines and available to members, these clubs offer couches, TVs, telephones, bar service,

ORLANDO AIRPORT SHOPPING MAP

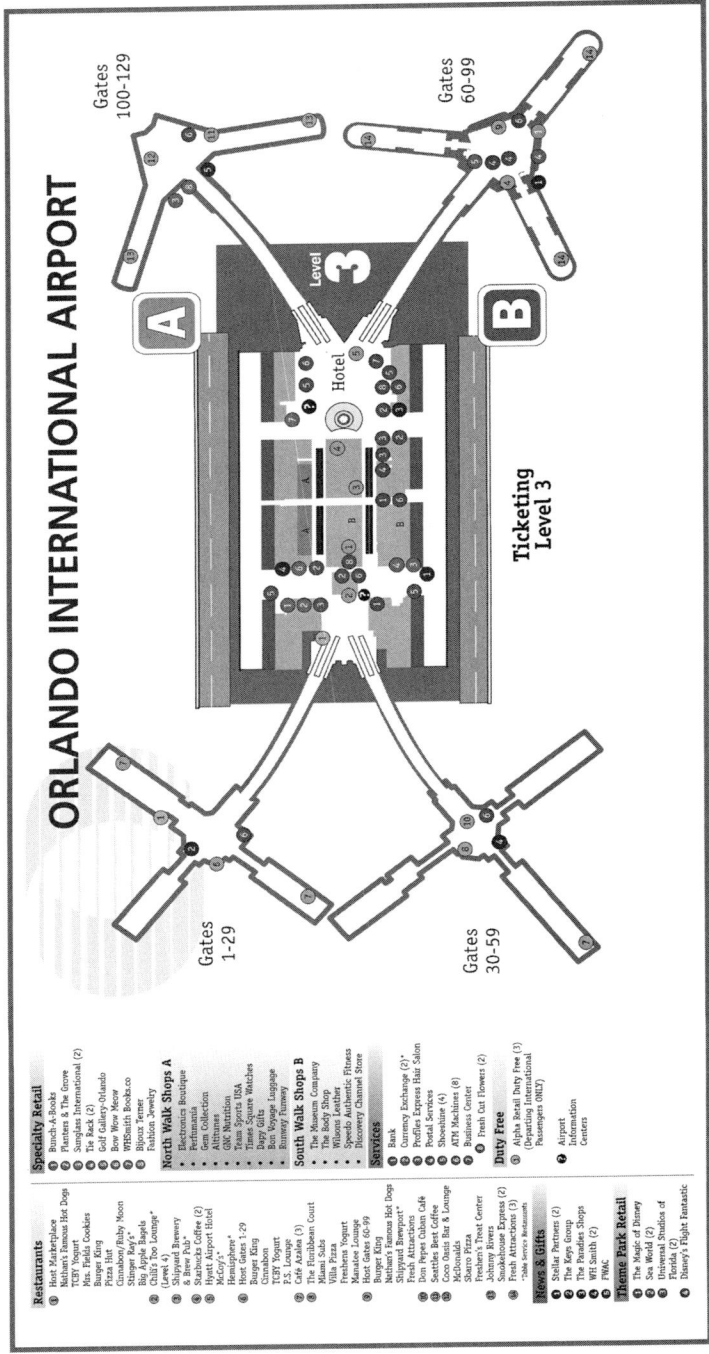

Map courtesy of Greater Orlando Aviation Authority.

complimentary newspapers and magazines, copiers, fax machines, internet access, clean restrooms, and other amenities, making these areas especially attractive if you have an extended wait at the airport. Fully equipped, private meeting rooms can also be rented.

AIRLINE CLUB	LOCATION
United Airlines Red Carpet Room	Near Gate 42
Delta Crown Room Airlines	Near Gate 60

For an annual fee, you can join Priority Pass, which offers access to more than 500 airport lounges worldwide, regardless of what airline you're traveling with. For more information, point your web browser to www.prioritypass.com or call (800) 352-2834. Annual membership prices range from $99 to $399.

Stuck at the Airport?

Located within a short drive from Orlando International Airport are dozens of hotels, motels, and resorts. Many of these properties offer free shuttle service to and from the airport. If your flight gets canceled, or you have a last-minute change of plans, you can contact any of these hotels to arrange for nearby overnight accommodations. The most convenient accommodations option, however, is the Hyatt Regency located in the center of the airport itself (see Section III, "Where to Stay while in Orlando," for details about this business-friendly hotel). Following is a sampling of the nearby accommodations. All addresses are in Orlando.

HOTELS LOCATED NEAR THE AIRPORT	
Best Western Airport Inn	8101 Air Center Court
(407) 581-2800	1.5 miles from the airport
Comfort Suites	7900 Conway Road
(877) 424-6423	1 mile from the airport
Courtyard Orlando Airport	7155 North Frontage Road
(407) 240-7200	1 mile from the airport
Crowne Plaza Orlando Airport	5555 Hazeltine National Drive
(407) 856-0100	1 mile from the airport
Fairfield Inn Airport	7100 Augusta National Drive
(407) 888-2666	.5 miles from the airport

HOTELS LOCATED NEAR THE AIRPORT	
Hampton Inn (407) 888-2995	5767 TG Lee Boulevard 1 mile from the airport
Hilton Garden Inn (407) 240-3725	7300 Augusta National Drive 1 mile from the airport
Holiday Inn Select (407) 851-6400	5750 T.G. Lee Boulevard 1 mile from the airport
Hyatt Regency Orlando International Airport (407) 825-1234	9300 Airport Boulevard Located in the airport's main terminal building
Renaissance Orlando Airport (877) 784-6835	5445 Forbes Place 1 mile from the airport

If you get stuck overnight at an airport because of a canceled flight, if the cancellation is a result of bad weather, you will be responsible for covering the cost of your accommodations, meals, and ground transportation. If, however, the airline canceled your flight because of mechanical problems (or any reason that was the airline's fault), you're probably entitled to have the airline pay for your overnight accommodations as well as provide you with vouchers for meals.

The Marriott near the Orlando airport (7499 Augusta National Drive, Orlando, 407-851-9000) is one of the few business-friendly hotels in the area to offer a lovely outdoor swimming pool. You'll also find the Porterhouse Restaurant and a Starbucks Coffee here.

MONEY SAVER
To save money on last-minute hotel accommodations near the airport or anywhere in the Orlando area, consider accessing the Hotels.com web site (www.hotels.com) or calling (800) 246-8357.

GROUND TRANSPORTATION OPTIONS

Information about rental cars, taxis, limos, buses, and trains can be found in Section IV, "Getting Around Town." For getting to and from MCC and any hotel, for example, a variety of shuttle bus services, shared-van services, taxis, and private town car (limo) services are available. Many of these companies offer door-to-door service from the airport to your hotel, resort, or any address within Orlando, Kissimmee, or the surrounding areas.

If you're staying at one of the hotels or resorts located at the Walt Disney World Resort, one easy option for traveling to and from the airport is to take advantage of Disney's Magical Express transportation service. When you use this service, your bags will be picked up at the airport's baggage claim area upon your arrival to Orlando and then delivered to your hotel room upon check-in. Guests are transported from the airport directly to their hotel in a luxury, air-conditioned bus. When you're ready to depart the Walt Disney World Resort, you can precheck your bags and obtain your airline boarding passes at your hotel. In addition to the convenience of not having to carry your own luggage, this service will save you considerable time upon your arrival to and departure from Orlando. Disney's Magical Express transportation is offered free of charge to guests at any of the more than 20 Walt Disney World Resort hotels.

Shared-Van, Bus, and Other Ground Transportation Options

The following are bus and shared-van services that offer transportation to and from the Orlando International Airport. Utilizing a shared-van service will take a bit longer than riding in a taxi (because multiple stops are made), but the rates are less than half of what a taxi or limo would cost.

- *MCO Express*—www.mcoexpress.com, (877) 626-9773. This company offers private and shared-van service to and from MCO.
- *Lynx.* Operated by the Central Florida Regional Transportation Authority, this scheduled bus service travels

from the airport to downtown Orlando or the International Drive area. The fare is only $1.50 per person and the ride takes between 40 and 60 minutes, depending on your destination. The bus stop at MCO is located on Level 1, outside of the main terminal building (in commercial lane parking spaces A31 through A34). For more information, visit www.golynx.com or call (407) 841-LYNX.

- *Mears Transportation Group*—www.mearstransportation.com, (407) 423-5566. This company offers a wide range of transportation services to and from the airport, as well as throughout the Orlando area. Shared-van service offers more economical transportation to and from the airport, while the company's private sedan (limo or town car service) offers a more luxurious way to travel. Traditional taxi service is also available. For large groups, charter bus service is available.

TIP
The most convenient and luxurious way to get to and from the airport is via a private chauffeured limousine or town car. More than 100 limousine companies, including Mears Transportation Group (407-423-5566, www.mears transportation.com) and Carey Transportation of Orlando (407-855-0442), operate in the Orlando area (see Section IV, "Getting Around Town," for a listing). Plan to spend between $50 and $85 per hour (plus tolls and tip) for a chauffeured limo.

Taxi Service

The Orlando area is serviced by more than a dozen privately owned and operated taxi companies. Just outside of the main terminal building at the airport, on level 1, you'll find a taxi dispatcher and designated taxi stand where you can hail a cab to any location within the Orlando area. See Section IV, "Getting Around Town," for more information about traveling within Orlando via taxi.

TIP
When riding in a taxi, be sure to write down the medallion number of the vehicle. If you need to file a complaint or retrieve lost items, this information will be helpful. Be sure to ask for and keep your receipt.

AVERAGE TAXI FARES BETWEEN POPULAR DESTINATIONS AND MCO

Mears Transportation, which provides luxury sedan, shuttle bus and van, motor coach (bus), and taxicab services to and from the Orlando International Airport and throughout the Orlando area, offers an online fare estimator, which you can utilize by visiting www.mearstransportation.com/TaxiFareEstimator.asp. You can also call (407) 422-2222 for information. Mears operates a fleet of more than 530 taxicabs in the Orlando area.

AVERAGE TAXI FARES FROM MCO

DESTINATION	AVERAGE TAXI FARE (excluding tolls and tips)
Downtown Orlando	$35
Gaylord Palms Convention Center	$45
Hyatt Grand Cypress	$43
International Drive area	$33 to $39
Kissimmee	$43 to $60
Lake Buena Vista	$47
Nearby airport hotels	$12
Orange County Convention Center	$31
Peabody Hotel (International Drive)	$31
Port Canaveral	$105
Portofino Bay Hotel at Universal Orlando	$37
Walt Disney World Resort	$52 to $60

TIP
Private car and chauffeured limousine service is available from multiple companies to and from MCO. Listings for limousine and town car services can be found in Section IV, "Getting Around Town."

Rental Cars

The following popular rental car companies have customer service counters located on level 1 of the airport's main terminal building. While it's best to reserve your car in advance in order to ensure availability and get the best rates, you can often rent a car simply by approaching one of these companies customer service counters at the airport.

Allow between 20 and 45 minutes for checking in and picking up your car, depending on crowds. When applicable, rental car shuttle buses board from outside of the main terminal building (Level 1). Follow the appropriate signs for your rental car company.

- Alamo—(800) 832-7933
- Avis—(800) 230-4898
- Budget—(800) 527-0700
- Dollar—(800) 800-4000
- Enterprise—(800) 736-8222
- L&M Car Rental—(800) 277-5171
- Hertz—(800) 654-3131
- National Car Rental—(800) 227-7368
- Thrifty—(800) 367-2277

While all of these rental car companies have customer service counters on-site, some companies, like Hertz, require travelers to take a short complimentary shuttle bus ride to actually pick up or drop off their vehicle. Companies like Alamo, Avis, Budget, Dollar, and National allow you to pick up and drop off your vehicle in the parking garage located directly across the street from the main terminal building. Additional rental car companies are listed in Section IV, "Getting Around Town."

Amtrak Service to and from Orlando

Phone number: (800) USA-RAIL
Web site: www.amtrak.com

Yet another popular, convenient, efficient, and cost-effective way to travel to Orlando from various nearby cities and states is via Amtrak train. The Amtrak railroad station in Orlando is located at 1400 Sligh Boulevard. Depending on where you're traveling from, Amtrak's Sunset Limited or Silver Service (Palmetto) makes stops in Orlando.

The Amtrak Sunset Limited offers coast-to-coast service between Los Angeles, California, and Orlando, with stops in the following cities: Los Angeles, Pomona, Ontario, and North Palm Springs, California; Yuma, Maricopa, Tucson, and Benson, Arizona; Lordsburg and Deming, New Mexico; El Paso, Alpine, Sanderson, Del Rio, San Antonio, Houston, and Beaumont, Texas; Lake Charles, Lafayette, New Iberia, Schriever, and New Orleans, Louisiana; Bay Saint Louis, Gulfport, Biloxi, and Pascagoula, Mississippi; Mobile and Atmore, Alabama; and Pensacola, Crestview, Chipley, Tallahassee, Madison, Lake City, Jacksonville, Palatka, Deland, Winter Park, and Orlando, Florida. Three trains depart weekly in each direction. Services on the Sunset Limited include Superliner sleeping and dining car accommodations. The trip between Los Angeles and Orlando takes approximately 68 hours.

The Amtrak Silver Service (Palmetto) travels up and down the East Coast, starting at New York City's Pennsylvania Railroad Station and continuing to Miami, Florida (with stops in both Orlando and Kissimmee). From New York City, this train also makes stops in Newark and Trenton, New Jersey; Philadelphia, Pennsylvania; Wilmington, Delaware; Baltimore, Maryland; Washington, DC; Alexandria, Richmond, and Petersburg, Virginia; Rocky Mount, Wilson, Selma, and Raleigh, North Carolina; Fayetteville, Dillon, Florence, Kingstree, North Charleston, and Yemassee, South Carolina; Southern Pines and Hamlet, North Carolina; Camden, Columbia, and Denmark, South Carolina; Savannah and Jesup, Georgia; and Jacksonville, Palatka, Deland, Winter Park, Orlando, and Kissimmee, Florida. The train departs daily in both directions. The duration of the trip between New York City and Orlando is approximately 28 hours. Sleeper and dining car services are available.

Be sure to make Amtrak reservations in advance, especially if you're looking to reserve a sleeper car.

TIP
Between Lorton, Virginia, and Sanford, Florida, Amtrak offers its Auto Train service, which allows you to take your car, van, motorcycle, SUV, small boat, or other vehicle from just outside Washington, DC, to Sanford, Florida (a short drive from Orlando). Trains depart daily. The trip duration is approximately 16.5 hours.

Bus Service to and from Orlando

In addition to driving, taking the train, or flying to Orlando (from nearby cities), another option is to take a bus. This is one of the least expensive travel options, but it is also often one of the least convenient and slowest forms of travel.

For more information about bus service to and from Orlando, call Greyhound Bus (800-231-2222), Bonanza Bus (800-556-3815), Grayline Bus (212-397-2620), or Peter Pan Lines (800-343-9999) directly.

The Lynx (www.golynx.com, 407-841-LYNX) is the public bus transportation system that operates throughout Orlando and surrounding areas.

FREQUENT FLIER MILES—A BUSINESS TRAVELER'S BEST FRIEND

If you find yourself doing a considerable amount of personal and/or business travel, you may be able to take advantage of one of the best perks offered by airlines, hotels, rental car companies, and some major credit card issuers—the ability to accrue frequent flier miles. Simply by flying with the same airline, staying at the same name hotel, or using the same rental car company when you travel, you can acquire miles or points that can later be redeemed for free airline tickets, upgrades, free accommodations at hotels, or other perks.

Virtually every major airline offers its own frequent flier program, which you can register for, free of charge, by filling out a form online (by visiting the airline's web site) or at the airport (speak with an airline representative at the ticket counter). Contact your favorite airline for details. In addition to earning miles by flying, you can also earn miles by doing business with the airline's promotional partners, which include specific credit card companies, hotels, rental car companies, and a wide range of other businesses.

Once you accrue a predetermined number of frequent flier miles with each airline, you'll also receive preferred status, which entitles you to additional perks, such as the ability to use special airport check-in counters (with much shorter lines), special toll-free reservation numbers (which don't require you to wait on hold), and complimentary upgrades to first class when you travel using a coach ticket.

Many hotel chains and rental car companies offer their own frequent traveler programs that allow customers to earn free accommodations, upgraded rooms, free meals, and other benefits, or automatic upgrades to their rental car. The points you receive from these programs can also often be redeemed for airline frequent flier miles and used for free travel.

Savvy business travelers learn how to maximize their frequent flier points by doing the majority of their travel with one airline (and then utilizing their favorite airline's partners to earn extra miles). Simply charging everyday business expenses to a specific credit card that awards frequent flier miles, for example, is another quick way to build up additional mileage or points.

TIP
As you travel for business or pleasure, be sure to register for frequent flier program of each airline that you travel with plus register for frequent traveler programs offered by the hotel chains and rental car companies you utilize. Be sure to keep a list of your membership numbers handy so you can receive credit for all of your travels and earn rewards faster. You can use the worksheet on page 284 in the Appendix to organize this information.

To help manage all of your frequent flier and frequent traveler memberships, or to obtain details about the various special offers from airlines, hotels, and rental car companies, visit the FrequentFlier.com web site (www.frequentflier.com). From this free site, you can review the terms of each popular frequent flier or traveler program, learn how to maximize your mileage or point collection by using travel partners and affiliates associated with each program, and subscribe to a free newsletter.

It's important to understand that when you join any of these programs, the ultimate goal is not to collect the miles or points themselves, but to trade in or redeem the points for the most valuable perks and benefits possible—whether it's free travel or upgrades, for example. One way to earn extra miles is to carefully read the membership newsletter published by the airline or hotel chain to learn about special promotions that allow you to quickly earn miles or points. If you utilize certain flights, travel dates, or promotional partners, you could earn double or triple miles for your travel.

WARNING
Every airline's frequent flier program has various rules and limitations. For instance, most airlines won't award frequent flier miles for airline tickets purchased through a

discounted online travel service. Also, it is possible for accrued miles or points to expire after a predetermined period. To avoid losing the points or miles you've collected, be sure to redeem them in a timely manner.

The following is a list of the popular frequent flier or frequent traveler programs offered by the major airlines and hotel chains. Ideally, you want to join the appropriate rewards program prior to booking your travel reservations; however, you can also often be credited for miles or points if you join after completing your travel.

Once you join one or more of these programs and begin accruing miles or points, you too will see how much fun and addictive it can be, especially when you get to reap the benefits of your frequent traveling and start to receive free travel, perks, and rewards.

POPULAR FREQUENT TRAVEL PROGRAMS

AIRLINE/HOTEL CHAIN	PROGRAM NAME	WEB SITE
Air Canada	Aeroplan	www.aeroplan.com/home.do
AirTran	A Plus Rewards	www.aplusrewards.com/a_rewards_more_rewarding.aspx
Alaska Airlines	Mileage Plan	www.alaskaair.com/mileageplan/
American Airlines	AAdvantage	www.aa.com/apps/AAdvantage/AAdvantageHome.jhtml
ATA	Travel Awards	www.ata.com/awards/index.html
Continental	OnePass	www.continental.com/web/en-US/content/onepass/default.aspx
Delta	SkyMiles	www.delta.com/skymiles/index.jsp
Independence Air	iClub	www.flyi.com/iclub/iclub_home.jsp
JetBlue	TrueBlue	www.jetblue.com/trueblue
Northwest Airlines	WorldPerks	www.nwa.com/freqfly/
Southwest Airlines	Rapid Rewards	www.southwest.com/rapid_rewards/rapid_rewards.html
United Airlines	Mileage Plus	www.united.com/page/middlepage/0,1454,1136,00.html
U.S. Airways	Dividend Miles	www.usairways.com/awa/content/dividendmiles/default.aspx
Best Western	Gold Crown Club	www.goldcrownclub.com

AIRLINE/HOTEL CHAIN	PROGRAM NAME	WEB SITE
AmeriHost, Days Inn, Howard Johnson, Knights Inn, Ramada, Super 8, Travelodge, Villager, Wingate Inn	TripRewards	www.triprewards.com
Hilton	HHonors	http://hhonors.hilton.com/en/hhonors/index.jhtml
Hyatt Hotels	Hyatt Gold Passport	http://goldpassport.hyatt.com/gp/en/index.jsp
InterContinental, Crowne Plaza, Holiday Inn, Holiday Inn Express, Staybridge Suites	Priority Club Rewards	www.ichotelsgroup.com/h/d/pc/1/en/home
Marriott, Renaissance, Courtyard, Residence Inn, Fairfield Inn, TownePlace Suites, Ritz-Carlton, Ramada	Marriott Rewards	http://marriott.com/rewards/rewards-program.mi
Westin, Sheraton, Four Points, St. Regis, Luxury Collection, W Hotels	Preferred Guest	www.starwoodhotels.com/preferredguest/index.html
Wyndham, Summerfield Suites	ByRequest	www.wyndham.com/wbr/wbr_signin.wnt?

Donate Your Miles and Help a Worthy Cause

Many of the major airlines, including American Airlines, Continental, Delta, Midwest Express, United, and Virgin Atlantic, allow frequent fliers to donate their accrued miles to charities, such as the Make-a-Wish Foundation, the United Way, the Red Cross, the Special Olympics, the Adam Walsh Children's Fund, and CARE. When you donate your miles, free airlines tickets and other benefits are granted to people who need them. In many cases, the airline will match your miles donation. For details about these programs, contact your airline's frequent flier membership office.

Manage Your Miles

To help you keep track of your frequent flier and frequent traveler memberships, use the Frequent Traveler Program Worksheet in the Appendix. Otherwise, you'll need to travel with and keep all of your individual membership cards handy.

TRAVEL NOTES

SECTION II

©Norman Pegson

PACKING FOR YOUR
BUSINESS TRIP

When you're traveling for business, preparation is one of the keys to enjoying a stress-free trip. One way to prepare is to select the most suitable luggage and then carefully pack everything you'll need. Finding suitable luggage that's rugged, well built, and designed for what you are transporting is important, but not always as easy as it may seem. As you start shopping for luggage, you'll quickly discover many similar-looking bags at vastly different price points.

SHOPPING FOR THE PERFECT LUGGAGE

The first step to choosing appropriate luggage is to determine your needs. Figure out what you'll be carrying and how long you typically travel (from one to three days, from three to five days, or a week or longer). In your checked luggage, will you be packing several business suits that can easily get wrinkled, or more casual attire? Knowing this will help you determine the size, design, and number of bags you should purchase to meet your unique needs.

TIP
Many pieces of luggage designed for business travelers by high-end companies, such as Zero Halliburton (www.zerohalliburton.com) and Tumi (www.tumi.com), have special compartments designed to hold suits and other clothing that you want to remain wrinkle free. The Zero Halliburton 24-inch Expandable Upright with Suiter, for example, is made from extremely durable material and has a separate compartment for two or three business suits, as well as built-in wheels and an expandable handle. It is ideal for a trip of between three and seven days. Similar designs are also available in 20-, 22-, 27-, and 29-inch sizes to accommodate a wide range of packing needs. You can mix and match bag styles to create a luggage set that's ideal for you.

The luggage you select should be easy to transport. After all, you'll need to navigate your way through busy airports, down long hotel hallways, and in and out of cars or taxis. Doing this with poorly designed luggage can put added stress on your back, neck, and arms. Plus, you don't want your luggage to fall apart midtrip.

Soft-sided luggage with durable wheels is often ideal for businesspeople on the go. This type of luggage tends to weigh less than traditional hard-bodied suitcases, which is important, since all major airlines now have strict weight restrictions for checked luggage. Bags weighing more than 50 pounds are each subject to a surcharge of $25, $50, $100, or more, depending on the airline.

Passengers are also limited to checking only two or three bags (depending on the airline). Each additional bag is subject to a fee of $50, $100, or more. It's important that the luggage you choose be able to hold everything you'll need to have with you yet meet your airline's requirements.

The construction of a bag is as important as its design. Ideally, you want luggage designed to take a beating yet remain strong.

You'll pay a bit extra for bags with strong and padded handles, durable wheels that glide smoothly, well-sewn seams, and heavy-duty zippers, and that are made from extra-strong material, such as ballistic nylon or napa leather. But over the long term, these bags will last much longer than their less expensive counterparts and keep their contents safer.

TIP
When evaluating luggage, consider the interior design of each bag. Does the luggage have enough pockets and compartments to accommodate your needs? Will it allow you to keep your toiletries separate (in case of spillage)? Also, is the bag comfortable to carry or pull? Are the handles durable, padded, and located in the best possible places?

By visiting a specialty luggage store or high-end department store, you'll be able to see top-quality, name-brand luggage from a variety of manufacturers. Remember, when it comes to the price of the bag, make sure you're paying for top-quality construction, not just for a designer name. Each popular luggage manufacturer typically offers several product lines with different looks, color schemes, designs, and levels of construction quality. If you take only one business trip per year, you may be able to purchase less expensive and lower-quality luggage. However, if you travel often, you should invest in durable luggage that will last.

TIP
If you're buying luggage with wheels, make sure the wheels are well made, spin smoothly, are quiet when they roll, and don't wobble. Remember, when the bag is full, you'll be pulling or carrying up to 50 pounds. Also, focus on the durability of the bag's handles and zippers, as well as the material used for the bag's overall construction.

The last factors to consider are the look of the bags and the color scheme, as well as how the various bags in the set interconnect for easy transport. Many larger bags on wheels have hooks that allow you to easily attach smaller bags. Just because the manufacturer offers a set of luggage with five or six bags in different sizes and styles, this doesn't mean you need to purchase all of these bags. Pick and choose the bag styles that best meet your needs.

TIP
As soon as you've purchased your luggage, make sure you fill out and securely attach luggage tags with, at least, your full name and phone number. (Listing your address and cell phone number is optional.) It's also important to place your contact information *inside* each checked bag. This will make it easier to recover your belongings if the bag gets lost in transit or the luggage tag falls off.

When shopping for luggage, check out luggage sets by several manufacturers. Be sure to ask about the luggage's warranty and determine the process for getting bags repaired. Some luggage companies charge a minimum of $100 per bag (plus shipping), even for a basic repair. Remember, many bags from different manufacturers look very similar but have very different construction quality and overall value. It's important to carefully evaluate luggage firsthand to make sure it fits your needs before purchasing it.

Zero Halliburton (www.zerohalliburton.com) and Tumi (www.tumi.com) are two manufacturers that offer multiple lines of high-end, well-constructed, and extremely well-designed luggage that's ideal for business travelers. Both offer pieces created from durable ballistic nylon (also used to create bulletproof vests), as well as premium-quality, ultra-soft, yet very durable napa leather.

TIP
Because many pieces of luggage look similar, creative travelers often use brightly colored luggage tags or place colorful ribbons around their bags' handles to set them apart. This will help ensure the wrong person doesn't accidentally retrieve any of your luggage at an airport's baggage claim area, for example.

Some of the other popular luggage manufacturers that offer designs for frequent business travelers include:

- American Tourister (www.americantourister.com)
- Delsey (www.delseyusa.com)

- Hartmann (www.hartmann.com)
- Kipling (www.kipling.com)
- Louis Vuitton (www.louisvuitton.com)
- Samsonite (www.samsonite.com)
- Skyway Luggage Company (www.skywayluggage.com)
- TravelPro USA (www.travelpro.com)

WARNING
Because of heightened airport security, it is no longer advisable to lock your luggage, even with TSA-approved luggage locks. If your luggage is hand searched, the locks will be cut off and discarded by security personnel. Never pack any valuables in your luggage that could be lost or stolen. Valuables should be kept in a carry-on bag or shipped in advance. In addition, when staying at a hotel, instead of locking your luggage, take advantage of the in-room safe available at most high-end hotels to protect your valuables.

PACKING TIPS FOR BUSINESS TRAVELERS

Now that you've selected the ideal luggage for your trip, you want to ensure that you pack everything you'll want and need while you're away. This section offers useful packing tips and a detailed packing list.

Most business travelers have one or more large pieces of luggage that will be checked with the airline plus one carry-on bag (and a personal item, such as a laptop case or purse).

In your carry-on, be sure to pack anything and everything you'll need during your flight or immediately after you land. If you are landing at your destination and immediately attending an important meeting, have everything with you for that meeting. It's become an all-too-common occurrence for checked luggage to get lost or temporarily delayed, and you don't want this to affect your meeting.

As a general rule, refrain from overstuffing your bags to the point where they're difficult to close or, when opened, your belongings spill out. When TSA officers search your bags, they should be easy to open and close.

When packing casual clothes, rolling them (as opposed to folding them) helps save space and prevent wrinkles. For your business attire, use luggage with a special "suiter" compartment. For items you want to keep wrinkle free, learn how to properly fold them, then place them within the bag in an area where they won't be crushed. As an added precaution, consider wrapping liquid or gel items (such as shampoo, perfume, toothpaste, or liquid cosmetics) in individual sealable plastic bags or in sealable plastic containers, like Tupperware®.

WARNING
Be mindful of the changing list of items the TSA does not permit within checked or carry-on luggage. For an up-to-date list of prohibited items, point your web browser to www.tsa.gov/travelers/index.shtm.

Shoe polish or dirt from your shoes can easily rub off onto your clothing and create permanent stains. Wrapping your shoes in a soft shoe bag, separate from your clothing, can help prevent this. To help maintain the shape of your shoes and keep them from getting crushed, insert a wooden shoe tree or stuff rolled socks into each shoe.

TIP
If you're packing books, printed brochures, or other heavy paper-based items, spread them out in your luggage. Don't pile them in a corner, for example. You want to keep the weight evenly distributed within your luggage.

ORLANDO WEATHER

The weather in Orlando is typically mild, although it can be extremely sunny, humid, and hot in the summer months (June, July, and August). During the spring and fall months, the climate in Orlando tends to be very pleasant, although you can expect sudden (albeit short) rain showers or even thunderstorms in the afternoons. During the winter, the temperature can drop into the high 40s or low 50s, especially at night, so be sure to pack accordingly.

TIP
For up-to-date weather forecasts, point your web browser to www.weather.com, www.orlandoinfo.com/other/weather/index.cfm, or www.cnn.com/weather.

Before packing, obtain an extended weather forecast for Orlando, and if necessary, pack an extra sweater, windbreaker, or sweatshirt. To protect yourself from the sun, even on overcast days, be sure to wear a hat, sunglasses, and sunscreen whenever you're outdoors.

The following chart lists the average temperatures in Orlando throughout the year.

AVERAGE TEMPERATURES FOR ORLANDO, FLORIDA				
Month	High Temperature (Fahrenheit)	Low Temperature (Fahrenheit)	Precipitation (in inches)	Humidity (%)
January	70.8	48.6	2.30	56
February	72.7	49.7	3.02	52
March	72.7	49.7	3.02	52
April	83.0	59.4	1.80	46
May	87.8	65.9	3.55	49
June	90.5	71.8	7.32	57
July	91.5	73.1	7.25	58
August	91.5	73.4	6.78	60
September	89.7	72.4	6.01	60
October	84.6	65.8	2.42	56
November	78.5	57.5	2.30	56
December	72.9	51.3	2.15	57

TIP
Regardless of the temperature outside, inside the hotels, restaurants, theaters, and convention centers you'll probably encounter air-conditioning. So pack accordingly.

PACKING FOR YOUR TRIP

The following is a comprehensive list you can use when packing for your trip. Don't forget to pack any additional work-related items not already listed here.

Remember: Never pack any personal electronics, a laptop computer, a camera, important business papers, jewelry, eyeglasses, antiques, business equipment, or other expensive items within your checked luggage. These items are *not* covered by the airline if they're lost, damaged, or stolen.

PACKING CHECKLIST

Packed	Item/Garment	Quantity Needed
❏	Airline tickets, travel itinerary, confirmation letters	
❏	Allergy medication	
❏	Bathing suits and poolwear	
❏	Batteries	
❏	Belt(s)	
❏	Blouses	
❏	Books and magazines	
❏	Boots	
❏	Business cards	
❏	Business organizer	
❏	Camera and film (or memory cards and batteries)	
❏	Casual shirts	
❏	Cell phone (including charger and headset)	
❏	Coat	
❏	Cufflinks	
❏	Data CDs	
❏	Day planner/appointment book/address book	
❏	Deodorant	
❏	Dress shirts	
❏	Dress shoes	
❏	Dresses and gowns	
❏	Eyeglasses and contact lenses	
❏	Golf clubs	
❏	Hair care products	
❏	Hairbrush and grooming products	
❏	Hat or cap	
❏	Health insurance card	
❏	ID (driver's license or passport)	
❏	iPod (MP3 player) and headphones	
❏	Jacket or windbreaker	
❏	Jewelry and fashion accessories	
❏	Laptop and accessories (including charger)	
❏	Lingerie	
❏	Makeup and cosmetics	
❏	Moisturizer	
❏	Nail care items	
❏	Neckties	
❏	Over-the-counter medications and vitamins	
❏	Perfume or cologne	
❏	Personal digital assistant (including charger)	
❏	Prepaid calling cards	
❏	Prescription medications	
❏	Product brochures, press kits, and sales literature	

PACKING CHECKLIST

Packed	Item/Garment	Quantity Needed
❏	Purses	
❏	Scarf	
❏	Shaver (razor) and blades, shaving cream, etc.	
❏	Shorts	
❏	Sleepwear	
❏	Sneakers	
❏	Socks (white and colored)	
❏	Sport coat	
❏	Suits (formal business attire)	
❏	Sunscreen/sunblock (high SPF rating)	
❏	Sunglasses	
❏	Tampons and sanitary napkins	
❏	Toothbrush, toothpaste, and dental floss	
❏	Travel alarm clock	
❏	Trousers (pants, jeans, etc.)	
❏	T-shirts	
❏	Undershirts	
❏	Underwear	
❏	Video camera (including charger and accessories)	
❏	Walking shoes	
❏	Wallet (credit cards, cash, traveler's checks)	
❏	Watch	
❏	Workout clothes	
❏	Work-related papers, reports, proposals, and files	
❏	Other:	
❏	Other:	
❏	Other:	
❏	Other:	
❏	Other:	
❏	Other:	
❏	Other:	

TIP

If you have multiple pieces of consumer electronics that will need to be charged, such as your laptop, cell phone, headset, PDA, and iPod, consider packing your own power strip. Few hotels offer an ample number of conveniently located and accessible electrical outlets to meet the needs of most business travelers.

TIP
Whether you're attending a convention or exploring Orlando and the theme parks, you'll be doing a lot of walking! You'll want to wear extremely comfortable walking shoes or sneakers.

TIP
Business meetings, conventions, and seminars are all excellent networking opportunities. Don't forget to pack a large supply of your business cards and carry a nice business card holder. The business card holder should also have a pocket for storing the business cards you collect from others. If you need business cards printed quickly while in Orlando, refer to Section IX, "Business Services."

Packing Checklist for Your Carry-On Bag

Remember, anything you may want or need during the flight should be placed in your carry-on and brought with you onto the aircraft. Use this checklist to help you make sure you have all you might need.

CARRY-ON BAG PACKING LIST	
❏	Airline tickets, boarding passes, and your travel itinerary
❏	All personal electronics (iPod, PDA, etc.)
❏	Business equipment
❏	Business papers and work-related items
❏	Camera
❏	Cell phone (and charger)
❏	Change of clothing
❏	Eyeglasses or contact lenses
❏	Headphones
❏	Jewelry
❏	Keys
❏	Laptop (including DVDs you might want to watch during the flight)
❏	Paper and pen
❏	Photo identification
❏	Prescription medications
❏	Reading material (books and/or magazines)
❏	Wallet (money, credit cards, traveler's checks, etc.)

WARNING
The TSA has imposed restrictions on bringing more than three ounces of liquids or gels aboard flights. This includes everything from drinks to shampoo. (Prescription medications can still be carried onto the plane but are subject to inspection.) Other items—such as lighters, chemicals, and any sharp instruments (including pocketknives, scissors, tools, and nail clippers)—continue to be prohibited. See the TSA's web site (www.tsa.gov) to learn about the latest restrictions. Drinks, including bottled water, may be purchased at the airport *after* you pass through security.

Optional Items

To make a long flight more relaxing, consider investing in a pair of noise-canceling headphones. These headphones can be connected to your iPod, laptop, or the aircraft's in-flight entertainment system to reduce most outside noise, such as babies crying and the roar of the aircraft's engine.

Noise-canceling headphones may allow you to sleep better during a flight or better enjoy whatever in-flight entertainment you have planned. The cost of noise-canceling headphones is between $100 and $400. They're available from companies such as Bose (www.bose.com), Shure (www.shure.com), Sharper Image (www.sharperimage.com), and Brookstone (www.brookstone.com). This is a must-have accessory for frequent business travelers.

Several different models of Shure Sound Isolating Earphones are now available. Each offers superior sound quality and allows you to truly enjoy what you're listening to. These Shure products are also lightweight and extremely comfortable to wear. Similar products from Bose, for example, are more cumbersome to travel with because of their size and shape.

TIP
If you find your ears getting clogged during flights, EarPlanes by Cirrus Air Technologies (800-EAR-6151 or www.cirrushealthcare.com) offer an inexpensive solution. These reusable earplugs are designed to regulate air pressure in your ears naturally. They sell for about $5 per pair and are available from pharmacies nationwide. They're particularly useful if you're suffering from a cold, flu, or allergies.

Keeping Healthy

Worried about catching a cold or getting sick while traveling? One way to help prevent this is to take Airborne, an all-natural herbal supplement designed for business travelers. Simply add one of these orange-flavored tablets to a glass of water and drink. You can take Airborne every three hours, as needed, as a dietary supplement. It's an excellent tool if you're starting to feel the onset of cold- or flu-like symptoms, or as a preventive measure. For more information, point your web browser to www.airbornehealth.com.

BEFORE-LEAVING-HOME CHECKLIST

The following are some tasks you may want to complete before leaving on your business trip:

BEFORE-LEAVING-HOME CHECKLIST	
Completed	Task
❏	Adjust the thermostat
❏	Arrange for the care and feeding of your pet(s)
❏	Call a taxi or limo service to schedule ground transportation to and from the airport
❏	Contact the post office and put your mail on hold
❏	Discard any refrigerated items that will spoil while you're away
❏	Double-check your packing list and ensure everything you need is packed in your suitcase or carry-on
❏	Go to the bank to get cash and/or traveler's checks
❏	Leave a copy of your travel itinerary with a friend, relative, your secretary, boss, and/or co-workers (as appropriate)
❏	Lock your windows and doors
❏	Pay your household bills
❏	Record your "away" voice-mail message at work
❏	Take out the trash
❏	Set the burglar alarm
❏	Set your at work e-mail account's auto responder with an "away" message
❏	Set your TiVo, VCR, or DVR to record your favorite shows while you're away
❏	Stop any deliveries to your home while you're away
❏	Turn off all unnecessary appliances and electronics
❏	Water your plants

SECTION III

Photo © TheSupe87

WHERE TO STAY WHILE IN
ORLANDO

When it comes to accommodations in the Orlando area, you'll find a vast selection. In addition to hundreds of inexpensive chain motels and hotels that offer nicely furnished rooms for under $100 per night, you'll find a wide selection of upscale, business-friendly hotels plus many world-class resorts (many of which have their own golf courses and day spas). Orlando also offers time-share resort properties (that also offer nightly accommodations) as well as the opportunity to stay in a fully furnished, multibedroom townhouse or apartment.

In the Orlando area, the average room rate at a three-star, business-friendly hotel is $100 to $150 per night. For a luxury suite or townhouse at a top-rated hotel or resort (such as the Peabody or the Ginn Reunion Resort), it's easy to spend $300 to $800 (or considerably more) per night for accommodations.

For the past several decades, Orlando has been primarily a vacation destination. Hence, while many of the hotels, resorts, and motels offer comfortable accommodations, only recently have some of these properties begun to target business travelers by offering amenities and services like high-speed internet access, an on-site business center, concierge-level business suites, and/or a desk and work area (with plenty of nearby electrical outlets) within the guestrooms. While most properties offer plenty of comforts for vacationers and tourists, if you'll be visiting Orlando for business purposes, be sure that the accommodations you choose include the business-related amenities and services you want and need; otherwise, you could find yourself in an extremely comfortable and luxurious guestroom, but not be able to access the internet or conduct an important conference call from the room's telephone.

If, like many business travelers, you're planning to bring your family along to Orlando to make this a "working vacation," be sure the accommodations you choose cater both to your business needs as well as to your family's needs. As you'll discover, there is a wide range of resort properties, like the Ginn Reunion Resort, JW Marriott, and Rosen Shingle Creek Resort, that expertly cater to business travelers and vacationers alike.

One thing to consider when choosing your hotel is its location. The majority of hotels are located in one of the following areas:

- Downtown Orlando
- International Drive (near the Orange Country Convention Center, Universal Orlando, and SeaWorld)
- Kissimmee
- Lake Buena Vista (Walt Disney World) and Celebration
- Orlando International Airport

Consider where you will be conducting the majority of your business while visiting the Orlando area. If you'll be attending a trade show at the Orange County Convention Center and dining at some of the fine restaurants along International Drive, for example, you can save a lot of time by choosing a hotel (such as the

Peabody) that's close by. Likewise, if you're attending an event at the Walt Disney World (WDW) Resort, you can choose from dozens of hotels and resorts located near the Disney theme parks. Staying at a hotel or resort that's not close to the event, meeting, trade show or convention you'll be attending will result in a lot of extra traveling, for which you will definitely need a rental car.

Room rates within the Orlando area are based on a variety of factors, including:

- *The type of guestroom or suite requested.* Most basic hotel guestrooms consist of a single bedroom containing one king-size or two queen-size beds, a small desk (work area), a TV, a dresser, a closet, and a bathroom. Larger suites might contain a separate sitting area, foyer, living room, kitchenette, terrace, one or more bathrooms, plus one or more separate bedrooms.
- *The view offered from the guestroom.* Rooms overlooking a lake, golf course, or one of the theme parks, for example, typically cost more.
- *Whether the room is located on the concierge floor (offered only at some hotels).* Rooms or suites on these floors cost more, but as a guest you're entitled to visit an exclusive VIP lounge where drinks, snacks, and sometimes full meals are served. Additional amenities and services for business travelers are also provided.
- *The overall quality of the hotel and the services and amenities offered.*
- *The time of year.* Expect to pay premium rates during peak travel times, such as holidays and during the winter months.
- *The overall current occupancy of the hotel and neighboring hotels.* The overall supply and demand for rooms in the area impact the cost of accommodations.

MONEY SAVER

If you use an online service, such as Hotels.com (www.hotels.com), Travelocity.com (www.travelocity.com), or Hotwire.com (www.hotwire.com), it's often possible to obtain accommodations in Orlando at top-rated hotels for up to 30 to 60 percent off. When making your reservation, be sure to check the hotel's own web site for current rates, ask about discounts for AAA or AARP members, for example, then check the rates being offered on the popular online travel-related services. Keep in mind that each online travel service uses different criteria for categorizing a hotel as a three-, four-, or five-star property. Make sure you understand the criteria being used.

CHOOSE YOUR ACCOMMODATIONS BASED ON AMENITIES AND SERVICES OFFERED

In Orlando, accommodations come in the form of basic (low-cost) motels, traditional (moderately priced to expensive) hotels, luxury resorts, and mid- to high-priced time-share and vacation rental properties. Your choices are plentiful regardless of your needs, wants, and budget.

Most upscale hotels and resorts in Orlando proudly offer a wide range of amenities and services that are in demand by business travelers, such as high-speed internet access, a fitness center, a business center, concierge services, in-room flat-screen televisions (with cable TV programming), extremely comfortable beds, ample desk space in the guestrooms for working, multiple phone lines, and 24-hour room service. Thus, what sets the most luxurious hotels apart is their commitment to customer service, their overall décor, their location, and the collection of services and amenities they offer.

MONEY SAVER
At the same time you determine which services and amenities are being offered by the hotel you select, determine if you'll be charged extra to utilize them. For example, many hotels charge extra for high-speed (or Wi-Fi) internet access, overnight parking, and use of the hotel's fitness center. You could wind up spending $50 to $100 or more per night on basic amenities.

Business Amenities and Services to Look For

When choosing where to stay in Orlando, consider the amenities and business services you want and need. The following checklist will help you evaluate your needs and find accommodations that'll make your stay as comfortable as possible. Many of the *Business Traveler* Top 15 Business-Friendly Hotels listed later in this section provide most or all of these services and amenities.

Within the nicer Orlando-area hotels, you'll find the majority of the following popular amenities and services being offered. Expect to pay extra, however, for amenities like high-speed internet access, valet parking, pay-per-view in-room movies, long-distance telephone calls, and dry cleaning services, for instance.

The following is a list of amenities to look for that can help make your hotel stay more convenient and comfortable.

BUSINESS AMENITIES CHECKLIST

- ❏ Ability to earn frequent flier miles for your stay
- ❏ Ample work space (including a desk) within the room
- ❏ Business center (equipped with computers, printers, fax machines, and copiers, in addition to the ability to ship packages via UPS, FedEx, DHL, etc.)
- ❏ Cell phone reception within the room
- ❏ Close proximity to the convention center, banquet hall, or meeting facility hosting your event
- ❏ Coffee machine (in room)
- ❏ Complimentary soaps, shampoo, and toiletries
- ❏ Concierge service (available 24 hours)
- ❏ Dry cleaning and laundry service
- ❏ Easy access to public transportation
- ❏ Express check-in and checkout
- ❏ Fax machine (in room)
- ❏ Hair dryer (in room)
- ❏ Health club and workout facility (open 24 hours)
- ❏ High-speed internet and Wi-Fi wireless internet (expect to pay between $9.95 and $19.95 per 24-hour period for internet access in most Orlando-area hotel guestrooms)
- ❏ Iron and ironing board (in room)
- ❏ Meeting room availability
- ❏ Minibar/refrigerator (in room)
- ❏ Multiple electrical outlets in the room (with several located near the desk)
- ❏ Multiple in-room phone lines
- ❏ Newspaper delivery to your guestroom
- ❏ Night-time turndown maid service
- ❏ On-site restaurant(s)
- ❏ Cotton or terry cloth robes (in room)
- ❏ Room service (available 24 hours)
- ❏ Spa and salon
- ❏ Starbucks Coffee or coffee shop in the lobby (or nearby)
- ❏ Valet parking

TIME SAVER
If the services and amenities you want or need aren't readily available at your hotel, see Section IX, "Business Services," and Section X, "Personal Services," within this guide for details on how and where to quickly find what you need. You could also contact your hotel's concierge.

THE *BUSINESS TRAVELER* TOP 15 BUSINESS-FRIENDLY HOTELS IN ORLANDO

Out of all the hotels in the area, listed here (in alphabetical order) are the *Entrepreneur Magazine's Business Traveler* Top 15

BROADBAND INTERNET ACCESS FROM ANYWHERE

If you're a frequent business traveler, you've probably gotten used to paying $15 to $30 per day for high-speed internet access from your hotel room, assuming the hotel where you're staying offers internet access and you're able to configure your laptop computer to connect properly. After three or four days staying at hotels, your internet charges start really adding up.

One way to lower your internet access charges while traveling, plus virtually guarantee you'll have high-speed access to the web from wherever you're staying, is to purchase a wireless broadband modem or PC card for your laptop, and subscribe to wireless internet service from a company like Sprint PCS (www.sprint.com), Verizon Wireless (www.verizonwireless.com), AT&T/Cingular Wireless (www.cingular.com), or T-Mobile (www.t-mobile.com). While rates vary by provider, for between $49 and $89 per month, you can obtain unlimited, high-speed wireless internet access from your laptop computer from almost anywhere. Thanks to mail-in rebates and other incentives, the cost of the modem itself is typically under $100. The main drawback, however, is that you must sign a two-year service agreement with the wireless service provider, and a hefty early-termination fee typically applies.

For frequent business travelers who need reliable internet access from hotel rooms, airports, their vehicle, or while on the go, a wireless high-speed internet service plan can be a cost-effective and extremely convenient option. New service plans offered by the major providers no longer require that you also have a wireless voice plan with the same carrier.

Business-Friendly Hotels in the Orlando area. The properties on this list were selected based on the services and amenities offered, overall value, location, and comfort.

While nightly accommodation rates vary greatly throughout the year, and many of these properties also offer luxury suites that cost hundreds or thousands of dollars per night, each of the following properties is ranked based on its average price range for standard guestrooms.

Understanding the Hotel Ratings

Each business-friendly hotel featured in this section is rated with between one and four stars based on comfort, amenities, service, business-friendly environment, and overall value. Here's a description of each rating:

- *One Star (☆)—Below Average.* Not up to the standards of other hotels in the Orlando area.
- *Two Stars (☆☆)—Average.* There's nothing luxurious offered, but the property is clean, functional, and adequate for business travelers.
- *Three Stars (☆☆☆)—Above Average.* You'll definitely enjoy your stay here as a business traveler looking for a comfortable, clean, friendly, and quiet environment.
- *Four Stars (☆☆☆☆)—Superior.* This is the best that Orlando has to offer to business travelers. You may pay a bit extra, but it's worth it. Expect to enjoy a good night's sleep plus have access to a wide range of services and amenities designed to offer luxury, comfort, and convenience. Many of the four-star hotels in the Orlando area have a full-service day spa on site, along with a selection of upscale restaurants and lounges.

An average nightly price for a standard guestroom at each featured hotel is also included in the following descriptions. (Expect to pay considerably more for multibedroom suites.) The average price range rating is as follows:

- *One dollar sign ($).* Less than $100 per night
- *Two dollar signs ($$).* Between $100 and $200 per night
- *Three dollar signs ($$$).* More than $200 per night

WARNING

Because of high occupancy rates, most Orlando-area hotels strictly adhere to their posted check-in and checkout times. If you require early check-in (before 3 P.M.), or need to check out after 11 A.M. or noon on your day of departure, contact the hotel's front desk in advance to avoid extra charges and hassles. Upon request, all hotels will happily store your luggage after the posted checkout time until your actual departure later that day. Call the hotel's bell desk or concierge for details.

TIP
Few hotels offer in-room fax machines. If you travel often and need to send and receive faxes while on the go, consider registering for the eFax service (www.efax.com). For a flat monthly fee, you'll be given your own unique fax number and be able to send and receive faxes via the internet. Incoming faxes show up as e-mails and can be viewed on-screen or printed using a computer.

Listed here are our picks for the Top 15 Business-Friendly Hotels in Orlando. These are, however, just a sampling of the hundreds of hotels and resorts you'll find within the area. No matter what your taste, chances are you'll easily find accommodations to meet your needs and budget.

1. Celebration Hotel

Address: 700 Bloom Street, Celebration, FL 34747
Reservations phone number: (888) 499-3800
Main phone number: (407) 566-6000
Web site: www.celebrationhotel.com
Accommodations classification: Hotel

Comfort	Amenities and Services	Customer Service	Business-Friendly Environment	Overall Value	Average Price Range
☆☆☆☆	☆☆☆☆½	☆☆☆☆	☆☆☆	☆☆☆☆½	$$$

DESCRIPTION
Celebration, Florida, is a lovely, small, but extremely upscale gated community that was originally conceived by Walt Disney himself, but built decades after his death. Located within the heart of the town, the Celebration Hotel is an elegant and luxurious property that offers all of the comforts you'd expect from a boutique hotel. With its 115 guestrooms and suites, it is, however, considerably

smaller and more intimate than many of the luxury resort properties in the area.

The Celebration Hotel is ideal for business travelers looking to relax, plus it is perfect for a romantic getaway. It's not, however, the best place to stay with kids. Guestroom amenities include triple-sheeted beds, dual-line telephones, high-speed internet access, and a 25-inch television with cable programming. There's also a 24-hour business center, concierge service, laundry service, valet parking, and free shuttle bus transportation to the Walt Disney World Resort, the Celebration Golf Course and the Celebration Fitness and Day Spa.

For lunch and dinner, the Plantation Room (in the hotel) offers an upscale, business-friendly environment that serves award-winning cuisine. Several additional fine-dining restaurants can be found within walking distance.

If you're looking for a luxurious hotel where you can relax after a long day of meetings or attending a trade show, try the Celebration Hotel; it offers the comforts and amenities most business travelers want in a beautiful, quiet, and intimate setting. Staying within Celebration is very different than staying in the much more commercial International Drive area, or the WDW Resort area, which is inhabited by countless tourists and vacationers.

The town of Celebration is located just minutes from the Walt Disney World Resort. When you visit this quaint community, you'll feel as if you're existing within a Norman Rockwell painting that's come to life right before your eyes. Yet all of the resort activities (golf, tennis, swimming, movies, etc.), fine-dining, and shopping you might desire are within walking distance.

2. Disney's Grand Floridian Resort and Spa

Address: 4401 Grand Floridian Way, Lake Buena Vista, FL 32830

Reservations phone number: (407) 939-7429 (resort)/(407) 939-7675 (vacation packages)

Main phone number: (407) 824-3000

Web site: http://disneyworld.disney.go.com/wdw/index

Accommodations classification: Resort

Comfort	Amenities and Services	Customer Service	Business-Friendly Environment	Overall Value	Average Price Range
☆☆☆☆	☆☆☆☆	☆☆☆☆	☆☆☆	☆☆☆☆	$$/$$$

DESCRIPTION

As one of the premier company-owned-and-operated resorts on the Walt Disney World Resort property, the Grand Floridian

The Grand Floridian offers 867 guestrooms and suites, including 74 concierge-level rooms, which are ideal for business travelers, thanks in part to the added amenities offered. The resort features an extremely elegant and traditional Victorian-style décor.

Resort and Spa offers the most well-rounded, sophisticated, and luxurious accommodations available. This hotel is definitely suitable for upscale business travelers and vacationers alike.

All guestrooms and suites offer either a lagoon or garden view plus a wide range of amenities, including evening turndown service, 24-hour room service, and high-speed internet access. Several different guestroom configurations are available to accommodate business travelers, or people traveling with their families. Standard guestrooms start at $375 per night. Club Concierge Rooms start at $490 per night. Spacious and nicely furnished one- and two-bedroom suites are also available, starting at $1,080 per night.

Like many of the on-property Disney resorts, this one offers a wide range of activities, from a lavish outdoor swimming pool area to a full-service day spa, which is one of the finest in Orlando. The business center can assist with all of your work-related needs, plus the resort itself offers more than 40,000 square feet of meeting and convention space. The on-site concierge staff is also extremely knowledgeable and delivers top-notch service.

TIP

The Grand Floridian Spa and Health Club (407-824-2332) offers a state-of-the-art fitness center (available to all resort guests) plus a world-class day spa and salon that's open to the general public by appointment. As you'd expect from one of the finest day spas in Orlando, a wide range of massage, plus full body and skin care treatments are available, including facials, water therapies and body wraps. Private personal trainers are available by appointment. This luxurious day spa offers the perfect way to relax and pamper yourself after a long day of work.

In addition to featuring all the benefits and perks of staying at an on-property WDW resort, this one is nicely located and offers easy access to the Disney theme parks via the monorail system, water taxis, and the bus system. Plenty of self-parking and valet parking is also available.

If you're looking for a more traditional business-oriented hotel on Disney property, the Swan and Dolphin hotels are probably a better choice (and they are more affordable). If, however, you want a nice selection of business-friendly amenities plus the opportunity to stay at a truly luxurious and comfortable resort (with service and amenities like what you'd find at a Four Seasons or Ritz-Carlton, for example), the Grand Floridian is the perfect option. You'll also experience the top-notch and friendly hospitality and attention to detail that Disney is famous for.

3. Disney's Yacht and Beach Clubs

Address: Disney's Yacht Club, 1700 Epcot Resort Boulevard, Lake Buena Vista, FL 32830

Disney's Beach Club, 1800 Epcot Resort Boulevard, Lake Buena Vista, FL 32830

Reservations phone number: (407) W-DISNEY

Main phone number: (407) 934-7000 (Yacht Club), (407) 934-8000 (Beach Club)

Web site: www.disneyworld.com

Accommodations classification: Resort

Comfort	Amenities and Services	Customer Service	Business-Friendly Environment	Overall Value	Average Price Range
☆☆☆☆	☆☆☆☆	☆☆☆☆	☆☆☆	☆☆☆☆	$$$

DESCRIPTION

Located in the WDW Resort complex, within walking distance of Epcot, Disney's Yacht and Beach Clubs are two separate, upscale hotel properties that feature a New England nautical theme reminiscent of the 1800s.

Offering some of the most luxurious accommodations you'll find anywhere in Orlando, these two resorts don't specifically cater to business travelers, but boast a wide range of services and amenities designed to ensure that someone engaging in business while in Orlando will have the resources he or she needs for a successful trip. Both resorts offer excellent accommodation options for those who are traveling on business and bringing their family along for a vacation. A business center, high-speed internet access, and concierge service are available at both properties.

Disney's Yacht Club Resort features 621 bright and cheerfully decorated, extremely comfortable and spacious guestrooms and suites. The hotel was built around a 25-acre manmade lake. All rooms offer French doors that open onto porches or balconies. Between the Yacht and Beach Club, 73,000 square feet of meeting and convention space is available. There's also a 36,000-square-foot grand ballroom, which can seat up to 2,800 people for dinner. Disney's Beach Club Resort contains 576 guestrooms and suites. The Beach Club is a low-rise, luxury hotel located along the lake. It has a nautical theme and a large and unique sand-bottom swimming pool, along with a manmade beach along the lake. The hotel is ideal for family travelers and adults traveling without kids.

Because these are Disney-owned hotels, guests can enjoy a wide range of special perks, such as free transportation around the entire WDW Resort and the ability to take advantage of Disney's Magical Express airport transportation service.

TIP

Both Disney's Yacht Club and Disney's Beach Club offer several fine-dining restaurants. For reservations at any restaurant located anywhere on WDW Resort property, call (407) WDW-DINE or contact your hotel's concierge.

4. Gaylord Palms

Address: 6000 West Osceola Parkway, Kissimmee, FL 34746
Reservations phone number: (407) 586-2000
Main phone number: (407) 586-0000
Web site: www.gaylordhotels.com/gaylordpalms
Accommodations classification: Resort

Comfort	Amenities and Services	Customer Service	Business-Friendly Environment	Overall Value	Average Price Range
☆☆☆☆	☆☆☆☆	☆☆☆☆	☆☆☆☆	☆☆☆☆	$$$

DESCRIPTION

Not only was the Gaylord Palms Resort built in 2002 from the ground up to be the ultimate business-friendly resort and convention center the Orlando area, but it also incorporates numerous activities, services, and amenities to make it the perfect vacation destination, all under one roof.

The resort and convention center is located in Kissimmee, a five-minute drive from the Walt Disney World Resort and a 12-minute drive from the International Drive area (where the Orange County Convention Center is). The 63-acre complex offers 1,406 guestrooms and suites, multiple restaurants and lounges, many unique shops, the Florida location of the famous Canyon Ranch day spa, plus more than 400,000 square feet of convention, meeting, and exhibition space.

Each of the guestrooms is decorated and furnished based around a specific Florida theme (inspired by various regions of the sunshine state). The Emerald Bay section of the resort is designed to be a separate hotel within the resort, providing guests with a more intimate, boutique hotel experience. The 362 guestrooms and suites in the Emerald Bay section are more upscale and lavishly decorated, featuring higher-end amenities, like marble entries, high-fidelity sound systems, walk-in showers, as well as additional desk and work space.

All of the guestrooms, however, are designed with business travelers in mind. All include luxurious beds, high-speed internet access, multi-line telephones, in-room safes, and plenty of electrical outlets near the desk area. On the property, there's also a full-service business center and concierge.

When you're ready to relax and pamper yourself, there's no better place to do this than at the Canyon Ranch Spa (407-586-4SPA/www.canyonranch.com), a 20,000-square-foot fitness, beauty salon, and day spa facility. Here, a wide range of luxurious and unique massage, facial, body, and skin treatments are offered.

Located just one mile from the resort is Falcon's Fire Golf Club, a beautiful course designed by Rees Jones, which Gaylord Palms Resort guests have access to. This is a 6,900-yard course that plays to a par 72. In addition to 24-hour room service, the resort has several upscale steak and seafood fine-dining restaurants, each of which provides the perfect setting for important business lunches or dinners.

Many small- to-mid-size corporate events and trade shows are held entirely at Gaylord Palms Resort and Convention Center throughout the year. The meeting, convention, banquet, and exhibition facilities are all state-of-the-art. For details about hosting an event at this convention center, visit www.gaylordhotels.com/gaylordpalms/meetings.

CITY FACTOID
Gaylord Palms is owned and operated by Gaylord Entertainment, which also owns the Grand Ole Opry in Nashville, Tennessee.

Knowing that many business travelers opt to take their families on their trips to Orlando, Gaylord Palms also offers a wide range of activities for kids and families, including the La Petite Academy Kids Station, a full-service, professionally staffed childcare center.

For business travelers, this is definitely one of the most comfortable and best-equipped resorts to stay at, regardless of where you'll be conducting your business while in the Orlando area. Plus, when you're ready to relax and have fun after work, plenty of activities are available right on the property.

5. Ginn Reunion Resort

Address: 1000 Reunion Way, Reunion, FL 34747
Reservations phone number: (888) 418-9611
Main phone number: (407) 662-1100
Web site: www.reuniuonresort.com
Accommodations classification: Resort

Comfort	Amenities and Services	Customer Service	Business-Friendly Environment	Overall Value	Average Price Range
☆☆☆☆	☆☆☆☆	☆☆☆☆	☆☆☆☆	☆☆☆☆	$$$

DESCRIPTION
For the Orlando business traveler looking for accommodations that go well beyond a traditional hotel room or suite, the Ginn Reunion Resort provides the ultimate opportunity to stay at a 2,300-acre, world-class resort complex that's complete with its own restaurants, 54 holes of championship golf, a tennis complex, multiple swimming pools, and a day spa. Instead of tradition hotel guestrooms, this resort offers one-, two-, or three-bedroom villas (most of which overlook the golf course) and luxurious multibedroom homes (many with a private swimming pool).

All accommodations provide the experience of staying at a world-class luxury hotel, but the living areas are significantly more spacious. All of the villas and homes are filled with lavish and comfortable furnishings and extremely tasteful décor, and they feature premium bedding, flat-screen TVs, separate dining room areas, fully equipped kitchens, complimentary high-speed internet access, daily maid service, personal concierge service, in-room dining, and access to all of the resort's services, restaurants, and other upscale amenities.

The resort offers 22,000 square feet of ballroom and meeting space; however, the stand-alone homes are the ideal setting for smaller meetings, events, and retreats. Even though this resort is located just five to ten miles from Orlando's top attractions, unless you have a specific convention to attend at the Orlando Convention Center, for example, you'll be hard-pressed to find reasons to leave this beautiful resort's grounds.

The 54 holes of championship golf were designed by such greats as Arnold Palmer, Tom Watson, and Jack Nicklaus. The resort also offers the Annika Sorenstam Golf Training Academy, a driving range and practice green, a golf shop, plus ongoing tournaments and events. Other activities available at the resort include a full-service day spa (407-662-4772), horseback riding, a water park, multiple swimming pools, and several fine-dining restaurants.

Ginn Reunion Resort offers an extremely high level of luxury and comfort, affordable rates, an excellent location, plus a wide range of services and amenities that are ideal for business travelers. With so many resort complexes in the Orlando area to choose from, this is definitely among the very best and well worth experiencing. You won't want to leave!

What's really surprising is that the luxury accommodations featured at the Ginn Reunion Resort are surprisingly affordable (equivalent to a guestroom at an upscale hotel). Depending on the season, the rate for a lovely and spacious one-bedroom villa, for example, starts at just $179 per night. One thing that makes a stay at this resort extra convenient is that all of your dining and activity reservations and needs will be personally attended to by the extremely friendly and professional concierge staff.

6. Hard Rock Hotel at Universal Orlando (Loews)

Address: 5800 Universal Boulevard, Orlando, FL 32819
Reservations phone number: (800) BE-A-STAR
Main phone number: (407) 503-7625
Web site: www.hardrock.com/locations/hotels2/orlando
Accommodations classification: Hotel

Comfort	Amenities and Services	Customer Service	Business-Friendly Environment	Overall Value	Average Price Range
☆☆☆½	☆☆☆	☆☆☆☆	☆☆½	☆☆☆	$$/$$$

Featuring California mission-style architecture, the hotel has a Hard Rock Café, a much more elegant Palm Restaurant for fine dining, and three other restaurants. There's even a Starbucks Coffee located in the lobby.

DESCRIPTION

Following in the footsteps of its sister property in Las Vegas, this Hard Rock Hotel is designed to be a hip and trendy place to stay and be seen. Targeting young business professionals and vacationers alike, the overall theme of this hotel is rock 'n' roll. You'll find over $1 million worth of music memorabilia on display throughout the property, which is part of the Universal Orlando Resort complex.

Guestrooms are comfortable and modern in design and include basic amenities (like high-speed internet access) that business travelers will appreciate. The average guestroom offers 375 square feet of living space. Business travelers, however, should consider the Hard Rock Club Lounge rooms, which offer additional space and amenities plus access to an exclusive seventh floor lounge, separate concierge service, and free use of the property's fitness center.

The hotel contains a total of 650 guestrooms, including 29 spacious suites. When you're ready to enjoy the Florida sunshine, this hotel offers a 12,000-square-foot, manmade sand beach and a lovely pool area. If you happen to be staying at the hotel on the last Thursday of any month, you'll also be treated to a live concert by a well-known recording artist. To see a schedule of performances, visit www.velvetsessions.com.

This isn't a business hotel per say, but it does offer a business center, and meeting and banquet rooms are available. The Hard Rock Hotel has a boutique hotel atmosphere that's unique, upbeat, and fun.

TIP
One perk of being a guest at the Hard Rock Hotel is that when you visit either the Universal Studios or Islands of Adventure theme park, you'll be granted VIP access to the popular rides and attractions, which will dramatically decrease your waiting times.

---

7. Hyatt Regency Grand Cypress Resort

Address: One Grand Cypress Boulevard, Orlando, FL 32836
Reservations phone number: (888) 591-1234
Main phone number: (407) 239-1234
Web site: www.hyattregencygrandcypress.com
Accommodations classification: Resort

Comfort	Amenities and Services	Customer Service	Business-Friendly Environment	Overall Value	Average Price Range
☆☆☆☆	☆☆☆½	☆☆☆☆	☆☆☆½	☆☆☆☆	$$$

DESCRIPTION

Located close to the International Drive area and the Walt Disney World Resort (about 18 miles from the Orlando International Airport), the Hyatt Regency Grand Cypress Resort nicely meets the needs of demanding business travelers while at the same time providing a luxurious vacation resort atmosphere. In addition to the lavish furnishings, the resort is decorated with more than 1,000 pieces of fine art.

To help meet your work-related needs, the full-service business center (407-239-3865) offers secretarial services, plus there's concierge service available 24 hours per day. The business center is staffed between 7 A.M. and 7 P.M. on weekdays and between 8 A.M. and 4 P.M. on weekends.

When you're ready for some recreation, the resort has its own golf course, tennis complex, a day spa, a beauty salon, a fitness

This 1,500-acre Hyatt Regency contains 750 spacious guestrooms and suites, each with a private balcony, a marble bathroom, high-speed internet access, dual-line telephones, an in-room safe, a minibar, and a large work area. The average guestroom offers 360 square feet of living space and a stunning view of the surrounding landscaping. More than a dozen different guestroom configurations are available to accommodate businesspeople traveling alone or with their families.

center, an equestrian center, multiple swimming pools, plus a variety of different water sports. The 45-hole golf course was designed by Professional Golfers' Association (PGA) legend Jack Nicklaus. If you need to brush up on your game, the Grand Cypress Academy of Golf offers private instruction.

TIP
Members of Hyatt's Gold Passport program will earn points for their stay at this resort (or can redeem their points for room upgrades or free stays).

If you're looking for fine-dining experiences suitable for hosting even your most important clients, you have several different restaurants to choose from, including the White Horse Bar and Grill (steakhouse) and Hemmingway's (seafood), on the premises. A lovely Sunday brunch is also served.

The resort contains 65,000 square feet of meeting and function space, 29 meeting rooms, plus several outdoor function areas. Complete meeting and function planning services are available. For business travelers and vacationers alike, this is one of the most nicely equipped and luxurious full-service resorts in the Orlando area. In addition, it offers the fine service you'd expect from a Hyatt Regency property.

TIP
The hotel can coordinate private town car service to and from Orlando International Airport for a fee of $60 each way. Call the hotel's ticket and transportation desk (407-239-1234, ext. 4149) for details.

8. Hyatt Regency Orlando International Airport

Address: 9300 Airport Boulevard, Orlando, FL 32827
Reservations phone number: (888) 591-1234
Main phone number: (407) 825-1234
Web site: http://orlandoairport.hyatt.com/hyatt/hotels
Accommodations classification: Hotel

Comfort	Amenities and Services	Customer Service	Business-Friendly Environment	Overall Value	Average Price Range
☆☆☆½	☆☆☆½	☆☆☆	☆☆☆☆	☆☆☆½	$$$

DESCRIPTION

Most major airports have a handful of hotels and/or motels located nearby, making it convenient for travelers to find last-minute accommodations if their flight is delayed. Orlando International Airport, however, has an upscale Hyatt Regency hotel located right in the center of the airport. It's actually part of the main terminal building. Featuring all of the services and amenities you'd expect from a luxury hotel, this Hyatt also offers the ultimate in convenience for business travelers wishing to stay at the airport. Of course, the building has been soundproofed, so guests don't hear airplanes taking off or landing, but are treated to an excellent view of airport operations from their room or suite.

The Hyatt Regency Orlando International Airport is a modern, business-friendly hotel offering a full-service business center, concierge service, meeting and conference rooms, high-speed internet access, multiline telephones in the guestrooms, and plenty of

Unlike the Hyatt Regency Grand Cypress Resort, this property is designed to be exclusively a business-oriented hotel, not a vacation destination. There is, however, an outdoor pool (with an airport runway view) and an on-property fitness center. If you're flying into Orlando for a quick business trip, or plan to stay a few days but don't want to experience the hassle of driving to and from the airport, this hotel is an excellent option. It's also ideal if you experience a last-minute change in travel plans and are already at the airport.

in-room work space, especially if you reserve one of the hotel's Business Plan guestrooms. The beds feature Hyatt's signature pillow-top mattresses and feather blankets to ensure comfort. Most guestrooms also have a balcony.

The hotel is located between 20 and 30 minutes from the Orange County Convention Center and the Walt Disney World Resort (depending on traffic).

TIP

Members of Hyatt's Gold Passport program will earn points for their stay at this resort (or can redeem their points for room upgrades or free stays).

---

9. JW Marriott Orlando Grande Lakes

Address: 4040 Central Florida Parkway, Orlando, FL 32837
Reservations phone number: (800) 576-5750
Main phone number: (407) 206-2300
Web site: www.grandelakes.com
Accommodations classification: Resort

Comfort	Amenities and Services	Customer Service	Business-Friendly Environment	Overall Value	Average Price Range
☆☆☆	☆☆☆☆	☆☆☆☆	☆☆☆☆	☆☆☆☆	$$$

DESCRIPTION

Imagine a 500-acre, $600 million Marriott resort that's relatively new (it opened in July 2003), modern, and located less than 15 minutes from the Orlando International Airport and just five minutes from the Orange County Convention Center and the International Drive area. In addition to focusing on the needs of business travelers planning to work while in Orlando, this resort also caters to travelers looking to enjoy their leisure time. The resort offers an 18-hole championship golf course designed by Greg Norman, plus a 40,000-square-foot day spa and fitness center.

What's unique about the 1,000-guestroom JW Marriott Orlando is that it shares its property and facilities with the luxurious Ritz-Carlton. This 26-floor resort offers guestrooms and suites with marble bathrooms, extremely comfortable beds, high-speed internet, dual-line telephones, a 27-inch flat-screen television (with DVD or VCR and CD player), and plenty of work space, making it ideal for business travelers. More than 72,000 square feet of indoor meeting and banquet space, 43 meeting rooms, and 62,000 square feet of outdoor function space are also available.

On the property, you'll find several award-winning restaurants, including Primo (serving contemporary Italian cuisine prepared by Chef Melissa Kelly) and Citron (offering American cuisine for lunch and dinner). There's also a Starbucks Coffee located in the lobby.

While the JW Marriott may appeal to business travelers because of its services and amenities, it's also one of the most prestigious resorts in Orlando, providing comfort and lavish accommodations surrounded by breathtakingly beautiful landscaping. Because it's a resort, it offers much more than a traditional hotel in terms of activities. The property participates in the Marriott Rewards program for frequent travelers and is entirely nonsmoking. It's an excellent choice if you're planning to relax or have some fun during your Orlando trip, especially if you play golf.

10. Peabody Hotel

Address: 9801 International Drive, Orlando, FL 32819

Reservations phone number: (800) PEABODY

Main phone number: (407) 352-4000

Web site: www.peabodyorlando.com

Accommodations classification: Hotel

Comfort	Amenities and Services	Customer Service	Business-Friendly Environment	Overall Value	Average Price Range
☆☆☆☆	☆☆☆☆	☆☆☆☆	☆☆☆☆	☆☆☆☆	$$$

DESCRIPTION

For business travelers planning to attend a meeting, trade show, or convention at the Orange County Convention Center (or around the nearby International Drive area), there's no better place to stay than the Peabody, a luxurious hotel located directly across the street.

The Peabody offers a variety of different guestroom and suite configurations, designed to meet a wide range of budgets and space needs. All accommodations, however, feature luxurious amenities, comfortable furnishings, and a Peabody Dream Bed by Simmons Beautyrest®. You'll also find at least two dual-line telephones, a flat-screen television, high-speed internet access, and plenty of work space in every guestroom and suite.

In addition to a large swimming pool, tennis courts, and a fitness center, the hotel has a day spa, a beauty salon, an on-site Hertz rental car desk, a full-service business center, complimentary self-parking,

The Peabody opened in Orlando back in 1986. The original Peabody opened in 1925 in Memphis, Tennessee. While the hotel is located within a five-minute walk of the convention center, it offers 57,000 square feet of flexible meeting space on two levels, a 27,000-square-foot ballroom, and two 8,600-square-foot junior ballrooms, along with 32 meeting rooms.

optional valet parking, and concierge service. The large, 27-floor hotel prides itself on delivering top-notch service.

For the perfect fine-dining restaurant to host an important meal with clients or co-workers, try either the Capriccio Grill (an Italian steakhouse) or the Dux (the hotel's award-winning signature restaurant), located near the main lobby. Both restaurants share the famous Peabody Wine Cellar.

While the Walt Disney World Resort may have Mickey Mouse as its mascot, the Peabody has its own team of beloved mascots that delight guests on a daily basis. The famous Peabody ducks (yes, they're real Mallard hens) participate in the march of the Peabody ducks from the Royal Peabody Duck Palace to the atrium lobby fountain every day at 11 A.M. and 5 P.M. It's a fun tradition at this hotel that shouldn't be missed. Don't let this "attraction" fool you. The Peabody is definitely one of the most well-equipped, most conveniently located, and nicest business-oriented hotels in Orlando.

TIP
Afternoon tea, the perfect midday break, is served weekdays between 3 P.M. and 4:30 P.M. This is an excellent setting for an informal business gathering.

---

11. Portofino Bay Hotel at Universal Orlando (Loews)

Address: 5601 Universal Boulevard, Orlando, Florida 32819

Reservations phone number: (800) BE-A-STAR

Main phone number: (407) 503-1000

Web site: www.loewshotels.com/en/Hotels/Portofino-Bay-Hotel/Overview.aspx

Accommodations classification: Hotel

Comfort	Amenities and Services	Customer Service	Business-Friendly Environment	Overall Value	Average Price Range
☆☆☆½	☆☆☆	☆☆☆☆	☆☆☆	☆☆☆½	$$$

DESCRIPTION

As a sister property to the Hard Rock Hotel the Portofino Bay Hotel, located in the Universal Orlando complex, offers a more sophisticated, traditional, and upscale experience. This 750-room business-friendly hotel is capable of hosting meetings and functions.

Because this hotel is designed for vacationers who need to conduct business while away, it does offer a business center and internet access in the guestrooms. The focus, however, is on leisure activities. Here, you'll find three themed swimming pools, the luxurious Mandara Spa and fitness center, and a variety of

If you're looking for a luxurious place to stay near the Universal theme parks, the Portofino is an excellent choice. Members of the Loews First frequent traveler program (www.loews-first.com) can earn points for their stay here.

other on-property activities. It's also a short walk from Universal City Walk, which features a variety of shops and restaurants.

12. Ritz-Carlton Orlando Grande Lakes

Address: 4012 Central Florida Parkway, Orlando, FL 32837
Reservations phone number: (800) 241-3333
Main phone number: (407) 206-2400
Web site: www.grandelakes.com
Accommodations classification: Resort

Comfort	Amenities and Services	Customer Service	Business-Friendly Environment	Overall Value	Average Price Range
☆☆☆☆	☆☆☆☆	☆☆☆☆	☆☆☆☆	☆☆☆☆	$$$

DESCRIPTION

Until the Four Seasons opens in 2010 (as part of the WDW Resort), the Ritz-Carlton will remain the only ultraluxurious chain hotel in the Orlando area. Sure, there are other extremely luxurious resorts and hotels, like the Peabody and the Ginn Reunion, for example, but the Ritz-Carlton is known around the world for its incredible service, lavish accommodations, and ability to expertly cater to the needs of business travelers and vacationers alike.

By sharing its 500-acre property and some of its amenities (like its championship golf course, swimming pool with lazy river, and day spa) with the JW Marriott, the Ritz-Carlton is able to provide a world-class resort experience yet maintain the feeling of a small hotel that offers highly personalized service. The architecture is inspired by the grand palazzis of Italy. This Ritz-Carlton contains 584 spacious and nicely decorated guestrooms, including 64 suites and 56 Ritz-Carlton Club Rooms (ideal for business travelers), plus two Ritz-Carlton Suites.

Each guestroom and suite offers a slew of amenities that cater to a business traveler's needs, ranging from dual-line telephones to high-speed internet access, a 27-inch flat-screen television, a spacious work area, plus a marble bathroom and a private balcony (in most rooms and suites). You'll also find a business center on-site as well as multiple meeting rooms and plenty of function and banquet space. Between the Ritz-Carlton and the JW Marriott, the resort complex has 11 dining establishments, many of which are ideal for hosting important business lunches or dinners.

If you're a business traveler accustomed to fine accommodations and have enjoyed stays at the Ritz-Carlton hotels in other cities, this Orlando location will definitely live up to expectations.

13. Rosen Plaza Hotel and Rosen Centre Hotel

Address: 9700 International Drive, Orlando, FL 32819
Reservations phone number: (800) 336-9700
Main phone number: (407) 996-9700
Web site: www.rosenplaza.com
Accommodations classification: Hotel

Comfort	Amenities and Services	Customer Service	Business-Friendly Environment	Overall Value	Average Price Range
☆☆☆	☆☆☆	☆☆☆	☆☆☆	☆☆☆	$$$

DESCRIPTION

Located right next to the Orange County Convention Center in Orlando, the Rosen Plaza Hotel and Rosen Centre Hotel (located across the street) are top-quality, business-oriented hotels that offer their own convention, banquet, and meeting facilities on the premises. Both facilities combined offer 800 luxurious guestrooms and suites, featuring high-speed internet access and a wide range of other amenities sought by business travelers. A standard guestroom consists of 330 square feet of living space, while some of the larger suites contain more than 1,000 square feet of living space.

Just one of the services offered at the Rosen Plaza Hotel is the Bags service, which allows guests to check in with their airline and check their luggage at the hotel prior to their departure. This saves time and the hassle of waiting in long airport ticket counter lines.

The Rosen Centre is one of two Rosen business-friendly hotels located across the street from the Orange County Convention Center (along International Drive).

A full-service business center and a concierge staff are also on hand to provide assistance with reservations, ground transportation, or help dealing with other work-, leisure-, or travel-related issues you encounter.

The hotels are located about 15 minutes from Orlando International Airport and 10 minutes from the WDW Resort. Either of these properties is a perfect choice if you're traveling on business, especially if you'll be attending an event at the Orange County Convention Center.

14. Rosen Shingle Creek

Address: 9939 Universal Boulevard, Orlando, FL 32819
Reservations phone number: (866) 996-6338
Main phone number: (407) 996-9939
Web site: www.shinglecreekresort.com
Accommodations classification: Resort

Comfort	Amenities and Services	Customer Service	Business-Friendly Environment	Overall Value	Average Price Range
☆☆☆☆	☆☆☆☆½	☆☆☆☆	☆☆☆	☆☆☆☆	$$$

DESCRIPTION

Offering luxury accommodations in a full-service resort complex, the Rosen Shingle Creek features a wide range of leisure activities, such as fine dining, golf, the Spa at Shingle Creek (407-996-9SPA), swimming, basketball, fishing, hiking, and tennis. This resort is

The 1,500 guestrooms and suites feature stunning views of either the 18-hole championship golf course or the pool area. The course was designed by David Harman and is named by *Golfweek* as one of America's Top 40 New Courses, and one of Central Florida's Top Ten Toughest Courses by *Orlando Business Journal*.

primarily for upscale vacationers, but it has a wide range of services and amenities that business travelers will appreciate.

Each guestroom and suite includes the resort's signature Creek Sleeper bed, a 32-inch flat-screen television, high-speed internet access, two telephones, plus a selection of other lavish amenities.

One nice feature of this hotel is that the in-room televisions offer NXTV technology, which allows guest to utilize an online concierge service for making dining reservations, scheduling tee times, viewing on-site meeting schedules, and accessing personal e-mail. The televisions can also be connected to a laptop computer and used as a monitor for in-room presentations or connected to an iPod and used as a personalized stereo system. Like the Rosen Plaza Hotel, this resort also offers the Bags service, which allows guests to check in for their departing flight from the hotel and check their bags with the airline from the resort's lobby.

The resort offers several fine-dining establishments, including Cala Bella (an Italian bistro featured in Section V, "Where to Dine in Orlando"). This is a great place to stay if you're planning to do some business while in Orlando but can set aside some time for fun as well. The 230-acre resort opened in September 2006 and offers 445,000 square feet of meeting and banquet space. A full-service business center is located on the property. It's situated about one mile from the Orange County Convention Center and ten minutes from the Orlando International Airport.

15. Walt Disney World Swan and Dolphin

Address: 1500 Epcot Resort Boulevard, Lake Buena Vista, FL 32830
Reservations phone number: (888) 828-8850
Main phone number: (407) 934-3000 (Swan)/(407) 934-4000 (Dolphin)
Web site: www.swandolphin.com
Accommodations classification: Resort

Comfort	Amenities and Services	Customer Service	Business-Friendly Environment	Overall Value	Average Price Range
☆☆☆☆	☆☆☆☆	☆☆☆☆	☆☆☆☆	☆☆☆☆	$$$

DESCRIPTION

Located in the heart of the WDW Resort complex, you'll find two massive business-friendly hotels adjacent to each other. The Walt Disney World Swan and Dolphin offer the ideal accommodations for upscale business travelers. The Swan is a Westin hotel, while the Dolphin is a Sheraton property. Both are owned and operated by

BUSINESS TRAVEL ADVICE FROM A TOP ORLANDO RESORT CONCIERGE

Timothy Allen Morse is the lobby concierge at the Rosen Shingle Creek Resort (866-996-9939, www.shinglecreekresort.com) in Orlando. For more than seven years, his daily responsibilities have involved catering to the needs of the resort's guests and helping them deal with any problems that have arisen during their travels. To accomplish this successfully, he has developed vast and up-to-date knowledge about Orlando, local restaurants, ground transportation options, and all area attractions.

On a daily basis, Morse is asked to recommend fine-dining restaurants to resort guests. "Before I recommend a restaurant, I always inquire about what the guest is looking for in particular, in terms of atmosphere, type of cuisine, price, etc. For business travelers, I tend to recommend top-quality restaurants that offer private dining areas, as well as excellent service and food. My personal top picks for restaurants include Moon Fish, Christini's Ristoranti, Chatham's Place Restaurant, Cala Bella, and the Capital Grille. These restaurants are all located within 3.5 miles from our resort," stated Morse.

Morse's Top Five Business-Friendly Restaurant Picks

(Listed in alphabetical order. For additional business-friendly restaurant recommendations, see Section V, "Dining in Orlando.")

1. *Cala Bella*—http://calabellarestaurant.com, (407) 996-FOOD, 9939 Universal Boulevard, Orlando
2. *The Capital Grille*—www.thecapitalgrille.com, (407) 370-4392, 9101 International Drive, Orlando
3. *Chatham's Place Restaurant*—www.chathamsplace.com, (407) 345-2992, 7575 Dr. Phillips Boulevard, Orlando
4. *Christini's Ristoranti*—www.christinis.com, (407) 345-8770, 7600 Dr Phillips Boulevard #84, Orlando
5. *Moon Fish*—www.fishfusion.com, (407) 363-7262, 7525 West Sand Lake Road, Orlando

Aside from being asked to make last-minute dining reservations for guests, one of the most common travel-related problems Morse helps resolve is when a guest's luggage is lost by an airline. "I am constantly being asked to use my extensive contacts to make last-minute restaurant reservations for small groups, coordinate last-minute ground transportation, or help someone get back their lost luggage," Morse said. "We also help guests obtain items they

BUSINESS TRAVEL ADVICE, continued

might have forgotten at home, such as specialized toiletries, a charger for their cell phone, or collar stays for their dress shirts. I need to have instant answers and know where to go in order to quickly and efficiently address every guest's needs or requests."

When asked to help with a luggage-related situation, Morse immediately gets on the phone with the guest's airline, tracks down the appropriate "property irregularity report number," and then tries to determine how quickly the luggage can be found by the airline and delivered to the hotel. "If an airline loses your luggage, immediately go to the airline's staffed luggage counter located near baggage claim and file a report. You will need to describe your lost bags in detail. You will then be provided with a property irregularity report number. This will be your reference number with the airline until your bags are delivered to you. Hopefully, the airline will be able to quickly track your bags, determine their whereabouts, and provide an estimate in terms of when you can expect them to be delivered to you," said Morse.

While you're waiting for your lost luggage to arrive, utilize the services of your hotel's concierge to help you obtain specific items, such as toiletries or a change of clothing, that you may need right away. "If your bags remain lost for more than 24 to 48 hours, depending on the airline, you're entitled to receive financial compensation. We try to help travelers get everything they're entitled to from the airline, plus help to speed up the process for getting the lost luggage returned. One thing you can do to speed up the process is to return to the airport and pick up the bags yourself when they arrive in Orlando. Otherwise, you'll have to wait, sometimes an extra eight to ten hours or longer, for the delivery service [that] represents all of the airlines to deliver your bags."

If someone is looking for fun and interesting activities to experience while in Orlando, but doesn't want to visit a theme park, Morse recommends visiting the Winter Park area (located about 14 miles west of Orlando), which offers a handful of indoor and outdoor museums and cultural attractions.

For business travelers planning to fit a few rounds of golf into their busy schedule, a hotel concierge can help them obtain last-minute tee times at a variety of different courses. "The various golf courses and golf clubs extend courtesies to concierges and can often fit in a last-minute tee time reservation when requested by a concierge from a nearby hotel. As a golfer myself, I really like the course we have here at Rosen Shingle Creek, as well as what's

BUSINESS TRAVEL ADVICE, continued

offered at Falcon's Fire Golf Club and Metro West Golf Club, all of which have a PGA professional feel to them. In addition to the golf shops at each course, you can rent or buy clubs and equipment at the nearby Edwin Watts Golf Shop [407-351-1444, www.edwinwattsgolf.com, 8330 International Drive, Orlando] which has a tremendous selection of well-known brands," Morse said.

Morse recommends travelers prebook all ground transportation, such as limousines or a rental car, as well as any advance dining or golf tee time reservations that are appropriate, before leaving home for Orlando. Your hotel's concierge can help you make these reservations before you arrive in Orlando. When booking your travel, determine if there are other big events happening in the area at the same time. If, for example, you're planning to visit Orlando during the Daytona 500, it'll be extremely difficult to find a hotel room and secure a rental car, unless you make your reservations very early. During big Daytona events, people fly into and stay in Orlando, then drive to the event in Daytona. This also causes a lot of extra traffic in the area. There is a huge lack of hotel space and rental car availability in Daytona, so Orlando winds up accommodating these travelers, as well as those coming specifically to Orlando for business or pleasure.

Also, if you have a specific room request where you'll be staying, you'll want to confirm or reconfirm this with the hotel or resort prior to your arrival. "As you pack, take a quick inventory to make sure you have everything you need, from your toiletries to your cell phone accessories and laptop computer charger. Think about what you'll wear each day and each night, and don't forget to pack a bathing suit. I find a lot of business travelers needing to purchase bathing suits once they arrive here. It may be cold and snowing in your home city, but in Orlando, it's probably sunny and 85 degrees," he said.

If you happen to forget a cell phone or laptop computer charger, accessory, or cable, for example, Morse recommends visiting Electronics Plus, located at the Pointe Orlando shopping area (407-447-4979, 9101 International Drive, Orlando). Morse explained, "They have the largest selection of chargers, adapters, cables, and accessories in the area for all types of consumer electronics, cell phones, and laptop computers."

Once you check in at your hotel, be sure to provide the front desk with your cell phone number. "Businesspeople often receive urgent or emergency work or personal calls while they're away. If an

> ## BUSINESS TRAVEL ADVICE, continued
>
> important call comes in and the front desk has your cell phone number, we can track you down and forward that important call to you," Morse added.
>
> As a matter of convenience and to save time and money, Morse recommends that business travelers who are traveling with one or more other people rent a car as opposed to taking shuttle buses or other forms of ground transportation to and from the airport. The shuttle bus to many of the hotels in the area will cost $20 or more per person and can take an hour or longer. It's cheaper and faster to utilize a rental car or taxi. "Orlando is very spread out. I personally recommend that business travelers obtain a rental car during their stay. Otherwise, simply going out to lunch or dinner, or going to and from the convention center, can generate a $20 to $40 round-trip taxi fare. Having a rental car available also makes it easier to make quick trips to Staples, OfficeMax, or Wal-Mart to purchase last-minute items you need for a meeting, for example," said Morse.
>
> A hotel's concierge can help with virtually all of your needs before and during your stay. This includes helping guests obtain tickets to sold-out theatre or sporting events, helping to retrieve luggage lost by an airline, booking last-minute travel reservations, and helping to find and purchase forgotten items. "Our job is to make a guest's trip more comfortable and to eliminate some of the stress associated with travel. For some things, however, waiting until the last minute can make things difficult. For example, it's extremely difficult to get a clothing item same-day dry-cleaned if you drop off that item after 11 A.M.," Morse said.

Starwood Hotels and Resorts Worldwide. Of the 32 hotels on WDW Resort property, these are the two best business-friendly options.

TIP
Planning to host a business meeting or gathering of any size at the Swan or Dolphin? These hotels offer 329,000 square feet of meeting, convention, and banquet space. Visit www.swandolphinmeetings.com to help you preplan your event.

The 87-acre Swan and Dolphin complex unto itself includes the Mandara Spa (a world-class day spa), 17 restaurants and lounges, five swimming pools, a white sand beach (manmade), two health clubs, tennis, an on-site laundry center (plus a valet laundry service), a National Car Rental branch, shopping, two full-service business centers, a top-notch concierge service, access to complimentary Disney transportation (for getting around the WDW Resort), plus a wide range of other services and amenities.

Designed by award-winning architect Michael Graves, the Swan and Dolphin combined offer 2,265 luxurious and spacious guestrooms and suites, each featuring at least one Heavenly Bed adorned with a custom-designed pillow-top mattress set, cozy down blanket, three crisp sheets, a duvet, and five fluffy pillows to provide the maximum comfort while you sleep. Each room is also equipped with a 27-inch television, a spacious desk and work area, plus high-speed internet access.

Guestrooms and suites are available in a variety of configurations, starting with a Standard Guest Room, which is suitable for most business travelers. More spacious, Junior Suites and single- or multi-bedroom full-size suites plus Presidential Suites are also available. Basic guestrooms start at $199 per night.

Within these two hotels are several business-friendly fine-dining restaurants, including Il Mulino (407-934-1609), which serves Italian cuisine and is modeled after the famous New York City restaurant of the same name. You'll also find Todd English's Bluezoo (407-934-1111), an award-winning seafood restaurant; Shula's Steak House (407-934-1362); and Kimonos (407-934-1609), a Japanese and sushi restaurant, right on the premises. Each of these restaurants is an ideal setting for a business lunch or dinner.

TIP
Want to pamper yourself, relax, and unwind during your stay? To book your treatments at the world-class Mandara Spa, located in the Swan and Dolphin complex, call (407) 934-4SPA or visit www.swandolphin.com/mandaraspa.

Staying at the Walt Disney World (WDW) Resort Offers Many Perks

The WDW Resort currently offers 22 Disney-owned-and-operated resorts, plus an additional 10 resorts operated by third parties.

You'll pay a premium to stay at any of these resorts, but most travelers find the experience to be well worth it. The overall WDW Resort property is home to more than 31,000 guestrooms and suites as well as 784 campsites. Each of the resorts has a unique theme and decor, and most are located close to at least one of Disney's theme parks.

All of the on-site hotels are serviced by the expansive and convenient Disney transportation system, which offers free transportation around the WDW Resort using buses, water taxis (boats), and the Disney monorail system. A variety of other special perks and service are also made available exclusively to guests.

CITY FACTOID
Some of the resorts located at the WDW Resort are timeshare properties that are part of the Disney Vacation Club (http://dvc.disney.go.com/dvc/index). Accommodations at these properties are available on a limited basis to nonmembers.

Especially if you're visiting Orlando on business but bringing your family along for a vacation, staying at any of the resort hotels located within the WDW Resort offers a wide range of helpful perks, along with the excitement of staying at one of the most popular vacation destinations in America.

Guests of the WDW Resort can enjoy the incredible convenience of stepping off their airplane at the Orlando International Airport and experiencing Disney's Magical Express. This service picks you up at the airport, collects your luggage for you from the airline's baggage claim area, and takes you directly to your hotel. Your luggage is promptly delivered directly to your guestroom. Upon checkout, Disney's Magical Express will precheck you in with your airline, collect your baggage and deliver it to your airline, plus provide you with luxury motor coach transportation back to the airport—all on a complimentary basis. This is a tremendous time saver and eliminates the need to carry your own luggage and wait in long airport lines to check in.

Guests of any WDW Resort hotel are also entitled to utilize all of the various methods of resort transportation to get around the massive property. This includes the monorail system, air-conditioned buses, and water taxis. Resort guests can also enjoy extended operating hours at the various Disney theme parks throughout the week, which means shorter ride and attraction lines.

Another perk allows guest to participate in the Magic Your Way dining package (for an additional fee) and save up to 40 percent off all dining at more than 100 restaurants located throughout the Walt Disney World Resort property. Of course, guests of any WDW Resort are guaranteed to enjoy the world-class service and hospitality Disney is famous for. All of these benefits make the added cost associated with staying at the WDW Resort well worth it.

MONEY SAVER

If you're staying at any WDW Resort hotel, you will not need a rental car if you plan to stay on Disney property throughout your visit.

The WDW resorts are divided into categories, based on price and luxury. The Disney Value Resorts (which are not at all business friendly and are more suitable for families on a budget) start at just $82 per night. A guestroom at a Disney Moderate Resort will start at around $145 per night, while a guestroom at a Disney Deluxe Resort will cost $215 or more per night. Disney Vacation Club Resorts (which are typically timeshare properties) offer fully furnished, multibedroom apartments or townhouses that are ideal for families. Prices start at $279 per night, based on availability for nonmembers.

The following is a summary of popular WDW resorts. Plans are under way for Disney to open or expand several resorts over the next few years. For example, at Disney's Animal Kingdom, between 2007 and 2009, Disney's Animal Kingdom Villas will open, providing homelike amenities in fully furnished apartments and townhouses.

SUMMARY OF SELECT WDW RESORTS

Resort	Price	Location	Business-Friendly Rating
Disney's Pop Century Resort	$	Near Disney's Wide World of Sports area	☆
Disney's All-Star Movies Resort	$	Near Disney's Animal Kingdom area	☆
Disney's All-Star Music Resort	$	Near Disney's Animal Kingdom area	☆
Disney's All-Star Sports Resort	$	Near Disney's Animal Kingdom area	☆

SUMMARY OF SELECT WDW RESORTS

Resort	Price	Location	Business-Friendly Rating
Disney's Caribbean Beach Resort	$$	Epcot area	☆☆
Disney's Coronado Springs Resort	$$	Near Disney's Animal Kingdom area	☆☆
Disney's Port Orleans Resort— French Quarter	$$	Near downtown Disney area	☆☆
Disney's Port Orleans Resort— Riverside	$$	Near downtown Disney area	☆☆
Disney's Animal Kingdom Lodge	$$$	At Disney's Animal Kingdom	☆☆½
Disney's Beach Club Resort	$$$	Epcot area	☆☆☆½
Disney's Boardwalk Inn	$$$	Epcot area	☆☆½
Disney's Contemporary Resort	$$$	Magic Kingdom area	☆☆½
Disney's Grand Floridian Resort	$$$	Magic Kingdom area	☆☆☆☆
Disney's Polynesian Resort	$$$	Magic Kingdom area	☆☆
Disney's Wilderness Lodge	$$$	Magic Kingdom area	☆
Disney's Yacht Club Resort	$$$	Epcot area	☆☆☆½
Walt Disney World Swan	$$$	Near MGM-Studios	☆☆☆☆
Walt Disney World Dolphin	$$$	Near MGM-Studios	☆☆☆☆

Plans are also under way to open another luxury resort in partnership with the Four Seasons by 2010. This 900-acre resort will offer single- and multi-family vacation homes and its own 18-hole golf course.

To learn more about any WDW Resort property or to make a reservation, call (407) W-DISNEY or visit www.disneyworld.com.

MAJOR HOTEL CHAINS IN THE ORLANDO AREA

In addition to the Top 15 Business-Friendly Hotels listed in this section, virtually every major hotel chain has at least one property (many have several) in the Orlando area. Often, these chain hotels allow you to earn points and/or frequent flier miles for your stay.

The following is a list of the popular hotel chains with properties in and near Orlando. Many of these chains offer less luxurious and more affordable accommodations than the Top 15 Business-Friendly Hotels listed earlier in this section.

AREA ACCOMMODATIONS

Hotel or Motel	Phone	Web Site
Best Western	(800) 780-7234	www.bestwestern.com
Clarion Hotels	(800) 258-4290	www.choicehotels.com
Comfort Inn	(877) 424-6423	www.choicehotels.com
Courtyard by Marriott	(800) 321-2211	www.marriott.com
Crowne Plaza	(800) 980-6429	www.crowneplaza.com
Days Inn	(866) 331-3414	www.daysinn.com
Econo Lodge	(800) 4-CHOICE	www.choicehotels.com
Embassy Suites	(800) EMBASSY	www.embassysuites.com
Four Points by Sheraton	(866) 837-4258	www.sheraton.com
Hampton Inn	(800) HAMPTON	http://hamptoninn1.hilton.com/en_US/hp/index.do
Hilton	(800) HILTONS	www.hilton.com
Holiday Inn	(888) HOLIDAY	www.holidayinn.com
Howard Johnson Express Inn	(800) 446-4656	www.hojo.com
Hyatt	(800) 233-1234	www.hyatt.com
La Quinta	(800) 567-7720	www.lq.com
Loews	(800) 23-LOEWS	www.loewshotels.com
Marriott	(800) 242-8685	www.marriott.com
Omni Hotels	(800) THE-OMNI	www.omnishorehamhotel.com
Ramada Inn	(800) 567-7720	www.ramada.com
Renaissance	(800) HOTELS-1	http://marriott.com/renaissance-hotel/travel.mi
Residence Inn	(800) 331-3131	www.residenceinn.com
Ritz-Carlton	(800) 241-3333	www.ritzcarlton.com
Sheraton	(800) 223-6550	www.sheraton.com

AREA ACCOMMODATIONS

Hotel or Motel	Phone	Web Site
Super 8	(800) 567-7720	www.super8.com
Westin	(800) WESTIN-1	www.westin.com
Wyndham	(800) 847-8232	www.wyndham.com

ALTERNATIVE ACCOMMODATIONS FOR BUSINESS TRAVELERS

More and more business travelers, especially those who travel to Orlando with their families, are opting to forego the hotel or traditional resort accommodation experience in favor of renting a private, luxury home, condo, or townhouse. These properties offer a more homelike environment, but with the amenities you'd expect from a top hotel or resort.

The homes, condos, and townhouses available for rent from companies like All-Star Vacation Homes (800-592-5568, 407-997-0733, www.allstarvacationhomes.com) are all fully furnished and offer two to seven bedrooms and accommodations that come complete with a full-size and fully equipped kitchen (with new and modern appliances), multiple bathrooms, in-home laundry facilities, a dining room, a living room, a private patio, and a work area. Each rental property offered by All-Star Vacation Homes is carefully selected for its perfect combination of luxury, living space, amenities, and location.

For example, an All-Star Vacation Homes condo that's located within the prestigious Vista Cay Resort provides lavish accommodations in a private, upscale, residential community that's less than a quarter of a mile from the Orange County Convention Center. It's also located just minutes from Universal Orlando and SeaWorld and less than 15 minutes from the Orlando International Airport and the Walt Disney World Resort. Situated on a private lake, the Vista Cay Resort offers its own resort-style clubhouse, swimming pool and Jacuzzi, the availability of meeting rooms and a theater (which seats about 20), a fitness center, and plenty of free parking.

For a business traveler, a stay at the Vista Cay Resort (www.vistacay.com) provides the perfect location, plus a quiet, comfortable, and homelike environment. One difference between staying at this type of rental property as opposed to a hotel or resort is that

> ## ALTERNATIVE ACCOMMODATIONS, continued
>
> guests are not offered daily housekeeping services. Each property is equipped, however, with clean and luxurious linens, towels, dishes, pots, pans, laundry detergent, and toiletries (excluding shampoo). For an additional fee, a midstay housecleaning service is available. This is recommended for stays longer than four or five days.
>
> All-Star Vacation Homes offers dozens of unique properties, each of which has been carefully selected because it has exactly what business travelers want and need to enhance their travel experience. The company works with an interior designer to ensure that all furnishings and in-home amenities combine to create the most comfortable and functional accommodations possible. Most vacation homes, townhouses, and condos available through All-Star Vacation Homes are equipped with a high-end PC-based computer, printer, and high-speed wireless internet access. Each is also equipped with a comfortable desk and work area plus cordless telephones. Most properties also have a swimming pool and/or other resortlike amenities.
>
> All-Star Vacation Homes offers properties for a minimum of a three-night stay. Rates vary based on location, property, and time of year; however, they are extremely competitive with traditional mid-range to high-end resorts and hotels. The company includes a free mid-size rental car (through Enterprise) with each seven-night reservation.
>
> While there are many companies like All-Star Vacation Homes in the Orlando area that rent short-term properties to vacationers and business travelers, this company has been in operation since January 1998 and offers a selection of only high-end, luxury properties, plus top-notch and extremely attentive guest services (available 24 hours per day).

NEED ADDITIONAL HELP FINDING A HOTEL?

If you need additional help finding occupancy at a hotel you can afford during your travel dates, in addition to visiting the popular online travel-related services (such as www.hotels.com), point your web browser to the Orlando/Orange County Convention and Visitors Bureau's web site (www.orlandoinfo.com) or call (800) 972-3304 or (407) 363-5872. For the best selection of available hotels and guestrooms (at the lowest prices), don't wait until the last minute to make your reservations, especially during peak travel times.

TIP

If you're traveling to Orlando with your family, the Staybridge Suites Orlando offers nicely-furnished and very spacious two bedroom/two bath suites, priced between $119.95 and $145.95 per night. These suites are clean, comfortable, and include a full kitchen and dining area, living room area, and bedrooms. The bedrooms and living rooms each have a television. Two locations: 8480 International Drive, Orlando (800-465-4329), which is close to the convention center, SeaWorld, and Universal Studios; and 8751 Suiteside Drive, Orlando (800-972-2590), which is one mile from the Walt Disney World Resort. These resorts contain about 150 suites each in a cluster of three-story buildings that surround an outdoor swimming pool. For details, visit www.ichotelsgroup.com.

TAKE ADVANTAGE OF CONCIERGE SERVICES OFFERED AT YOUR HOTEL

Especially at upscale hotels and resorts, the concierge has been trained to accommodate or fulfill virtually any type of need or request you might have. In addition to suggesting restaurants and making your dining reservations, a concierge can help you obtain golf tee times, spa appointments, and theater or sporting event tickets, even if they're sold out.

You can also consult a concierge for driving directions or to help you coordinate ground transportation, such as limo service, or help you track down and acquire a product or service you need, even if it's on a last-minute basis. For example, if you need to purchase or rent an outfit for a black-tie event, your hotel's concierge can suggest where to shop, then help you line up a tailor or seamstress so your purchase can be ready to wear in time for the event. The concierge can also help you recover luggage misplaced by an airline or run errands that you don't have time to do yourself.

The services offered by a hotel's concierge are typically free of charge. However, for the attention and personalized service you receive, you are expected to tip the concierge staff. If you anticipate having a handful of needs before leaving home, once you book your hotel reservation, contact the concierge in advance of your arrival and begin tapping the services offered in order to save time and make your trip planning easier.

SECTION IV

Bus stop. Photo © Felix Casio

GETTING AROUND
TOWN

Because things throughout the Orlando area are spread out, most business travelers find it the most convenient to either acquire a rental car during their stay or utilize taxis and/or private limousines. However, depending on where you're staying and where you'll be going while in the area, you may be able to save money by utilizing only shuttle buses and shared-van services.

For example, if you'll be staying at the Peabody and the main purpose of your trip is to attend a trade show at the Orange County Convention Center (located across the street), you could simply take a shuttle bus or arrange for transportation to and from the airport, and forgo a rental car since every place you'll be visiting while in Orlando is within walking distance (or can be reached using a free shuttle bus).

Also, if you'll be visiting the Walt Disney World Resort and staying on the resort's property during your entire stay, you won't need a rental car, since you can utilize the free Disney transportation system to get around the WDW property. If you're staying at an on-property resort, you can also utilize the free Disney Magical Express for transportation to and from the airport.

If, however, you'll need to get around a bit, whether it's between several different hotels or locations to attend meetings, dinners, or other events, a rental car (which you'd pick up and drop off at the airport upon your arrival and departure) is probably the most convenient and cost-effective option available to you. You'll find that in Orlando, taxi service is readily available, but fares tend to be rather high. The cost of a private limousine or town car will range between $50 and $80 (or more) per hour.

This section focuses on your various ground transportation options while in the Orlando area. Especially during busy travel times, it's best to make your ground transportation reservations in advance, to ensure the best rates and that the transportation you require will be available. You'll find that during holidays and other peak travel times (or when a major NASCAR event is happening in Daytona Beach), rental cars tend to sell out quickly and go for premium rates.

TAXIS

The benefit of utilizing taxis is that they're readily available, 24 hours per day, and they provide convenient door-to-door service. Taxi stands are located at the Orlando International Airport, at all of the major hotels, theme parks, and attractions, as well as at the Orange County Convention Center. You can also call a taxi company directly to schedule a pickup in advance or ask your hotel's concierge for assistance in hailing a taxi when you need one. Be sure to call 20 to 40 minutes prior to when you'd like to leave.

TIP
It's important to know the exact address where you're headed. There are literally hundreds of hotels, motels,

resorts, restaurants and tourist attractions in the Orlando area. While most taxi drivers will know exactly how to get to the convention center, the WDW Resort and some of the popular hotels and restaurants, don't expect your driver to know the exact location of less popular destinations.

Mears Transportation (407-422-2222, www.mearstransportation.com), operating under the names Yellow Cab Company, Checker Cab Company, and City Cab Company, has the largest fleet of taxis in Orlando (with more than 500 vehicles). But there are well over a dozen other privately owned and operated taxi companies that also offer service in and around the Orlando area. While the color, make, and model of the vehicles used as taxis vary greatly, make sure the taxis you hire have the familiar taxi light on the roof and are licensed.

MONEY SAVER
Mears Transportation's taxi service offers a free, online taxi fare estimator (www.mearstransportation.com/TaxiFareEstimator.asp). Enter your starting location and intended destination to determine an approximate fare in advance.

The following is a sampling of local taxi companies:

- AAA Yellow Cab Service and Shuttle—(407) 281-7111
- Ability Can Company—(407) 292-9291
- Ace Metro Cab Company—(407) 855-1111
- A1 Taxi—(407) 812-7252
- Airport Yellow Cab & Shuttle—(407) 298-4661
- All-Star Transportation—(407) 851-9727
- Airport Cab of Kissimmee—(407) 808-5555
- Celebration Cab Company—(407) 465-1100
- Chek a Cab in Lake Buena Vista—(407) 251-2222
- Gator Cab—(407) 855-0800
- Mr. Taxi—(407) 293-9616
- Orlando Cab—(407) 823-7214
- Standard Taxi—(407) 857-3433

Taxi Rates

The taxi companies in and around Orlando operate on predetermined metered fares, which are calculated based on distance traveled and waiting time (such as time stuck in traffic or moving very slowly). Tolls and other surcharges may also be added to the fare. The metered rates, however, vary by county or within the Orlando area. The rates charged by a taxi based in downtown Orlando will be different than those charged by a taxi company in nearby Kissimmee or Lake Buena Vista, for example.

Following are the rates for the taxi companies that are operated by Mears:

- $3.50 for the first mile
- $2 for each additional mile (or fraction thereof)
- $ .44 cents per minute of waiting time

RENTAL CARS

If you're traveling with multiple people, need to transport heavy or bulky items back and forth to a convention center, and/or want plenty of flexibility and convenience when you travel, renting a car can be worthwhile. While a rental car offers the ultimate in convenience, you'll wind up paying for parking, gas, and possibly rental car insurance in addition to the daily or weekly rental fee.

TIME SAVER
Always keep your vehicle rental agreement in the car with you. If you experience any problem with the vehicle, contact the rental car company immediately. Companies typically provide roadside service, towing, flat-tire repair, free vehicle replacement, or any other services required.

You can pick up and return your rental car at the Orlando International Airport or at any branch or satellite office operated by the rental car company you do business with. Companies like Hertz, Avis, and National, for example, have rental car counters at many of the major Orlando-area hotels and resorts.

WARNING
You are responsible for all parking tickets and/or fines for moving violations during the time you possess a rental car.

Through an online travel service (such as Hotwire.com, Travelocity.com, or Orbitz.com), you can often find competitive rates for car rentals. In some cases, however, your reservation made online cannot be changed or refunded. The rental fee charged by these online services does not include insurance, parking, or gas. All the popular rental car companies offer free unlimited mileage (except in some cases for high-end, premium cars).

TIP
When making your reservation directly with a rental car company, make sure you reserve any additional services or add-ons you'll want, such as a navigation system, satellite radio capabilities, or a smoking versus nonsmoking vehicle.

If you want to be able to change your reservation, contact the rental car company directly. Keep in mind, many of the rental car companies provide discounts to corporate travelers, members of AAA or AARP, or members of certain airline frequent flier programs. Regardless of which rental car company you do business with, the quoted rate will be for one primary driver over the age of 25 who has a major credit card in his or her name. All of the rental car companies charge an additional fee (up to $20 per person, per day) to add additional drivers to the rental agreement.

TIME SAVER
To obtain discounts and dramatically speed up the process of picking up and dropping off your rental car, when making your reservation, join the rental car company's frequent renters club (e.g., Hertz #1 Club or Avis Preferred Service). Membership is free, there's generally less paperwork to fill out when you arrive to pick up the car, and the vehicle will be waiting for you.

Like hotel guestroom rates, rental car rates fluctuate dramatically in Orlando based in part on current demand. During a slower travel time, finding a compact car for between $15 and $25 per day (plus insurance, tax, parking, and gas) is relatively easy. During peak travel times when demand is higher for cars, plan on spending upwards of $35 to $50 per day (plus insurance, tax, parking, and gas) for a compact rental car.

WARNING
When you pick up your vehicle, the rental car company will charge a $200 to $400 deposit to your credit or debit card. This is money that will be refunded when you return the vehicle undamaged, but that won't be available to you in the meantime for purchases, so plan your budget accordingly. Some rental car companies will rent vehicles only to people with a major credit card in their name; they will not accept a debit card.

Once you have picked up the rental vehicle, if you want to extend the rental period, be sure to contact the rental car company *before* the car is due to be returned. The appropriate phone number to call is listed within your rental agreement. Failure to do this will likely result in additional fees, since vehicles returned late are often charged by the hour, not by the day. The rental agreement lists the date and time by which the vehicle must be returned, as well as the return location. Any delay over one hour will likely result in extra fees.

For an additional per-day fee (which can double or triple the price of the rental), you can purchase a variety of insurance options from the rental car company to protect the vehicle, you, any passengers, your belongings, plus any victims of accidents. A loss damage waiver (LDW), for example, covers the cost to repair any damage to the rental vehicle, for any reason. This insurance alone will cost an additional $19.95 to $40 per day, depending on the vehicle type and the rental car company.

Some people automatically receive rental car coverage as part of their existing personal auto insurance policy, when they use a particular credit card, or through their business or employer. To save money, figure out what coverage you already have and purchase only the additional insurance you want or need, if any.

MONEY SAVER
Hertz offers a special discount program for small-business travelers. When masking your reservation, mention discount code CDP#1188888.

Rental Car Companies Servicing Orlando

All of the popular rental car companies have a presence at Orlando International Airport and operate satellite offices throughout the

Orlando area where cars can be picked up or dropped off. To avoid additional fees, you'll typically be required to pick up and drop off the vehicle at the same location.

Many of the hotels and resorts can also assist you with obtaining a rental car on-site regardless of whether a rental car company has a branch located at that hotel. In many cases, the hotel concierge or ground transportation desk can arrange to have a rental vehicle delivered to your hotel.

Rental Car Companies Servicing Orlando

The following are the major rental car companies with locations throughout the Orlando area. Some of these companies, including Alamo, Budget, Dollar, L&M Car Rental, and National, allow you to pick up your vehicle from the garage located right outside of Orlando International Airport. Others, like Hertz, require that you ride a free shuttle bus from the airport to the company's rental car facilities, located within a five-minute drive of the airport.

RENTAL CAR COMPANIES IN ORLANDO

Company	Phone	Web Site
Accessible Minivan Rental	(800) 308-2503	www.discountmobilityusa.com
Advantage/Eagle	(407) 397-9799	www.eagle-rent-a-car.com
Alamo	(800) 462-5266	www.alamo.com
Avis	(800) 331-1212	www.avis.com
Bargain Car Rental	(407) 381-1055	N/A
Budget	(800) 527-0700	www.budget.com
Dollar	(800) 800-3665	www.dollar.com
Enterprise	(800) 261-7331	www.enterprise.com
E-Z Rent-a-Car	(800) 277-5171	www.e-zrentacar.com
Hertz	(800) 654-3131	www.hertz.com
L&M Car Rental	(800) 227-5171	www.lmcarrental.net
National	(800) 227-7368	www.nationalcar.com
Payless Car Rental	(407) 856-5539	www.paylesscarrental.com
Thrifty	(800) THRIFTY	www.thifty.com

TIP

Luxury Rental Cars of Orlando (888-641-9211, 407-809-0800, http://luxrentals.com, 7822 West Irlo

Bronson Highway, Kissimmee, Florida) offers a fleet of high-end SUVs, sports cars, and luxury vehicles to drivers over the age of 25 who have a major credit card and proof of insurance. As of 2007, available vehicles included a Hummer H2, Hummer H2 Victory Red Limited Edition, Lincoln Navigator, Corvette convertible, Prowler, Mercedes-Benz CLK 430 Cabriolet, Mini Cooper convertible, and Cadillac Escalade. One-day, three-day, weekly, and monthly rates are available. A Hummer H2, for example, can be rented for $249 per day (plus gas and insurance). This includes 150 free miles per day.

When you pick up your rental vehicle, it will contain a full tank of gas. Depending on your rental agreement, either you can return the car on empty (because you have prepurchased the gas) or you must return the car with a full tank of gas. Failure to meet your obligations could result in significant extra charges.

TIP
Need driving directions? If you have a wireless Palm-OS or Pocket PC Smartphone, you can purchase a Bluetooth GPS navigation system (for about $300) that will help you find your way to and from any destination within the United States. Small stand-alone units that can be used with any vehicle (without any installation) are also available from companies such as TomTom (www.tomtom.com). These products can be extremely useful to business travelers driving in unfamiliar territories.

CHAUFFEURED LIMOUSINES AND TOWN CARS

For the upscale business traveler, getting around Orlando in a chauffeured limousine or town car is a preferred and convenient way to travel. Chauffeured stretch limousines, standard limos, and town cars can be rented by the hour, half day, or full day. Rates differ among the various companies, but the average rate ranges from $50 to $75 per hour for a basic limousine or up to $125 per hour for a superstretch limousine, plus tip and tolls. Some companies require a three-hour minimum.

Many of the hotels provide limo service upon request (for a fee), or you can book directly with any of the companies listed later in this section. You can also reserve limousine service online at www.limos.com.

All the limousine companies listed in this section offer airport pickup and drop-off service. Once you make your reservation, keep the limo company's phone number, reservation number, and pickup location address handy. You want to be able to contact the company if your travel itinerary changes or if the limo is late.

Reasons to rent a limousine include:

- To pamper and impress an important client or customer
- Convenience and comfort
- To travel in luxury to or from the airport, convention center, a restaurant, or a business meeting
- To celebrate a special event
- To enjoy extra comfort when sightseeing

MONEY SAVER

Especially if you're reserving limousine service for an extended period of time, prices and services are often negotiable.

Limousine Companies Servicing the Orlando Area

In addition to the fleet of more than 200 luxury, late-model sedans, plus 13 stretch limousines available for hire through Mears Transportation (407-423-5566, www.mearstransportation.com), there are over 100 independent limousine companies operating in Orlando and surrounding areas.

The rate for hiring a Mears sedan is $40 per hour (with a three-hour minimum), but the company offers flat rates with no minimum to and from a variety of locations, such as from Orlando International Airport to the Disney theme parks, Lake Buena Vista, 192 East, 192 West, International Drive, and the Universal Orlando area.

The following is a sampling of the other limousine and sedan companies operating in the Orlando area.

LIMOUSINE COMPANIES IN ORLANDO

Company	Phone
AAA Limo Inc.	(407) 383-4535
Ace Luxury Transportation	(407) 292-4444
A.D. Limousine	(407) 889-4727
All Luxury Transportation	(407) 414-4468

LIMOUSINE COMPANIES IN ORLANDO

Company	Phone
American Executive Town Car Service	(407) 341-8000
Celebrity Transportation	(407) 854-3891
Exotic Limousines	(407) 240-6010
Five Star Limousine Service	(407) 322-7005
Florida Town Car Service	(407) 277-5466
Four Shuttle	(407) 641-6580
Luxury Rides	(407) 493-9477
M&L Limousines	(407) 239-2818
1-800-BOOK-A-LIMO	(800) 266-5254
Orlando Carriers	(407) 936-0513
Superior Transportation	(407) 816-8606
Trans Orlando	(407) 898-9883
United Town Car Service	(407) 810-8387
Wheels to Wings Transportation	(407) 240-6655
Your Favorite Chauffeurs	(407) 206-0752
Zoom Transportation	(407) 491-5851

PUBLIC TRANSPORTATION

The Lynx (407-841-5969, www.golynx.com) is the public bus transportation system that operates in and around Orlando. From the web site, you can access a system map and route planner. The one-way, single fare to travel anywhere in the system is $1.50 per person. This is a relatively slow and inconvenient way to get around, but it's cost-effective.

The I-Ride Trolley

If you need to travel up and down International Drive (to and from your hotel to a restaurant, the convention center, the various shops, or an attraction), an alternative to taking a taxi is to ride the popular I-Ride Trolley (407-354-5656, www.iridetrolley.com). The bright green trolleys operate every 20 minutes, between 8 A.M. and 10:30 P.M. daily. The single ride (one-way) fare is $1. An unlimited day pass is available for just $3, and a three-day pass is available for $5. Passes can be purchased at more than 100 locations along International Drive.

The Main Line trolley route follows International Drive from the Prime Outlets Orlando to SeaWorld, then continues to the southern area of International Drive and ends at the Orlando Premium Outlets. There are 77 stops along the route. The Green Line trolley route stays more in the business district of International Drive. To see detailed route maps, visit www.iridetrolley.com/map.asp.

The Walt Disney World Resort Transportation System

Occupying more 25,000 acres (or 40 square miles), the Walt Disney World Resort is located in Lake Buena Vista, just outside the city limits of Orlando. To get around this resort complex, which is twice the size of Manhattan, visitors can drive their own car or utilize the Disney transportation system, which consists of a fleet of more than 200 air-conditioned buses, several water taxis, and the Disney monorail system. The bus system offers convenient and free transportation to and from any on-property resort to any of the theme parks or attractions. Bus stops are located outside every resort and in front of each attraction. Depending on your starting point and destination, follow the signs to utilize the best bus route.

For hotels and attractions located along Disney's lakes and waterways, water taxi (boat) transportation is also available. Hours of operation vary by route. Typically, buses traveling to and from one of the on-property hotels to one of the theme parks will begin to operate an hour before the theme park opens and continue until one hour after it closes. Depending on the route, buses operate

Connecting the Magic Kingdom to Epcot and several of the on-property resorts, the Disney monorail system is a fun, free, and convenient way to travel.

Taking a Disney bus is a much cheaper alternative than utilizing taxis, although a ten-minute taxi ride could take up to one hour via the bus system. The Disney transportation system is free to Disney hotel guests and Disney theme park ticket holders. The Disney airport transportation service is only for Disney resort guests. Both services are free of charge.

every 10 to 30 minutes. Plan on each trip taking anywhere from 10 to 60 minutes each way.

SHUTTLE AND CHARTER BUSES

If you're attending a large convention, your convention organizers may arrange for complimentary bus transportation between the convention center and the nearby hotels.

For a fee, shuttle bus and shared-van services are available to and from the Orlando International Airport. See Section I, "Welcome to Orlando," for details. You'll find a list of charter bus services (available for rent) within Section IX, "Business Services."

TIP
If you're staying at a resort located on the WDW Resort's property, you can take advantage of Disney's Magical Express airport transportation service to get to and from the airport. For details, see Section I, "Welcome to Orlando."

DRIVING AROUND ORLANDO

There are a few things to understand about driving around the Orlando area that will make your navigation easier. Several of the major roadways, including the following, have both numbers and names that are referred to interchangeably:

- International Drive is also called I-Drive. This is a heavily populated and popular tourist area where many hotels, motels, resorts, restaurants, and attractions are located.

- Interstate 95 is also called I-95. It travels along Florida's east coast, often along the Atlantic Ocean. It begins in Miami and extends to the northeastern states.
- State Road 192 (SR 192) is also called the Irlo Bronson Memorial Highway.
- State Road 408 (SR 408) is also called the East-West Expressway.
- State Road 417 (SR 417) is also called the Greenway.
- State Road 436 (SR 436) is also called Semoran Boulevard.
- State Road 482 (SR 482) is also called Sand Lake Road.
- State Road 528 (SR 528) is also called the Bee Line/Beach Line Expressway.
- Interstate 4 is also called I-4. This roadway bisects the Orlando area and travels from southwest Tampa (on Florida's west coast) to the northwest Daytona area along the state's east coast.

TIP
For real-time traffic information in Orlando, visit www.fl511.com.

Driving Distances from Orlando International Airport

The following chart offers approximate distances between the Orlando International Airport and popular destinations in the Orlando area.

DRIVING DISTANCES

Location	Distance from Airport
Cocoa Beach	46 miles
Daytona Beach	54 miles
Downtown Orlando	9 miles
Kennedy Space Center	54 miles
Kissimmee/St. Cloud	20 miles
Lake Buena Vista	20 miles
Miami	232 miles
Orange County Convention Center	20 miles
Port Canaveral	42 miles

DRIVING DISTANCES	
Location	Distance from Airport
SeaWorld	18 miles
Universal Studios	22 miles
WDW Resort	22 miles

Driving Directions to Popular Orlando-Area Destinations

The following are basic driving directions from the Orlando International Airport to popular destinations. For more personalized or detailed directions, consider utilizing MapQuest (www.mapquest.com) or Yahoo! Maps (http://maps.yahoo.com).

ORLANDO INTERNATIONAL AIRPORT TO ORANGE COUNTY CONVENTION CENTER

Go west on SR 528 to Exit 1 (International Drive). Take a right off the exit (proceed north) and go approximately one mile to the convention center. The West Concourse parking lot can be accessed by turning left at Convention Way (south entrance), Exhibit Way (north entrance), or by following Westwood Boulevard/West Entrance Drive (west entrance). The North/South Building parking lot can be reached by turning right at the South Concourse sign, or by continuing north on International Drive and turning right onto Convention Way. From Convention Way, turn right onto Universal Boulevard.

TIP

For quick driving directions between locations (theme parks, resorts, etc.) within the WDW Resort, visit www.wdwinfo.com/wdwinfo/transportation/transportation1.cfm.

ORLANDO INTERNATIONAL AIRPORT TO THE WALT DISNEY WORLD RESORT

To get to the Epcot or Disney's Hollywood Studios area, take the North Exit Road from Orlando International Airport to SR 528 West (Bee Line/Beach Line Expressway). Take SR 528 West to I-4 West, and follow signs to Walt Disney World. The trip is about 22 miles.

To get to the Magic Kingdom, Disney's Animal Kingdom, or Disney's Wide World of Sports area, take the South Exit Road from

Orlando International Airport to SR 417 West (Greenway). Follow signs to Walt Disney World. The trip is about 22 miles.

TIP

A detailed map of the WDW Resort can be found at www.kingdom-travel.com/Walt_Disney_World_Resorts/_ResortAssets/Walt_Disney_World_Map.pdf.

ORLANDO INTERNATIONAL AIRPORT TO UNIVERSAL STUDIOS FLORIDA

Take the North Exit Road from Orlando International Airport to SR 528 West (Bee Line/Beach Line Expressway). From SR 528 proceed to I-4 East and follow signs to Universal Orlando. The trip is about 18 miles.

TIP

Within the WDW Resort, there are three Hess gas stations. The first is located near the Magic Kingdom, on World Drive. A car care center (for minor car repairs) is located here. At this location there's also an Alamo and National Car Rental location, where vehicles can be picked up or dropped off. A second Hess gas station is located near Pleasure Island, with a third located near the area of MGM Studios and Disney's BoardWalk. All three are open 24 hours per day. Gas prices at these three gas stations are usually about five cents per gallon cheaper than at other gas stations located outside the Disney property.

TRAVEL NOTES

SECTION V

© Joy Brown

WHERE TO DINE IN
ORLANDO

In addition to offering dozens of tourist attractions and hundreds of hotels and resorts, Orlando is also where you'll find literally thousands of restaurants, featuring everything from fast food to multicourse gourmet meals—many influenced by cultures, countries, and cooking styles from around the world.

While it would be impossible to profile all of the amazing dining experiences the Orlando area has to offer, this section offers information about our 20 Top Business-Friendly Restaurants, where you can enjoy a top-quality meal in an environment that's conducive to conversation and entertaining important customers, clients, co-workers, or friends. But first, other types of more causal dining options are described in this section.

If you're staying at the WDW Resort, you'll find well over 100 restaurants on site, including a handful of fine-dining restaurants within the theme parks themselves plus multiple gourmet dining experiences within the various Disney resort hotels. For additional information about these restaurants or to make a reservation, call (407) WDW-DINE.

TIP

For more personalized restaurant recommendations, contact your hotel's concierge, who can offer suggestions based on the type of cuisine you're looking for, your location, and your budget, as well as assist you in making your dining reservations.

ORDERING ROOM SERVICE

Most midpriced to high-end Orlando hotels and resorts have at least one or two restaurants on the premises, which are often well worth experiencing for a "power breakfast," lunch, or dinner. However, if after a long day you just want to relax in your hotel room and dine in, consider ordering from your hotel's room service menu. The meals are typically prepared by the chefs from the hotel's inhouse restaurants and delivered to your hotel room within 30 to 45 minutes. Many business travelers opt for room service as opposed to dining out.

MONEY SAVER

Typically, the hotel will automatically add a 15 to 20 percent tip for the server to your room service bill. This will be itemized separately. There will, however, be an additional line on the bill to add an extra tip. Determine if a tip has already been included before adding another one.

When ordering room service, be prepared to pay regular menu prices, an extra delivery charge and service charge (which can each be as high as 20 percent of the total bill), in addition to local sales tax and a 15 to 20 percent tip for the server. While in-room dining is convenient, utilizing room service can almost double the price of your meal (as opposed to eating at the hotel's restaurant within its regular dining room).

Some of the reasons business travelers prefer room service include:

- To save time
- As a matter of convenience
- To get additional work done in their guestroom while waiting for the food to be delivered
- To be able to relax and enjoy watching TV or a movie while dining in the comfort of their guestroom
- To have a quiet and relaxing dining experience, without having to travel to a restaurant or make reservations
- To enjoy a fine-dining experience without having to dress up for the occasion (pajamas or a bathrobe are appropriate attire for private in-room dining)
- To host a small business meeting in their guestroom with top-quality food, so they can have access to important work documents, their computer, and a telephone, for example
- To avoid dining alone in public

THEME AND SPECIALTY RESTAURANTS

The following is a sampling of Orlando's many theme restaurants and midpriced dining experiences (for lunch or dinner) that offer something unique.

TIP
Located along International Drive, as well as Highway 192 (near the WDW Resort), you'll find literally hundreds of fast-food and franchise dining options plus many upscale dining establishments. Universal's CityWalk, Disney's Pleasure Island, and Pointe Orlando are additional places where you'll find multiple dining options in close proximity.

Buca Di Beppo
Address: 1351 Orlando Avenue, Orlando
Phone number: (407) 622-7663
Web site: www.bucadibeppo.com

DESCRIPTION

This family-style restaurant offers a festive atmosphere, an extensive menu chock full of classic Italian dishes, and extremely large portions. The restaurant serves great food at a relatively low price, with large tables and private dining areas able to accommodate parties of 2 to 50 (or more). This is not the place to go for a formal business dinner, but for a casual lunch or dinner, you can't go wrong. The restaurant is located within the Florida Mall. Hours: Monday through Saturday, 11 A.M. to 10 P.M.; and Sundays, 11 A.M. to 9 P.M.

ESPN Club

Address: Disney's BoardWalk, 2101 Epcot Resort Boulevard, Orlando

Phone number: (407) 939-1177

Web site: www.disneyworld.com

DESCRIPTION

Similar to the ESPN Zone restaurants located throughout the country, ESPN Club offers a casual sports bar and restaurant atmosphere. Featuring all-American cuisine, this is definitely a haven for sports fans. In addition to large-screen televisions showing sporting events, the restaurant offers interactive video games. Hours: Sunday through Thursday, between 11:30 A.M. and 1 A.M.; Friday and Saturday, between 11:30 A.M. and 2 A.M. During busy periods or when a major sporting event is taking place, the ESPN Club can get a bit loud and crowded. Plan on spending at least $20 per person (not including alcohol).

Hard Rock Café

Address: Universal CityWalk, 6050 Universal Boulevard, Orlando

Phone number: (407) 351-7625

Web site: www.hardrock.com

DESCRIPTION

On display here is an incredible collection of original music memorabilia. This is the largest Hard Rock Café in the world. While enjoying the midpriced American cuisine, you can't help but look around at the priceless pieces of memorabilia from the Beatles, Led Zeppelin, Billy Joel, Elvis Presley, Madonna, John Lennon, Jimi Hendrix, and countless other musical greats. You can always count on a loud and festive atmosphere. There's also a large gift and souvenir shop. Open seven days for lunch and dinner. Hours: 11 A.M. until "late." This restaurant also offers a 3,000 seat concert venue

The menu at the Hard Rock Café features burgers, salads, steaks, chicken, and seafood dishes, plus sandwiches and a wide range of other American favorites, like Texas chili and barbequed baby back ribs.

where live music is performed regularly. Advance reservation (but not same-day reservations) can be made online only.

The Grape Wine Bar

Address: Pointe Orlando, 9101 International Drive, Orlando
Phone number: (407) 351-5815
Web site: www.yourgrape.com

DESCRIPTION

Located across the street from the Orange County Convention Center and within a short walk of the Peabody Hotel, the Grape Wine Bar is a sophisticated, business-friendly place to enjoy an afternoon or evening cocktail. Between 120 and 150 different varieties of wine are served by the bottle (and many by the glass). Before purchasing any wine, you're invited to sample it. This is also an excellent place to enjoy a relatively inexpensive but classy Sunday brunch (between 11 A.M. and 2 P.M.). Outdoor patio seating is available, weather permitting. Hours: Monday through Thursday, between 11 A.M. and 11 P.M.; Friday and Saturday, between 11 A.M. and midnight; and Sunday, between noon and 9 P.M. If you're dining nearby, at the Capital Grille or Maggiano's Little Italy, for example, this is a great place to drop by afterward for a nightcap.

Hooters

Addresses: 8510 Palm Parkway, Lake Buena Vista; 9101 International Drive, Orlando (Pointe Orlando); and inside the Orlando International Airport
Phone number: (407) 239-0900
Web site: www.hooters.com

DESCRIPTION

This popular restaurant and bar chain caters primarily to a male clientele, with its cadre of world-famous (and scantily clad waitresses). The menu offers everything from fish and chips, soups, burgers, and steamed clams to sandwiches and salads. Hooters is also famous for its chicken wings and other appetizers, but most guys don't really come here just for the food. It's open for lunch and dinner. Hours vary.

House of Blues

Address: 1490 E. Buena Vista Drive, Lake Buena Vista
Phone number: (407) 934-2583
Web site: www.hob.com

DESCRIPTION

Serving up tasty, southern-inspired lunches and dinners daily, the House of Blues also contains its own concert venue where big-name artists perform regularly. Menu items include appetizers, "stock pot" entrees (such as New Orleans-style chicken gumbo), salads, sandwiches, southern specialties (such as Louisiana shrimp Creole and Cajun meatloaf with shrimp), chicken, Tasso ham, and brick-oven roasted pizza. House of Blues offers a midpriced, casual dining experience. Hours: Monday through Thursday, 7:30 P.M. to 2 A.M.; Friday and Saturday, 8 P.M. to 2 A.M.; and Sunday, 9 P.M. to 3 A.M.

Jimmy Buffet's Margaritaville

Address: Universal CityWalk, 6068 Universal Boulevard, Orlando
Phone number: (407) 363-8000
Web site: www.margaritavilleorlando.com

DESCRIPTION

Featuring a full bar that serves exotic drinks (along with margaritas), plus a full-service dining room, this is a popular nightspot. Specialties include chicken and broccoli pasta, bayou shrimp pasta, crab cakes, Jimmy's jammin' jambalaya, coconut shrimp, and jerk salmon. A wide range of appetizers, soups, salads, sandwiches, burgers, and desserts round out the eclectic menu. The atmosphere is typically loud and crowded, but the food is good. A casual dining and drinking experience is offered for lunch and dinner. Usually open until 2 A.M. daily. Limited menu after 10:30 P.M. If the restaurant is empty, it will close a bit earlier.

Medieval Times Dinner and Tournament

Address: 4510 W Irlo Bronson Highway, Kissimmee
Phone number: (407) 396-1518
Web site: www.medievaltimes.com

DESCRIPTION

This is one of several popular, family-oriented dinner shows in the Orlando area. Medieval Times features knights riding on real horses, special effects, and jousting tournaments as guests enjoy an extremely casual (average in quality) meal. The atmosphere is loud and extremely informal. Kids and teens will appreciate this experience much more than business travelers. One or two shows are presented nightly, typically at 6 P.M., 7:30 P.M., and/or 8:15 P.M. Tickets: $54.95 per adult and $34.95 per child.

The Melting Pot

Address: 7549 West Sand Lake Road, Orlando
Phone number: (407) 903-1100
Web site: www.meltingpot.com

DESCRIPTION

This fast-growing national chain of midpriced restaurants offers an unusual yet sophisticated dining experience. The menu's focus is on a wide range of fondue dishes. Intimate seating in plush booths is provided, but small-group dining is also available. Choose the four-course dining option ($82 to $92 per couple) to truly get the full fondue experience, from appetizer to dessert.

NASCAR Sports Grille

Address: Universal CityWalk, 6068 Universal Boulevard, Orlando
Phone number: (407) 224-7223
Web site: www.nascarcafeorlando.com

DESCRIPTION

Hard Rock Café has a rock 'n' roll theme, Planet Hollywood has a movie theme, while the ESPN Club offers a sports bar experience. The NASCAR Sports Grille offers all-American cuisine and a racing theme, complete with actual NASCAR vehicles on display. While you're waiting to dine (or afterward), you can experience state-of-the-art NASCAR simulators and video games. If you're a NASCAR fan, this is a casual lunch or dinner dining experience you won't want to miss. Hours: 11:30 A.M. until "late."

This restaurant recently underwent a massive, $10 million renovation and reopened in early 2007. Each table now has a built-in plasma TV screen, allowing you to choose the sports programming you want to watch.

NBA City

Address: Universal CityWalk, 6068 Universal Boulevard, Orlando
Phone number: (407) 363-5919
Web site: www.nba.com/nbacity

DESCRIPTION

Think Hard Rock Café or NASCAR Sports Grille, but with an NBA twist. For basketball fans, NBA City provides the ultimate casual, midpriced dining experience. All-American cuisine is served, including grilled steaks, hamburgers, fresh pastas, brick oven pizzas, salads, and sandwiches. All of the desserts are made from scratch. Private dining rooms are available for up to 25 people, but groups of up to 800 can be accommodated. As you dine on entrees that cost less than $15 each, you'll be surrounded by video monitors showing sports programming. Hours: 11:30 A.M. until "late."

Planet Hollywood

Address: Downtown Disney, 1506 East Buena Vista Drive, Lake Buena Vista
Phone number: (407) 827-7827
Web site: www.planethollywood.com

DESCRIPTION

This popular restaurant offers a festive atmosphere, an extensive, midpriced menu (featuring all-American cuisine), and a full bar. What makes it special, however, is the extensive collection of television and movie memorabilia displayed throughout the massive dining rooms. Television monitors broadcast entertainment news, movie trailers, and music videos. The menu includes a diverse range of entrees, all of which are expertly prepared and tasty. It's located in the heart of Downtown Disney and is open every day until late. The restaurant itself is housed within a giant blue globe-shaped building.

Rainforest Café

Address: 1800 E Buena Vista Drive, Lake Buena Vista; the second locations is at the entrance of Disney's Animal Kingdom theme park

Phone number: (407) 827-7827

Web site: www.rainforestcafe.com

DESCRIPTION

With two locations within the WDW Resort (including one near the entrance of Disney's Animal Kingdom theme park), Rainforest Café offers a vast menu featuring American cuisine. Everything from steak and chicken dishes, to salads, seafood, and sandwiches is available. It's a family-oriented, midpriced, casual restaurant that has been designed to look like a rain forest—complete with indoor, simulated thunderstorms and lifelike animatronic animals in the middle of the dining rooms. Rainforest Café also offers a full bar, serving exotic and tropical drinks. This restaurant is definitely more family friendly than business friendly, but the food and atmosphere are festive. Lunch and dinner are served. Hours vary. During busy periods, expect to wait. Reservations are not accepted.

Tommy Bahama's Tropical Café

Address: Pointe Orlando, 9101 International Drive, Orlando

Phone number: (321) 281-5888

Web site: www.tommybahama.com

DESCRIPTION

One of the most recognizable names in casual resort clothing is Tommy Bahama. This is a "lifestyle" clothing brand that promotes a laid-back attitude and is inspired by Caribbean destinations. This same attitude can be found at the Tropical Café, located across the street from the Orange County Convention Center. This is a casual, yet sophisticated, midpriced place to dine for lunch or dinner. A typical meal costs less than $30 per person. Island-inspired cuisine is served. Coconut shrimp and piña colada cake are the house specialties. A full drink menu is available. Hours vary.

Tony and Tina's Wedding

Address: 5795 West Highway 192, Kissimmee
Phone number: (866) 811-4111
Web site: www.tonyandtinaorlando.com

DESCRIPTION

This is an interactive comedy dinner show that recreates a large and extremely festive family wedding—and you are one of the guests. Get ready for a fun, lighthearted, and memorable evening. The admission price includes a full dinner and the show. Dinner performances are held nightly at 7 P.M. Price is $69 per adult, which includes the wedding ceremony, a full Italian dinner, a champagne toast, wedding cake, and dancing to a live band. A cash bar is available. Preferred seating is available for $99 per person. Reservations are required. This casual dinner theater experience lasts about two hours.

TIP

Orlando is home to a handful of other dinner shows, including Dolly Parton's Dixie Stampede Dinner and Show (Orlando, 407-239-4455), Hoop-Dee-Doo Musical Revue (WDW Resort, 407-939-3463), Makahiki Luau (SeaWorld, 407-363-2559), Pirates Dinner Adventure (Orlando, 866-544-6152), Sleuths Mystery Dinner Shows (Orlando, 407-363-1985), The Spirit of Aloha (WDW Resort, 407-939-3463), and Wantilan Luau (Universal Orlando, 407-503-3463), all of which offer family-oriented entertainment and include a casual dinner. Prices range from $45 to $55 per person. Show times vary. Private parties can be accommodated.

The Wine Room

Address: 270 Park Avenue South, Winter Park
Phone number: (407) 696-9463
Web site: www.thewineroom.com

DESCRIPTION

Featuring a classy atmosphere, the Wine Room is a place where wine enthusiasts can socialize, regardless of their level of experience. In addition to serving a vast selection of fine wines, this establishment holds winemaking sessions, during which participants can experience the excitement of handcrafting their very own wine from more than 25 varieties of select grapes brought in from California and Chile. Thus, the Wine Room offers a truly unique experience. All wines are made one barrel at a time and aged in American oak barrels. According to the management, "While most groups are comprised of two to ten people for each barrel of wine being made, the price is not based on the number of people you have participating. It is based on the variety and quantity of wine made, along with your choices of new or used barrels, bottles, corks, capsules and labels. The average total cost for making a half-barrel of wine is $1,100 and $2,100 for a full barrel. Since each barrel yields 20 cases (240 bottles), that breaks down to less than $10 per bottle. This is an extremely good savings, as you are handcrafting wine that is easily comparable to $25 bottles from a liquor store." Be sure to visit the company's web site to learn more about private parties and functions that can be hosted here. Reservations are required.

THE *BUSINESS TRAVELER* TOP 20 FINE-DINING RESTAURANTS IN ORLANDO

Out of the hundreds of fine-dining restaurants in Orlando, this guide describes a handful of options that were selected because they offer:

- A well-rounded menu, including steak, chicken, seafood, and a variety of other entrees.
- A business-friendly environment, featuring tables that can comfortably seat four, six, eight, ten, or more people (some of the restaurants offer private dining rooms).
- Delicious, top-quality food that's expertly prepared by celebrity, award-winning, and/or world-renowned chefs.
- Superior service.
- An extensive wine list and full bar service.

The Business Traveler *Restaurant Ratings*

The restaurants in this section are ranked between one (☆) and four (☆☆☆☆) stars in four categories: *food quality and variety, value, service,* and *business-friendly environment.* A final overall rating is also included, which takes all of these criteria into consideration.

Here's a description of each ranking:

- One Star (☆)—Below Average. Avoid, if possible.
- Two Stars (☆☆)—Average. There is plenty of room for improvement.
- Three Stars (☆☆☆)—Above Average. You'll definitely enjoy the dining experience.
- Four Stars (☆☆☆☆)—Superior. Best of the best! Well worth experiencing.

This section features our picks for the top 20 *Business Traveler* Fine-Dining Restaurants in the Orlando area, listed in alphabetical order. At any of these restaurants, you're virtually guaranteed to enjoy a memorable meal. This is just a sampling of the many fine-dining restaurants that offer a top-notch dining experience and business-friendly environment.

1. Benihana

Location: Hilton Hotel, 1751 Hotel Plaza Boulevard, Lake Buena Vista (the WDW Resort)

Phone number: (407) 827-4865

Web site: www.benihana.com

Reservations required: Strongly recommended

Meals served: Dinner

Price range: $15 to $50 per person

Food Quality and Variety	Value	Service	Business-Friendly Environment	Overall Rating
☆☆☆½	☆☆☆½	☆☆☆☆	☆☆☆	☆☆☆½

DESCRIPTION

World-famous for offering quality Japanese cuisine (including sushi) prepared at your table by expert chefs, Benihana offers a wonderful, fun, and upbeat dining experience. All Benihana restaurants are traditional Japanese-style hibachi steakhouses, called "teppanyaki." Guests dine at group tables (accommodating eight people each). The menu includes a large selection of steak, chicken. and fish entrees, served with rice, vegetables, salad, and soup. A full sushi menu and bar service are also available, as is a wide selection of exotic drinks.

According to the restaurant's management, during its 200-year history, the tabletop cooking offered at Benihana has developed into a highly refined and beautiful form of expression, characterized by an intricate combination of presentation and knife skills by the chef. In 1964, when Benihana opened its first restaurant in New York, the elegant art of teppanyaki cooking was introduced to America.

Benihana offers a casual dining experience that is highlighted by the food's preparation right before your eyes. Hours of operation are Monday through Thursday, 4 P.M. to 10 P.M.; and Friday, Saturday, and Sunday, 2 P.M. to 10 P.M.

2. Brown Derby

Location: Disney's Hollywood Studios (the WDW Resort)
Phone number: (407) WDW-DINE
Web site: www.disneyworld.com
Reservations required: Suggested, but not required
Meals served: Lunch and dinner
Price range: $25 to $75 per person (dinner)

Food Quality and Variety	Value	Service	Business-Friendly Environment	Overall Rating
☆☆☆½	☆☆☆½	☆☆☆½	☆☆☆½	☆☆☆½

DESCRIPTION

Located in the middle of the Disney's Hollywood Studios theme park, this is an upscale, business-friendly restaurant that serves

If you happen to be visiting the Disney theme parks with important clients or co-workers, this is one of the nicest places you'll find to eat within any theme park. The only drawback is that you must have a valid admission ticket to the Disney's Hollywood Studios to dine here.

truly excellent food. The restaurant itself is modeled after the classic Hollywood, California, landmark where the famous Cobb salad was invented. In addition to featuring the Cobb salad (which is excellent), the menu changes seasonally but offers a selection of steak, chicken, and seafood dishes. Soups, salads, appetizers, and desserts round out the menu. Hours: 11:30 A.M. to 4 P.M. (for lunch); 4 P.M. until the Disney's Hollywood Studios' closing time (for dinner). Full bar service is available. Casual (theme park) attire is acceptable.

3. Butcher Shop Steak House

Location: The Mercado, 8445 International Drive, Orlando

Phone number: (407) 363-9727

Web site: N/A

Reservations required: Yes

Meals served: Lunch and dinner

Price range: $40 and up per person

Food Quality and Variety	Value	Service	Business-Friendly Environment	Overall Rating
☆☆☆½	☆☆☆½	☆☆☆	☆☆☆	☆☆☆½

DESCRIPTION

Conveniently located along International Drive (about a five-minute drive from the Orange County Convention Center), the Butcher Shop Steak House is one of many steak restaurants that serve great food in a business casual environment.

All of the steaks served here are hand cut daily by the restaurant's butcher. Only USDA prime and choice grain-fed beef from the Midwest is served. To add flavor, the beef is aged four to six weeks. The signature entrée is the 24-ounce porterhouse steak, although a variety of steak, seafood, and chicken dishes are featured on the menu.

Hours: Sunday through Thursday, between 5 P.M. and 10 P.M.; Friday and Saturday, between 5 P.M. and 11 P.M. In the restaurant's lounge, Martini Night begins at 5 P.M. every Thursday. All martinis are priced at just $5, plus all appetizers are half price. Private dining is available for groups.

4. Cala Bella

Location: Rosen Shingle Creek Resort, 9939 Universal Boulevard, Orlando

Phone number: (407) 996-3663

Web site: www.shinglecreekresort.com

Reservations required: Yes

Meals served: Dinner

Price range: $40 (and up) per person

Food Quality and Variety	Value	Service	Business-Friendly Environment	Overall Rating
☆☆☆☆	☆☆☆☆	☆☆☆☆	☆☆☆☆	☆☆☆☆

DESCRIPTION

For the upscale business traveler and golfer, the Rosen Shingle Creek Resort offers all of the comfort and luxury you'd expect from a world-class resort (see Section III, "Where to Stay While in Orlando). It should come as no surprise that within this type of resort are several superior restaurants that combine a sophisticated and upscale dining atmosphere with excellent service and delicious food.

Salads, seafood dishes, steaks, pastas, vegetarian dishes, and a vast selection of fine wines are featured on the menu at this fashionable Italian bistro. Most entrees are classic Italian dishes with a Mediterranean and/or American influence. The restaurant's décor is classy and overlooks the resort's 18-hole golf course. The high ceilings, Italian artwork, and open kitchen provide a wonderful atmosphere for a business dinner.

The restaurant is open daily, starting at 5:30 P.M. Closing time varies. The dress code is resort casual. Even if you're not staying at this resort, dining at Cala Bella is well worth the trip.

5. Capital Grille

Location: 9101 International Drive, Orlando

Phone number: (407) 370-4392

Web site: www.thecapitalgrille.com

Reservations required: Yes

Meals served: Lunch and dinner

Price range: $50 and up per person (dinner)

Food Quality and Variety	Value	Service	Business-Friendly Environment	Overall Rating
☆☆☆☆	☆☆☆☆	☆☆☆☆	☆☆☆☆	☆☆☆☆

DESCRIPTION

Offering the ultimate upscale steakhouse dining experience, the Capital Grille boasts a selection of fabulous steak and seafood entrees, all expertly cooked to perfection and served in a lavish and

To accompany any meal at the Capital Grille, a nice selection of à la carte side dishes, including vegetables and the popular and extremely tasty lobster mac 'n' cheese, are offered.

sophisticated dining room. This is the perfect place to gather for an important business lunch or dinner. The restaurant is located across the street from the Orange County Convention Center, less than a five-minute walk from the Peabody Hotel, Rosen Plaza Hotel, and Rosen Centre Hotel. It can be found within the newly renovated Pointe Orlando shopping area.

For appetizers, the cold shellfish platter and Petrossian caviar are favorites. For main entrées, the chef's specialties include the filet Oscar (a ten-ounce filet mignon), a Kona-crusted dry-aged sirloin steak with caramelized shallot butter, and the porcini-rubbed delmonico steak with eight-year aged balsamic vinegar. Broiled lobster, fresh grilled swordfish, and fresh seared salmon round out the seafood portion of the menu.

The restaurant boasts a wine list containing more than 800 labels. The wait staff is trained to offer suggestions for perfect wine pairings and expertly explain how each steak entrée is dry aged for two weeks and then prepared, often with signature sauces.

Business casual attire is required. Hours: Monday through Thursday, 11:30 A.M. to 10 P.M.; Friday, 11:30 A.M. to 11 P.M.; Saturday, between 5 P.M. and 11 P.M. (dinner only); and Sunday, 5 P.M. to 9 P.M. (dinner only). If you're looking for a superior meal after spending a day at the Orange County Convention Center, trust the Capital Grille to provide a truly memorable dining experience.

6. Del Frisco's Prime Steak and Lobster

Location: 729 Lee Road, Orlando (Exit 88 off of the I-4 West)

Phone number: (407) 645-4443

Web site: www.delfriscosorlando.com

Reservations required: Yes

Meals served: Dinner

Price range: $50 and up per person

Food Quality and Variety	Value	Service	Business-Friendly Environment	Overall Rating
☆☆☆☆	☆☆☆☆	☆☆☆☆	☆☆☆☆	☆☆☆☆

DESCRIPTION

Del Frisco's Prime Steak and Lobster is definitely one of the very best restaurants in America (yes, the entire country—not just Orlando) in terms of food quality, preparation and service. In fact, the only problem is that this incredible restaurant is located about 30 minutes away from the convention center, WDW Resort, and Universal Orlando areas—but the drive is well worth it!

Since it opened in 1993, owners Russ and Carole Christner have worked every day to ensure only the freshest and highest-quality ingredients are used to prepare each and every meal. Much of the beef, seafood, and vegetables are personally hand selected by Russ or Carole on a daily basis. They've also assembled a truly dedicated and capable staff of servers and chefs, many of whom have been with the restaurant since opening day. This is a family-owned-and-operated business, which provides for a warm, welcoming, and friendly dining experience that you won't find at most chain restaurants.

Your dining experience will begin with freshly baked bread that's served hot. As you peruse through the menu, you'll discover a wonderful selection of prime, aged, corn-fed beef dishes that are expertly cut to order right off the loin. The restaurant's famous lobster tails (one of the signature dishes served here) are cold-water Australian tails flown in daily.

Even the salad dressings, steak sauces, and all side dishes and desserts are homemade and freshly prepared daily using the finest ingredients. To accompany your fine meal, the restaurant's wine room boasts a collection of more than 5,500 bottles and one of the largest selections of single-malt scotches in Florida.

Popular appetizers include a shrimp sampler, crab cakes, and lobster bisque. In addition to a excellent selection of steak entrées, including filet mignon, rib eye, New York strip, and porterhouse, the Australian cold-water lobster tails, veal porterhouse, shrimp scampi, swordfish, and salmon are all mouth-watering entrees that are expertly prepared.

The restaurant offers a sophisticated, business casual environment, featuring live piano music. Several private dining rooms are available. Dinner is served Monday through Saturday, starting at 5 P.M. (closed Sundays). The attire is "coat and tie optional." Reservations are definitely required, since Del Frisco's attracts a large local crowd of upscale diners, in addition to business travelers and vacationers.

If only one fine-dining experience fits into your schedule and/or budget while in Orlando, take the drive to Del Frisco's. You won't be disappointed!

7. DUX

Location: The Peabody Hotel, 9801 International Drive, Orlando

Phone number: (407) 345-4550

Web site: www.peabodyorlando.com

Reservations required: Yes

Meals served: Dinner

Price range: $50 and up per person

Food Quality and Variety	Value	Service	Business-Friendly Environment	Overall Rating
☆☆☆☆	☆☆☆☆	☆☆☆☆	☆☆☆☆	☆☆☆☆

DESCRIPTION

Located across the street from the Orange County Convention Center is Dux, the signature restaurant within the famous Peabody Hotel. This fine-dining restaurant is definitely one of the very best in the area, offering a formal and business-friendly environment, superior service, and expertly prepared food.

The menu includes a selection of appetizers, such as poached Key West shrimp, caviar, oysters, butternut squash bisque, and Maine lobster pasta au gratin, plus several unique and tasty salads. Main entrees include butter-poached Maine lobster, grilled beef tenderloin (USDA prime), sautéed halibut, salmon, free-range chicken crepinette, and rack of lamb.

In addition to the popular and extensive à la carte menu, Dux offers a delicious tasting menu ($65 per person) and a vegetarian tasting menu ($55 per person). Wine pairings can be added for an extra $35 per person.

Keeping with the Peabody Hotel's duck theme, tasteful duck-related artwork adorns the walls of the lovely dining room. With each meal, three kinds of freshly baked breads are served, along with duck-shaped, homemade butter. Dux offers a vast wine line, with more than a dozen fine wines served by the glass. The restaurant also serves several signature martinis (including the popular chocolate chip martini and spiced apple martini) plus specialty coffees.

Make sure you leave room for dessert. The Bailey's chocolate delight cake, trio of crème brûlée, and the cheesecake all make a wonderful ending to a delicious meal. Dessert wines are served by the glass. Dux is definitely one of the more formal restaurants you'll find in the Orlando area, so proper attire and reservations are required.

8. Emeril's Restaurant Orlando

Location: Universal CityWalk, 6000 Universal Blvd, Orlando
Phone number: (407) 224-2424
Web site: www.emerils.com
Reservations required: Strongly recommended
Meals served: Lunch and dinner
Price range: $30 and up per person

Food Quality and Variety	Value	Service	Business-Friendly Environment	Overall Rating
☆☆☆	☆☆☆	☆☆☆	☆☆☆	☆☆☆

DESCRIPTION

If you're a fan of celebrity chef Emeril Lagasse, or you're visiting the Universal Orlando theme parks and you're looking for an upscale, fine-dining experience for lunch or dinner, one good option in the CityWalk area is Emeril's Orlando. While this extremely popular restaurant offers a fun and upbeat atmosphere, plus tasteful décor and excellent food, the main dining room (which seats only 60 people) is small. Thus, a reservation (made as far in advance as possible) is almost always required. Walk-ins are accepted, but expect a significant wait. Several private dining rooms (able to seat between 16 and 60 guests) are available for business functions.

This restaurant serves what Lagasse refers to as new New Orleans-style cuisine, which includes New Orleans barbecue

Emeril's Orlando offers a unique cross between a theme restaurant (which you'll pay a premium to experience) and a fine-dining establishment that's located in the heart of a family-oriented tourist attraction.

shrimp, Creole marinated calamari, Kobe meatballs, blue crab remoulade and black mussels and clams as your appetizer choices. This can be followed up with tasty homemade soup or a salad, before you enjoy a specialty entrée.

For dinner, entrées include hickory-smoked, lemongrass-roasted duck, roasted Atlantic salmon with poached fennel, roasted filet mignon, and a grilled vegetable plate. More than eight of Emeril's favorite desserts are also served, including his own banana cream pie, New Orleans-style bread pudding, and caramelized white chocolate toffee crunch cheesecake. The wine list is also extensive and nicely displayed on the restaurant's wine wall.

Hours: 11:30 A.M. to 3 P.M. (daily for lunch); Sunday through Thursday, 5:30 P.M. to 10 P.M. (dinner); and Friday and Saturday, between 5:30 P.M. and 11 P.M. (dinner). A full service bar is also located within the restaurant.

9. Everglades Restaurant

Location: Rosen Centre Hotel, 9840 International Drive, Orlando
Phone number: (407) 996-2385
Web site: http://evergladesrestaurant.com
Reservations required: Recommended
Meals served: Dinner
Price range: $30 and up per person

Food Quality and Variety	Value	Service	Business-Friendly Environment	Overall Rating
☆☆☆½	☆☆☆½	☆☆☆☆	☆☆	☆☆☆½

DESCRIPTION

Located with the Rosen Centre Hotel (across the street from the Orange County Convention Center), Everglades offers a lovely, somewhat casual, midpriced dining experience in a dining room that promotes a tropical Florida feel. The décor includes a large fish tank, indoor palm trees, life-size animal statues, and colorful artwork. Booths and stand-alone tables are available.

Appetizers include Alligator Bay chowder, Caribbean crab cakes, Florida rock shrimp, and escargot. Broiled-to-order entrées include grilled angus filet, aged New York strip steak, Everglades free-range chicken, venison pepper steak, tenderloin of buffalo, and lamb chops. Seafood entrees include Spanish harbor swordfish, broiled Florida grouper, blackened red snapper, Chilean sea bass, and Maine lobster. A nice selection of soups, salads, side orders, and desserts round out the menu.

Hours: Dinner is served daily, starting at 5:30pm. Closing time varies.

10. Forte Restaurant

Location: Ginn Reunion Resort, 1000 Reunion Way, Reunion
Phone number: (407) 662-1100
Web site: www.reunionresort.com
Reservations required: Yes
Meals served: Breakfast, lunch, and dinner
Price range: $40 and up per person (dinner)

Food Quality and Variety	Value	Service	Business-Friendly Environment	Overall Rating
☆☆☆	☆☆☆	☆☆☆	☆☆☆	☆☆☆

DESCRIPTION

This luxurious and sophisticated fine-dining establishment is located within the Ginn Reunion Resort and overlooks one of its pristine golf courses. It's an excellent option for hosting an upscale business dinner, since the menu offers a diverse selection of entrees plus an extensive wine list.

The restaurant's signature appetizer is the chilled crustacean plateau, which include1s a selection of Mexican white gulf shrimp, lobster tail, oysters, and other seafood delicacies, priced between

While breakfast and lunch are casual at Forte, dinner offers a more upscale atmosphere. A weekend brunch is also served.

$65 and $95 (serves two). Domestic caviar and steak tartare also appear on the appetizer menu. Several soups and salads, including a popular lobster bisque, are served.

Entrées include six mouthwatering steak selections each served with your choice of signature sauces or flavored butters. If you're more in the mood for seafood, you'll find five main seafood entrees featured on the menu, including grilled yellow fin tuna and lobster. Entrees are served à la carte (with six choices of potatoes and six choices of vegetables offered).

Be sure to leave room for the tasty desserts, which include a chilled lemon soufflé, white chocolate and lemon mousse, tropical cheesecake, and crème brûlée. Dessert wines, brandy, whisky, and a selection of gourmet coffees and teas are the perfect way to end a delicious meal.

Dinner is served Monday through Saturday, between 6 P.M. and 10 P.M. Business casual attire is recommended.

11. Jack's Place

Location: Rosen Plaza Hotel, 9700 International Drive, Orlando
Phone number: (407) 996-1787

Web site: www.jacksplacerestaurant.com

Reservations required: Yes

Meals served: Dinner

Price range: $40 and up per person

Food Quality and Variety	Value	Service	Business-Friendly Environment	Overall Rating
☆☆☆☆	☆☆☆☆	☆☆☆☆	☆☆☆½	☆☆☆☆

DESCRIPTION

To pay homage to his father, resort president Jack Rosen has created Jack's Place, a lovely, fine-dining restaurant located within the Rosen Plaza Hotel (across the street from the Orange County Convention Center).

The elegant, midsize dining room contains about 50 tables, each capable of comfortably seating between two and eight guests (although much larger groups can be accommodated). The menu features a variety of chicken, pasta, vegetarian, steak, and seafood dishes that are all very reasonably priced. Menu highlights include a shrimp cocktail appetizer, Jack's house salad, Jack's grilled duck breast, fettuccini diablo, New York strip steak, filet mignon, fresh Florida grouper, and seared halibut. For dessert, toasted truffles,

Originally from New York, Jack Rosen spent his professional life working at the Waldorf-Astoria as a safety engineer. During his employment, which began in 1932, Rosen met and socialized with thousands of the hotel's distinguished and often famous guests. Using his talents as an artist, he often drew caricatures of the people he met and had them autographed by those people. Over the years his collection grew to more than 100,000 drawings, many of which adorn the walls of the Jack's Place dining room.

Jack's famous New York cheesecake, and the chocolate truffle gateau are well worth experiencing.

This is a less formal restaurant than Dux (found in the Peabody Hotel) or the Capital Grille (located across the street from the Rosen Plaza Hotel), but the food quality and service are outstanding. Plan on spending about $30 per person for a lovely dinner. An impressive wine and drink list is available. Hours are 5:30 P.M. to 10 P.M. daily.

12. LaCoquina's Chef Table

Location: Hyatt Regency, One Grand Cypress Boulevard, Orlando

Phone number: (407) 239-3853

Web site: http://grandcypress.hyatt.com/hyatt/hotels/entertainment/restaurants/index.jsp

Reservations required: Yes

Meals served: Dinner

Price range: $95 per person (prix fixe menu); $135 per person with wine pairings

Food Quality and Variety	Value	Service	Business-Friendly Environment	Overall Rating
☆☆☆☆	☆☆☆☆	☆☆☆☆	☆☆☆☆	☆☆☆☆

DESCRIPTION

The elegance and sophistication of the Hyatt Regency Grand Cypress Resort extend to this fine-dining opportunity where chef Orlando invites diners into his kitchen for a truly unique culinary experience that's created right before your eyes. A small, upscale, and intimate dining area (comprising of about six tables) has been set up within the private kitchen, where a personalized, seven-course tasting menu is served.

Prior to each course, the master chef personally visits each table to describe the upcoming course, which he and his staff expertly prepare in the open kitchen. Each table is serviced by a team of waiters and waitresses in order to ensure top-notch, friendly, and extremely attentive service throughout the meal.

While the tasteful décor of the dining room and the novelty of actually eating in the chef's kitchen offer a unique experience, it's the expertly prepared and presented food that makes this meal truly memorable.

Dinner is priced at $95 per person ($135 per person with fine wine pairings to accompany each course). The dining area is dimly lit, well decorated with fine art, and quiet, which makes it

During your meal, expect to experience a sampling of delicious seasonal entrees, including roasted veal tenderloin, seared ahi tuna, buffalo tenderloin, and red pepper-marinated duck. Substitutions can be made to satisfy personal tastes or dietary restrictions. (Photo courtesy of Hyatt Regency.)

ideal for hosting an intimate business dinner or a romantic evening. Formal or business attire is recommended. Dinner is served Thursday, Friday, and Saturday evenings only, between September and June. Hours vary. Reservations are definitely required. If you're not staying at the Hyatt resort, complimentary valet parking is offered.

13. Maggiano's Little Italy

Location: Pointe Orlando, 9101 International Drive, Building #5, Orlando
Phone number: (407) 241-8650
Web site: www.maggianos.com
Reservations required: Yes
Meals served: Lunch and dinner
Price range: $35 and up per person (dinner)

Food Quality and Variety	Value	Service	Business-Friendly Environment	Overall Rating
☆☆☆	☆☆☆	☆☆☆½	☆☆☆	☆☆☆½

DESCRIPTION

Italian cuisine is served "New York style" at this midpriced, business casual restaurant located within Pointe Orlando (across the street from the Orange County Convention Center). Featuring a festive atmosphere, Maggiano's serves classic Italian food for both lunch and dinner.

Appetizers include baked shrimp oreganata, calamari fritte, four-cheese ravioli, jumbo lump crab cakes, stuffed mushrooms, and mussels. Salad offerings include a classic Caesar, chopped salad, Maggiano's signature salad, and a tasty spinach salad. A chopped salad with chicken, Italian antipasti, and arugula salad are among the entrée offerings.

More than a dozen pasta options (featuring large and flavorful portions) are served, along with a handful of chicken dishes, steaks, veal, chops, seafood, and baked specialties. Some of the restaurant's Little Italy favorites include baked ziti and sausage, braised beef cannelloni, lobster ravioli, and chicken cacciatore.

Carry-out meals and private dining rooms are available. Open daily for lunch, between 11 A.M. and 3 P.M. Dinner is served Sunday through Thursday, between 3 P.M. and 10 P.M., and on Friday and Saturday, between 3 P.M. and 11 P.M.

14. McCormick & Schmick's Seafood Restaurant

Location: 4200 Conroy Road, Orlando

Phone number: (407) 226-6515

Web site: www.mccormickandschmicks.com

Reservations required: Yes

Meals served: Lunch and dinner

Price range: $40 and up per person (dinner)

Food Quality and Variety	Value	Service	Business-Friendly Environment	Overall Rating
☆☆☆☆	☆☆☆☆	☆☆☆☆	☆☆☆☆	☆☆☆☆

DESCRIPTION

McCormick & Schmick's has more than 50 locations nationwide; the Orlando restaurant is known for its vast selection of fresh seafood dishes, which typically includes more than 30 seafood varieties offered daily. The menu changes each day, based on fresh seafood deliveries. Alaskan halibut, Northwest salmon, Hawaiian mahi mahi, Oregon petrale sole, and oysters from the United States and Canada are among the house specialties at this upscale restaurant.

The service at McCormick & Schmick's is as exemplary as the food's preparation and presentation. This is a wonderful place to enjoy an elegant business lunch or dinner. Business casual attire is suggested. The restaurant also features a full bar. Hours: Monday through Thursday, between 11 A.M. and 11 P.M.; Friday and

Saturday, between 11 A.M. and midnight; and Sunday, between 11 A.M. and 10 P.M.

15. Morton's Steak House

Location: 7600 Dr. Phillips Boulevard #1, Orlando

Phone number: (407) 248-3485

Web site: www.mortons.com

Reservations required: Yes

Meals served: Dinner

Price range: $40 and up per person

Food Quality and Variety	Value	Service	Business-Friendly Environment	Overall Rating
☆☆☆	☆☆☆	☆☆☆	☆☆☆	☆☆☆

DESCRIPTION

Out of the 74 restaurants that constitute the Morton's Steak House chain, the Orlando location is definitely one of the busiest and most popular, especially among upscale business travelers looking for a hearty steak or seafood dinner.

Appetizers include tuna tartare, smoked Pacific salmon, Maine lobster cocktail, jumbo lump crabmeat cocktail, and oysters on the half shell. Five different salads, including Morton's signature house salad, are offered. The menu includes a large selection of à la carte beef entrées, including double-cut filet mignon,

Featuring a business casual but sophisticated setting, Morton's offers a large and tastefully decorated main dining room, which includes an open view of the main kitchen. Several private dining rooms and a separate bar and lounge are available.

porterhouse steak, New York strip steak, and Chicago-style bone-in rib eye steak. Domestic double-rib lamb chops, chicken Christopher, sesame-encrusted yellow fin tuna, broiled salmon fillet, and jumbo lump crab cakes are among the seafood offerings. All portions are large and expertly prepared.

If you're craving seafood, try either the lobster tail or the whole baked Maine lobster; both are definitely among the most popular and tasty offerings. A large selection of vegetable and potato side dishes are available.

What sets Morton's apart from all of the other fine-dining restaurants in Orlando (and in many other U.S. cities) is not just the expertly prepared and delicious food, but the fact that within the private dining rooms, Velocity Broadcasting's state-of-the-art, live satellite video conferencing service is available, linking any or all of the Morton's restaurant locations. Each private dining room is equipped with 7.2 cinema surround sound; a nine-foot drop-down screen; a digital, 16.9 high-definition projection system; and satellite reception in certified VelocityHD.

Since 1978, Morton's has created a reputation for offering a delicious, fine-dining experience that's complemented by superior service. Like all of the Morton's locations, this one includes tasteful décor (featuring dark wood tables and booths), subdued lighting, and white tablecloths. The walls are adorned with a collection of LeRoy Neiman serigraphs and photographs of local and national celebrities, plus lavish wine displays.

Morton's in Orlando is located about ten minutes from the Orange County Convention Center. Private town car service can be coordinated to and from the restaurant when making your reservation. Hours: Monday through Saturday, between 5:30 P.M. and 11 P.M.; Sunday, 5 P.M. to 10 P.M. The full-service bar opens at 5 P.M. daily.

16. Palm Restaurant

Location: Hard Rock Hotel, 5800 Universal Boulevard, Orlando (within Universal Orlando)

Phone number: (407) 503-7256

Web site: www.thepalm.com

Reservations required: Yes

Meals served: Dinner

Price range: $35 to $50 per person

Food Quality and Variety	Value	Service	Business-Friendly Environment	Overall Rating
☆☆☆½	☆☆☆½	☆☆☆½	☆☆☆½	☆☆☆½

DESCRIPTION

For more than 80 years, the Palm Restaurant has set the standard for fine dining with restaurants in more than 20 U.S. cities. This Palm Restaurant, which opened in 2001, serves huge cuts of prime beef, jumbo lobsters broiled to perfection, and a wide range of other tasty entrees. Veal, pasta dishes, salads, and lamb chops round out the extensive menu, which is accompanied by a vast selection of fine wines.

Like other Palm restaurants, this one is decorated on the walls with sketches of the famous people who have dined here. To accommodate small groups of business travelers, private dining rooms are available. This is an upscale restaurant, so casual business attire is appropriate. Hours: Monday through Thursday, between 5 P.M. and 10 P.M.; Friday through Sunday, 5 P.M. to 9 P.M.

17. Porterhouse Restaurant

Location: Orlando Airport Marriott, 7499 Augusta National Drive, Orlando
Phone number: (407) 851-9000
Web site: http://marriott.com/hotels/travel/mcoap-orlando-airport-marriott
Reservations required: Yes
Meals served: Dinner
Price range: $35 and up per person

Food Quality and Variety	Value	Service	Business-Friendly Environment	Overall Rating
☆☆☆½	☆☆☆½	☆☆☆☆	☆☆☆	☆☆☆½

DESCRIPTION

Located near the Orlando International Airport, you'll find a large cluster of low-end, midpriced, and upscale hotels and motels, some of which, like the Marriott at Orlando Airport, cater primarily to business travelers. Within the Marriott, for example, is an excellent, business-friendly restaurant that features a traditional American steakhouse menu and a lovely, business casual atmosphere.

This midsize restaurant (with an 80-person capacity) allows diners to view the open kitchen as the delicious meals are expertly prepared. Main entrees include a center-cut filet, blue ribbon free-range chicken, roasted gulf grouper, and red snapper. The signature dish is the expertly prepared and flavorful 22-ounce prime porterhouse steak. All steaks are served with a variety of sauce options that add flavor. The portions are large and the service is exemplary.

With more than 100 selections, the wine list is also impressive, and almost two dozen wines are served by the glass. Hours: 5 P.M. to 10 P.M. daily. If you're looking for an excellent, well-priced meal that's close to the airport, Porterhouse Restaurant is a great choice.

18. Portobello Yacht Club

Location: Downtown Disney, 1650 N Buena Vista Drive, Lake Buena Vista
Phone number: (407) 934-8888
Web site: www.disneyworld.com
Reservations required: Recommended
Meals served: Lunch and dinner
Price range: $40 and up per person (dinner)

Food Quality and Variety	Value	Service	Business-Friendly Environment	Overall Rating
☆☆☆	☆☆☆	☆☆☆½	☆☆☆	☆☆☆½

DESCRIPTION

Located in the downtown Disney area of the WDW Resort, Portobello Yacht Club features an upscale dining atmosphere (overlooking the water) and serves classic Italian cuisine, plus steak, seafood, pasta, and pizza dishes. Main entrees are served à la carte ($30 to $50 per person for dinner). Most are prepared in the restaurant's authentic Italian wood-burning oven. An extensive wine selection is also offered.

One of the restaurant's signature appetizers is fried calamari, while entrees include rib eye steak, salon, shrimp scampi, several types of pasta dishes, and red snapper. Casual attire is acceptable and reservations are recommended. The dining room has a warm and inviting Mediterranean flare.

Lunch is served daily, between 11:30 A.M. and 4 P.M., while dinner is served daily, starting at 4 P.M. (closing time varies). During busy travel times, advance reservations are recommended, although walk-ins can be accommodated.

19. Ran-Getsu of Tokyo

Location: 8400 International Drive, Orlando
Phone number: (407) 345-0044
Web site: www.rangetsu.com
Reservations required: Recommended
Meals served: Dinner
Price range: $30 and up per person

Food Quality and Variety	Value	Service	Business-Friendly Environment	Overall Rating
☆☆☆½	☆☆☆½	☆☆☆	☆☆☆	☆☆☆¼

DESCRIPTION

Conveniently located along International Drive, Ran-Getsu offers expertly prepared Japanese cuisine in a casual atmosphere. This restaurant has the largest sushi bar in the Orlando area, and it serves a variety of specialty dishes, including sukiyaki and shabu-shabu (sizzling slices of sirloin beef prepared tableside and accompanied by unique sauces, miso soup, green salad, and rice). A seafood yosenabe meal is also available, featuring Japanese-style bouillabaisse made with fresh seafood and vegetables.

More traditional entrees, including New York strip steak, filet mignon, Ran-Getsu bento, organic pork miso katsu, Chilean sea bass, salmon steak, shrimp tempura, and organic chicken teriyaki are also featured on the extensive menu.

The restaurant is open daily, between 5 P.M. and 11:30 P.M. Live entertainment, including a drum show, is presented throughout the week. The dining room is surrounded by an authentic Japanese garden, complete with koi fish pond.

20. Ruth's Chris Steak House

Location: 7501 West Sand Lake Road, Orlando

Phone number: (407) 226-3900

Web site: www.ruthschris.com

Reservations required: Yes

Meals served: Dinner

Price range: $35 and up per person

Food Quality and Variety	Value	Service	Business-Friendly Environment	Overall Rating
☆☆☆☆	☆☆☆☆	☆☆☆☆	☆☆☆☆	☆☆☆☆

DESCRIPTION

In addition to its famous steak entrées (such as the filet mignon, rib eye, New York strip, and porterhouse), house specialties at Ruth's Chris include ahi tuna steak, veal chop, stuffed chicken breast, fresh lobster, grilled portobello mushrooms, and cold-water lobster tail. An extensive wine list is also available. With any entrée, any of seven varieties of vegetables and/or jumbo shrimp, lobster tail, or other extras can be added. Be sure to leave room for dessert.

The crème brûlée, bread pudding with whisky sauce, and chocolate sin cake are among the popular selections.

One thing that sets the steak entrées served at Ruth's Chris Steak House apart is how they are prepared. All beef is corn fed and cooked in specially designed ovens at 1,800 degrees. Ruth's Chris Steak House is well known for offering a superior fine-dining experience. Private dining rooms are available. Hours: Monday through Saturday, 5 P.M. to 10 P.M.; Sunday, 5 P.M. to 9 P.M. Business casual attire is required and valet parking is offered.

TIPS FOR ORDERING FINE WINE WITH YOUR MEAL

One challenge many business travelers face is choosing an appropriate wine selection to go nicely with the entrees or desserts that are being ordered. Not only do you want to impress the people you're dining with (such as important clients), but you also want to order a quality wine that's within your budget.

To help make the wine-ordering process easier, Michael Salimone, the director of food and beverages at Rosen Shingle Creek in Orlando, along with Andy Myers, the sommelier at the Mandarin Oriental Hotel in Washington, DC, offer some valuable advice.

Salimone explained, "I think people are beginning to get away from the 'white with white meat' and 'red with red meat' thinking, and going more with personal preferences. When choosing an appropriate wine, the number of diners should be part of your decision. A 750 ml bottle, which is the size of a regular bottle of wine, will fill about four very nice-size glasses. Depending upon the diners, a party of four people could very easily put away two to three bottles of wine during dinner. Thus, it would be better to order both a white and red wine when ordering more than one bottle. Too much of one color doesn't offer much variety for everybody around the table, and wine is all about variety. If you are ordering for just two people, I would highly recommend ordering wine by the glass. Most restaurants today offer an extensive choice, so you can vary your selections. You may start off with a glass of white and then go with a glass of red, or even another glass of white. In this case, you are taking care of your own preferences and don't have to worry about the other person at the table, since they too will order based on their own personal preferences."

To ensure you make a great impression with the people you're dining with, Salimone adds, "If this is a make-or-break dinner, do

TIPS FOR ORDERING FINE WINE, continued

some research in advance. Get the wine list from the restaurant where you plan to dine, and predetermine your choices and the prices before you go. When you make your dining reservation, ask for the wine list to be emailed or faxed to you. Next, pick a couple of bottles that you are familiar with and that are within your budget. If you pick the wine to go with dinner by studying before you go, you can recite your choices very quickly to the waiter, which gives the impression you know what you are doing."

In addition to managing the hotel's massive wine collection, one of Andy Myers' responsibilities as the sommelier at the Mandarin Oriental Hotel in Washington, DC, is to help guests dining at the hotel's restaurants choose the best wine to accompany their meals.

Myers explained, "Ideally, the restaurant has a sommelier. If they do, then ask for that person, give them a basic budget for the evening, a feeling for how much your guests are likely to drink, and a rough idea of what kind of wines you like—fruity, earthy, full-bodied, light, etc. That'll solve most of your problems, as a good sommelier likes to have a clear, basic profile of the table, budget, and drinking habits. Using this information, we love it when you trust us to make the experience great."

If the restaurant you're dining at doesn't have a sommelier, Myers stated, "Assume that most people put away about a half a bottle of wine during dinner. This will help when figuring out how much to order. Next, as you'll never please everyone at the table, go for wines that work with lots of flavors. I recommend Sauvignon Blancs, Dry Rieslings, and Chenin Blancs for whites and Pinot Noirs and Rhône Varietals (Syrah, Grenache, Mourvedre) for reds."

Even if a sommelier is not available, most restaurants train their wait staff on how to assist guests in choosing appropriate wines. "Review the wine list to gather some ideas, and then ask your server or a manager what they think," added Myers.

It's important to understand that there are no hard-and-fast rules when it comes to pairing wines. "Very basically speaking, with beef go with big, chewy, tannic cabernets. Go to California if you like fruit, and go to Bordeaux if you want really dry. When ordering chicken, go with whatever wine you want, such as a white Burgundy, Chateauneuf-du-Pape blanc, or Oregon Pinot Noir.

TIPS FOR ORDERING FINE WINE, continued

Everything goes with chicken, as it has little flavor of its own to get in the way. Pairing wine with fish and seafood dishes is a bit tougher. For white wines, go with quirky Italian whites, such as Vermentino, Vernaccia, Falanghina, or Orvieto," recommended Myers.

Since you might not want to admit to the people you're dining with that you know little about wine, Myers recommends pulling your server or the restaurant's sommelier aside to initiate an open and honest conversation about your wine needs, taste, and budget. "Ask for their help and utilize their recommendations to ensure the best dining experience possible."

SECTION VI

Shamu show. Photo © Mike Liu

ENTERTAINMENT IN
ORLANDO

Aside from conducting the business you're traveling to Orlando for, hopefully you'll have time to enjoy some of what one of America's most popular tourist and vacation destinations has to offer, such as the Walt Disney World Resort theme parks, the Universal Studios and Islands of Adventure theme parks, SeaWorld, and the countless other attractions, activities, shopping opportunities, world-class day spas, and fine-dining restaurants you'll find in the area.

This section offers an overview of just some of the many ways you can enjoy your free time while visiting Orlando. If you'll need to entertain and impress important clients, business associates, or friends while in town, you'll find a wide selection of memorable ways to do this—from exclusive tours and VIP access to theme parks, to extremely memorable, unusual, and fun activities. If, like many business travelers, you're planning to bring your family along on the trip and transform at least some of your stay into a vacation, this section will help you decide how to entertain your family by helping you plan an exciting itinerary.

If you're planning to stay at any of the WDW Resort hotels, visit any of the theme parks, or attend or host a meeting or event at the WDW Resort, be sure to read Section VII, "Visiting the Walt Disney World Resort."

TIP
For an up-to-date listing of special events happening in the Orlando area during the dates of your visit, check out a current issue of *Where* magazine (distributed free at many hotels), or visit the Orlando/Orange County Convention and Visitors Bureau's events calendar at www.orlandoinfo.com/other/calendar.

TOP 15 ACTIVITIES AND ATTRACTIONS FOR BUSINESS TRAVELERS

In addition to the Walt Disney World theme parks, there are literally hundreds of fun, exciting, and memorable activities to experience in the Orlando area. The following is a sampling of 15 activities and attractions (listed in alphabetical order) that are specifically suitable for business travelers. Many of these activities and attractions can accommodate groups and/or host private functions, so they will work well if you're looking to host a business-oriented event or function (attended by employees, co-workers, or important clients, for example). The activities and attractions listed here can also be experienced on your own, during your free time in Orlando.

1. Around the World at Epcot Segway Tour

Location: Epcot (the Walt Disney World Resort)
Phone: (407) WDW-TOUR
Price: $35 to $85 per person (plus admission to Epcot)

The Segway HT is the world's first self-balancing, battery-powered human transporter that uses advanced technology, gyroscopes, and tilt sensors to emulate human balance. When a person leans slightly forward, the Segway HT moves forward. When she leans back, the Segway HT moves back. Riders can travel up to 12.5 miles per hour for a distance up to 24 miles on a single charge. Each Segway HT holds one person. No previous experience is necessary. For information about Segways, visit www.segway.com.

Time requirement: one to two hours (plus travel time)
Web site: www.wdwinfo.com/wdwinfo/tours.htm

Epcot is one of the most suitable WDW theme parks for adults. Here you'll find a wide range of attractions and rides designed to thrill, educate, and entertain you. Epcot offers a look at our future in a fun, interactive, and informative way. One way to experience the World Showcase or Innoventions area of this popular theme park is to participate in a one- or two-hour guided tour while riding a Segway Human Transporter (HT) vehicle.

The Around the World at Epcot tour allows guests to operate and ride a Segway HT throughout the World Showcase area of Epcot, before the park opens to the general public. The Around the World at Epcot tour is priced at $85 per person and departs daily at 8:30 A.M. and 9:30 A.M.

The Simply Segway tour ($35.00 per person) is a one-hour guided tour that takes guests around Epcot's Innoventions area. This tour departs daily (except Tuesdays) at 12:30 P.M. and 1:45 P.M. Both tours are limited to ten guests each, so advance reservations are definitely required. An admission ticket to Epcot is required (sold separately). See Section VII, "Visiting the Walt Disney World Resort," for ticket prices and information.

TIP
The Around the World at Epcot and Simply Segway tours are just two of over two dozen unique and behind-the-scenes tour opportunities offered at the WDW Resort. These tours are available to individuals or small groups, and most cater primarily to adults. For a listing of tours, visit www.wdwinfo.com/wdwinfo/tours.htm or call (407) WDW-TOUR. Participating in any one of these tours provides a vastly different experience than simply visiting one of the Disney theme parks.

2. Bob Carr Performing Arts Center

Location: West Livingston Street, Orlando, FL 32801
Event information: (407) 849-2001
Box office phone: (407) 849-2020
Ticketmaster: (407) 839-3900 / www.ticketmaster.com
Price: Varies by performance
Time requirement: Varies by performance
Web site: www.orlandocentroplex.com

Located in the downtown Orlando area, the Bob Carr Performing Arts Center is one of the city's premier venues where concerts (featuring well-known recording artists), touring Broadway shows, the symphony, ballets, and operas are performed throughout the year. This 2,518-seat theater is located within the Orlando Centroplex. If you're looking for an evening's worth of upscale entertainment, determine what events, concerts, or shows are being held at this venue during your visit.

During the 2006–2007 season, for example, some of the touring Broadway shows that were presented at the Bob Carr Performing Arts Center included the Tony Award-winning musical comedy *The 25th Annual Putnam County Spelling Bee* as well as *All Shook Up*. *The Lion King, Camelot, Sweet Charity,* and *Rent*. For a complete calendar of events, visit www.orlandocentroplex.com/calendar/calendar.php, call (407) 849-2001, or contact Ticketmaster.

MONEY SAVER
To save money and guarantee convenient parking when attending an event at the Orlando Centroplex, be sure to reserve a prepaid parking space at the venue (for an additional fee) when you purchase your show, concert, or event tickets.

3. Boggy Creek Airboat and Wildlife Safari Rides

Locations: Southport Park, 2001 East Southport Road, Kissimmee; East Lake
   Fish Camp, 3702 Big Bass Road, Kissimmee
Phone: (407) 344-9550, (407) 344-0018 (group reservations)
Price: $21.95 per person (airboat ride), $21.95 per person (land safari ride)
Time requirement: three to four hours, including travel time
Web site: www.bcairboats.com

Located about 30 minutes from the WDW Resort, in the Lake Toho area of Kissimmee, the Boggy Creek Airboat and Wildlife Safari Rides offer an up-close look at Florida's wildlife, including live alligators in their natural habitat (the everglades). Between 9 A.M. and 5 P.M. (seven days a week), 30-minute airboat tours are offered. During this high-speed, often turbulent adventure, you'll see exotic birds, turtles, snakes, and alligators.

Reservations are not required for either tour. For small groups (up to either 6 or 18 passengers), private, 45-minute airboat tours are available, but they must be reserved in advance. Both tours take place entirely outdoors, weather permitting. The tours have been operating since 1994 and have become must-see attractions for adventurous tourists. Nighttime tours are also available.

To continue your wildlife adventure on land, you can experience a one-hour swamp buggy nature tour. You'll ride in a custom-built monster land vehicle and travel through the largest cattle ranch in Florida. During this exciting expedition, you'll see eagles, turkeys, deer, cows, and wild hogs roaming free. Tours are operated continuously throughout the day. The safari tours are operated only at the Southport Park location.

The airboats are piloted by experienced master captains and are regularly inspected and approved by the U.S. Coast Guard.

4. Cirque du Soliel La Nouba

Location: Downtown Disney's West Side (Walt Disney World Resort)
Phone: (407) 939-1298
Show times: 6 P.M. and 9 P.M. (Tuesday through Saturday)
Ticket prices: $63, $79, $97, and $112 (plus tax)
Time requirement: Approximately two hours
Web site: www.cirquedusoleil.com

Prepare yourself for one of the most spectacular live shows you'll ever see. Within a custom-built theater (which is part of the show itself), the French-Canadian circus troupe known as Cirque du Soliel presents an extremely unique and exciting show that's exclusive to the Walt Disney World Resort. *La Nouba* features amazingly talented acrobats, aerialists, cyclists, clowns, performers, musicians, and singers.

During each performance, you'll see at least ten different acts, all perfectly synchronized to original music that's being performed live. Surrounding you and the performers are state-of-the-art sets, special effects, and lighting, all of which adds to the excitement. While you'll be at the edge of your seat watching the trapeze artists, the high-wire act, and the gymnasts on the trampolines, you'll also be entertained by the clowns and their unusual humor.

Even if you've already experienced a Cirque du Soliel touring production, or one of the resident Cirque du Soliel shows in Las Vegas, you'll find that *La Nouba* is very different and should not be missed. It's definitely one of the most impressive, entertaining, and exciting shows in Orlando—and well worth the price of admission!

Many people consider the highlight of La Nouba to be the diabolos act. It features four young girls who hold two sticks each that are connected by a string. The girls perform tricks with fast-spinning wooden spools (the diabolos) balanced on the strings, as they themselves execute extremely difficult and well-timed acrobatic maneuvers. (Photo courtesy of Cirque du Soliel.)

Be sure to reserve your tickets early. Reservations are taken up to six months in advance.

5. Comedy Warehouse

Location: Downtown Disney (Walt Disney World Resort)
Phone: (407) 934-7781
Show times: Multiple shows nightly, between 7 P.M. and 2 A.M.
Ticket price: $20.95 (includes admission to Downtown Disney)
Time requirement: Approximately one hour
Web site: http://disneyworld.disney.go.com/wdw/entertainment/entertainmentDetail?id=PleasureIslandEntertainmentPage

If you're in the mood for lighthearted, family-friendly, improvisational comedy that'll keep you laughing, you'll want to drop by the Comedy Warehouse during a visit to Downtown Disney. A troupe of four talented comedians takes ideas from the audience and spontaneously create skits, comedy, and songs based on suggestions. Every show is totally different. The Comedy Warehouse is open to people age of 21 and over. Full bar service is available. Seating is on a first-come basis, and lines begin to form about one hour prior to each performance.

TIP
To complete the night after a comedy show, if you're in the mood for a sing-along, consider visiting Jellyrolls, located at Disney's BoardWalk (about a five-minute drive from the Downtown Disney area; free shuttle bus transportation is available). Here, you'll find a live, ongoing dueling-piano show and full bar service. Audience members are encouraged to request songs and sing along to classics, TV show themes, and other popular hits. Performances begin at 7 P.M. nightly and continue until 2 A.M. The pianists are talented musicians, funny and extremely entertaining. This is a great place to unwind after a long day of meetings or after attending a convention.

6. Disney Fishing Excursions

Location: Various marinas throughout the WDW Resort
Phone: (407) 939-2277, (407) WDW-BASS
Excursion times: 7 A.M., 10 A.M., and 1:30 P.M.
Ticket price: $125 to $395
Time requirement: Between two and four hours, depending on excursion
Web site: www.wdwinfo.com/recreation/fishing.htm

What better way to relax and get away from the hustle and bustle of a hectic trade show or conference than to set off on a boat and enjoy a few hours of fishing? Several of the hotel properties located at the WDW Resort offer private, catch-and-release fishing excursions for up to five people. The price includes use of a boat, a tour guide, the rental of all needed fishing equipment (rod, reel, artificial bait, and shiners), plus beverages.

Several programs are available, utilizing different boats and lasting for different durations. For example, the Bass Nitro Fishing Excursion allows for a maximum of two guests per boat, lasts four hours, and includes the use of a tournament-style bass boat (price: $230 to $395 per boat). Reservations must be made at least 24 hours in advance. Guests are not allowed to bring their own food or beverages; however, they can bring their own fishing equipment. Fly-fishing excursions are also available.

7. Helicopter Tours

Location: Each company departs from a different private airfield or airport
Ticket price: $25 to $400 per person
Time requirement: 5 to 60 minutes

Tour operators:

- Legacy Grand Heliport—(407) 390-7502
- Orlando Helicenter—(407) 396-6006, www.orlandohelicenter.com
- Orlando Helitours—(407) 397-0226, www.orlandohelitours.com
- Universal Air Service—(407) 896-2966, www.universalhelicopter.com
- Air Florida Helicopters—(407) 354-1400, www.airfloridahelicopters.com

Several companies in the Orlando area offer aerial guided tours by helicopter. Depending on the heliport's location, you may get a bird's-eye view of Universal Orlando and the International Drive area or the WDW Resort and surrounding Lake Buena Vista area.

For about $25, you can experience a very quick two- to three-minute flight (which almost isn't worth the hassle). However, for between $150 and $400 per person, you can enjoy a 45-minute to one-hour tour. These longer tours offer a far more exciting and memorable experience that takes place aboard a five passenger, air-conditioned, luxury Bell Jet-Ranger helicopter.

Most of the tour operators offer flights starting around 9 A.M. and continuing until sunset. Advance reservations are definitely recommended. Private charter flights are available.

8. Kennedy Space Center

Location: Orsino (near Cocoa Beach)
Phone: (321) 449-4444
Hours: 9:00am to 7:00pm (Closing time varies by season)
Ticket price: $38 per person
Time requirement: Half day to full day
Web site: www.kennedyspacecenter.com

Located about 45 minutes from Orlando, the Kennedy Space Center offers visitors an up-close look at the National Aeronautics and Space Administration (NASA), the space shuttle program, as well as the history and future of space exploration. You'll experience interactive exhibits, see actual rockets and space shuttles, get a behind-the-scenes tour of the complex, see two IMAX movies, plus have the opportunity to meet an actual NASA astronaut. Since 1967, the Kennedy Space Center has continued to expand and has become one of Florida's most popular attractions. In addition to the walk-through and interactive exhibits offered at the visitors center, admission includes a narrated bus tour of the entire Kennedy Space Center complex, including the space shuttle launch pads.

One of the popular activities offered at the visitors center is the daily Astronaut Encounter program, where guests can participate in a question-and-answer session with a NASA astronaut.

For an additional fee of $22.99 per adult, visitors can enjoy lunch with an astronaut and hear firsthand stories of space exploration. A variety of dining options are available to the general public.

For the ultimate excitement, consider participating in the Astronaut Training Experience (ATX), a full-day program that provides a true taste of the space flight experience, including the opportunity to participate in simulator exercises. The program costs $225 per person. Space is very limited and reservations must be made in advance.

TIP
If you're lucky enough to be visiting the Orlando area when a space shuttle launch is scheduled, opportunities are also available to witness a launch event up close—from countdown to blastoff. The launch schedule is posted on the Kennedy Space Center's web site.

To reach the Kennedy Space Center from Orlando, take SR 528 East until you reach the SR 407 exit going to Kennedy Space Center and Titusville. Take SR 407 until it ends at SR 405. Turn right (east) onto SR 405, and follow the signs for Kennedy Space Center. You will travel approximately nine miles on SR 405. The KSC Visitor Complex will be on your right. Kennedy Space Center is open daily, except on December 25 and certain space shuttle launch days.

TIP
While in the area, consider spending time enjoying the shops, tourist sights, and restaurants located in nearby Cocoa Beach, which is about 45 minutes from the International Drive and WDW Resort areas.

9. Orlando Hot Air Balloon Rides

Location: Various locations near the WDW Resort
Phone: (800) 586-1884, (407) 894-5040
Hours: Sunrise flights are offered daily (weather permitting)
Ticket price: $175 per person
Time requirement: Approximately three to four hours
Web site: www.orlandoballoonrides.com

Each colorful hot air balloon is specifically designed for passenger comfort and safety. Orlando Balloon Rides boasts a 100 percent unblemished safety record. Weather permitting, flights depart 365 days per year at sunrise.

Even the most seasoned business traveler will have a memorable experience aboard a hot air balloon ride offered by Orlando Balloon Rides. Prepare yourself to float above the WDW Resort, Lake Buena Vista, and Orlando areas. Actual takeoff and landing locations, along with flight routes, vary daily, based on wind speed and direction.

Starting before sunrise, passengers meet at a designated location (about five minutes from the WDW Resort) and are transported by van to that day's launch site. You'll then participate in the setup and inflation of the hot air balloon, before climbing aboard with your licensed and experienced pilot for a once-in-a-lifetime flight that will last between 45 and 90 minutes. Upon landing, you'll be met by the ground crew. After packing up the balloon, you'll enjoy a champagne toast and be transported back to the original meeting site for breakfast.

Once airborne, you can expect an incredibly smooth flight as you float through the air. Each balloon holds four to six passengers, plus the Federal Aviation Administration (FAA)-certified pilot (who remains in constant contact with the land crew and other balloon pilots during the flight). No previous experience is necessary. The actual flight is very smooth and visually breathtaking. However, if you're afraid of heights, think twice about participating. Be sure to bring a camera! Private charter flights are available. Out of all the tours, rides, attractions, and experiences available in Orlando, this is definitely one of the most exciting and memorable!

10. Orlando Museum of Art

Location: 2416 North Mills Avenue, Orlando
Phone: (407) 896-4231
Hours: Tuesday through Friday, 10 A.M. to 4 P.M.; Saturday and Sunday, Noon to 4 P.M.; closed Mondays and major holidays
Admission price: $8 per person
Time requirement: Approximately one to three hours (or longer)
Web site: www.omart.org

Founded in 1924, the Orlando Museum of Art strives to "enrich the cultural life of Florida by providing excellence in the visual arts. To achieve this objective, the museum has dedicated itself to collecting, preserving and interpreting notable works of art; to presenting exhibitions of local, regional, national and international significance; to developing first-rate educational programs; and to presenting creative and inclusive programs to reach every segment of a diverse community."

Throughout the year, the museum presents 10 to 12 different exhibitions on-site, plus it offers a wide range of art enrichment programs, gallery tours, training programs, distinguished lectures, studio classes, and lecture and luncheon programs.

The museum's own collection includes paintings, drawings, prints, photographs, and sculptures from the 18th century to the present. For example, the museum's 18th-, 19th-, and 20th-century holdings include works by artists such as John Singer Sargent, Thomas Moran, George Inness, Georgia O'Keeffe, Ansel Adams, Suzanne McClelland, Robert Rauschenberg, Pat Steir, Morris Louis, John Chamberlain, and Dennis Oppenheim.

Other museums worth visiting while in the Orlando area include the Charles Hosmer Morse Museum of American Art (407-645-5311, 445 Park Avenue North, Winter Park), the Orange County Regional History Center (407-836-8500, 65 East Central Boulevard, Orlando), the Orlando Science Center (407-514-2000, 777 East Princeton Street, Orlando, www.osc.org), and the Zora Neale Hurston National Museum of Fine Arts (407-647-3307, 227 East Kennedy Boulevard, Eastonville).

You'll feel the engine roar, smell the fuel and exhaust fumes, and discover exactly what a NASCAR driver sees, hears, smells, and experiences on the track when strapped tightly in the race car and driving at ultrafast speeds.

11. Richard Petty Driving Experience

Location: Walt Disney World Speedway (Walt Disney World Resort)
Phone: (800) 237-3889
Hours: 9 A.M. to 4 P.M. daily
Prices: $99 to $1,249 per person
Time requirement: One hour to a full day (depending on the program)
Web site: www.1800BePetty.com

If you're a NASCAR fan or just enjoy driving fast, the Richard Petty Driving Experience is for you. You'll be in either the passenger seat or the driver's seat of an actual NASCAR racing car as you race around the Walt Disney World Speedway's track at speeds in excess of 100 to 140 miles per hour. This is a truly authentic NASCAR driving experience.

The Ride-Along program ($99 per person) allows you to sit in the passenger's seat of a two-seat stock car as a professional driver takes you for three extremely high-speed laps around the track for a simulated cup qualifying run. You'll wear an authentic racing uniform and helmet, be secured in the vehicle with a five-point harness, then experience the adrenaline rush associated with riding at speeds up to 140 miles per hour.

The Richard Petty Rookie Experience ($399 per person) is a three-hour program that includes in-depth driving instruction by a professional instructor. You'll then be secured in the driver's seat of an authentic, 600-horsepower stock car and take eight high-speed laps around the track (following a pace car). The actual speed you travel is based on your proficiency as a driver. You're in

For the ultimate racing encounter, the Experience of a Lifetime program ($1,249 per person) offers the chance to take a total of 30 solo laps around the track.

100 percent control over your vehicle while on the track. The instructors and pit crew will prepare you to make the most out of your driving experience, which will be exhilarating, scary, and challenging all at the same time.

The King's Experience ($749 per person) takes place over two separate sessions and includes a total of 18 high-speed, solo laps around the track, plus additional professional instruction, which should prepare you to drive at even faster speeds.

A professional photographer will document your experience and take a handful of full-color photos and a commemorative plaque available to you for an additional fee. A valid driver's license is required. Proficiency driving a standard transmission vehicle is also helpful, although not entirely necessary. This experience is not for the timid.

12. SeaWorld's Discovery Cove

Location: Intersection of Interstate 4 and SR 528 (Bee Line Expressway), Orlando
Phone: (877) 4-DISCOVERY, (407) 370-1280
Hours: 9 A.M. to 5:30 P.M. daily
Prices: $259 to $279 per person
Time requirement: Half day to full day
Web site: www.discoverycove.com

Discovery Cove is a sister theme park to SeaWorld, but it offers a vastly different experience. Here, you can interact directly with dolphins, fish, exotic birds, and rays in a manmade tropical hideaway.

The highlight of the day at Discovery Cove is the dolphin interaction session, which lasts about 30 minutes and is shared with no more than seven other guests.

For an all-inclusive fee, guests enjoy a full day at Discovery Cove, which has a maximum daily capacity of only 1,000 visitors. Advance reservations are required.

In addition to a unique "swim with the dolphins" interactive experience, a day at Discovery Cove includes snorkeling in an on-site coral reef, exploring the park's tropical river stream, interacting with rays, visiting the aviary to interact with exotic birds, swimming and relaxing by the private beach area. Lunch is also included. All equipment, including a wet suit and snorkel gear, is provided. Admission to SeaWorld is included with admission to Discovery Cove.

TIP
Be sure to bring a bathing suit, sunglasses, sunscreen, a camera, and a change of clothing along for your visit to Discovery Cove. While lockers are provided, you'll want to leave any valuables at your hotel.

Between April 25 and May 19, September 5 and October 7, and November 12 and December 20, if you're attending a convention in Orlando, you can participate in Discovery Cove's discounted, half-day Afternoon Escape program, which begins around 1 P.M. Convention attendees can call (866) 781-1333 to make a reservation.

Discovery Cove is far less crowded and less commercial than the other Orlando-area theme parks. It offers a unique experience that provides the opportunity to relax, enjoy the Florida sunshine, and get up close to exotic marine life in a totally safe and self-paced environment. With the exception of the dolphin interaction, your schedule is set entirely by you.

CITY FACTOID
In March 2008, SeaWorld will open an all-new water park adjacent to its other theme parks. This park will feature live animals, thrill rides, and sandy beaches. Aquatica will contain 36 water slides, six rivers and lagoons, and more than 80,000 square feet of manmade beach area.

GET CLOSE TO THE FISHES AT SEAWORLD ORLANDO

SeaWorld Orlando (800-327-2424, www.seaworld.com) has undergone a tremendous transformation in recent years. While this marine animal-themed park still offers a chance to get up close and personal with a vast array of aquatic wildlife, like dolphins, penguins, stingrays, whales, and all kinds of exotic fish, visitors to SeaWorld now also have the chance to experience exciting thrill rides (including several roller coasters) plus several different shows that are well worth seeing.

The *Blue Horizons* show features dolphins, exotic birds, plus a cast of world-class divers and aerialists. Every evening, don't miss *Mystify*, a larger-than-life fireworks and multimedia presentation, complete with special effects, flames, and shooting water.

Adults visiting SeaWorld will probably enjoy the Brewmaster's Club, which offers the opportunity to sample a wide range of beers. (SeaWorld is owned and operated by Anheuser-Busch.)

It's easy to spend a morning, afternoon, evening, or full day exploring SeaWorld Orlando and experiencing the various rides, shows, and attractions. The park is open daily starting at 9 A.M. Closing times varies by season (it's typically between 7 P.M. and 10 P.M.). A single adult admission ticket for SeaWorld Orlando is priced at

> ### GET CLOSE TO THE FISHES, continued
>
> $61.95; however, a variety of discounted ticket packages are available through the FlexTicket program (877-406-4836).
>
> SeaWorld Orlando is a 200-acre theme park located right off I-4 and the Bee Line Expressway, about 10 minutes from downtown Orlando and 15 minutes from Orlando International Airport.
>
>
>
> SeaWorld is famous for its popular Shamu killer whale show, now called *Believe*, which is presented several times daily. This show has been seen by more than 250 million guests.

TIP
To enhance your visit to this popular theme park, consider paying extra to experience Dine with Shamu, where guests eat alongside killer whales and dine with Shamu's trainers. Reservations are required (800-327-2424).

13. Skyventure Orlando Indoor Skydiving

Location: 6805 Visitors Circle, Orlando
Phone: (800) SKY-FUN-1, (407) 903-1150
Hours: 10 A.M. to 11 P.M. (Sunday through Thursday); 10 A.M. to midnight (Friday and Saturday)

Prices: $44.95 to $99.95 per person
Time requirement: Approximately 90 minutes
Web site: www.skyventureorlando.com

Image experiencing the thrill of skydiving out of an airplane without ever going more than 10 to 15 feet off the ground or having to worry about whether or not your parachute will actually open. Invented by Bill Kitchen and engineer Mike Palmer, Skyventure has allowed thousands of people to experience the very real sensation of skydiving, but in a much safer and more controlled, indoor environment since it opened in 1998.

Skyventure is not a ride simulator! When you step into the proprietary, custom-designed vertical wind tunnel, you'll actually be flying. Skyventure is a unique, indoor wind tunnel (powered by a jet engine) that creates a 125 mph column of air upon which you fly. With a bit of practice and training (provided), you'll be able to control how you move by adjusting your body's position.

The basic Skyventure experience ($44.95 per person) lasts about one hour and includes training, flight suit, helmet, and goggles. Your actual experience will include two exhilarating "flights" lasting about one minute each, which is equivalent to the free-fall portion of an actual skydive. The $99.95 Sports Package doubles your flight time. The AirXtreme Training package ($199.95) includes ten minutes of flight time, plus personalized coaching, in addition to the required training.

Skyventure offers a fun and exciting activity for yourself and friends. However, private parties are also available, making this a perfect activity for a memorable corporate event or function. For an additional fee, you can purchase a DVD and/or photos of your experience. Participants must weigh less than 250 pounds and be under six feet tall. No previous experience or special skills are required. During your flight, a professional instructor will accompany and supervise you. Reservations are strongly recommended.

14. Titanic: The Exhibition

Location: The Mercado, 8445 International Drive, Orlando
Phone: (407) 248-1166, ext. 3110
Hours: 9 A.M. to 9 P.M. daily
Prices: $19.95 per person (plus tax)
Time requirement: One to three hours
Web site: www.titanicshipofdreams.com

This interactive exhibit takes you back to April 14, 1912. You'll walk into full-scale reproductions of actual rooms and areas of the

RMS *Titanic* and see exactly how it looked the night it sank. You'll also see more than 200 priceless artifacts and historic treasures recovered from the ship, some of which are on display for the first time ever.

During your exploration of this exhibit, you'll also see movie memorabilia from *A Night to Remember, The Search for Titanic,* and *Titanic* (which starred Leonardo DiCaprio). In addition to the exhibits, *Titanic*: The Exhibition features short films, photos, and recordings that offer a very comprehensive look at the real-life *Titanic* and its tragic demise. Live actors, dressed in period costume, serve as informative and entertaining tour guides as you experience this unique and memorable exhibition.

After your visit to *Titanic*: The Exhibition, consider spending additional time at the Mercado (where the exhibition is located) to enjoy exploring the more than 60 unique shops and restaurants at this mediterranean-style marketplace. Free parking is available. You can also reach *Titanic*: The Exhibition via the I-Ride Trolley.

15. Universal Orlando Theme Parks—Universal Studios, Islands of Adventure, and CityWalk

Location: 6000 Universal Boulevard, Orlando
Phone: (407) 363-8000
Hours: Opens 9 A.M., Closing time varies throughout the year
Prices:
- One park, one day—$63 per adult
- Two parks, one day—$73 per adult
- Two-park, seven-day unlimited admission—$85.99 per adult
- Other discounted, multiday, multipark tickets and offers are available

Time requirement: One to two days per park
Web site: www.universalorlando.com

Back in 1999, Universal Studios opened a single theme park in Orlando that was loosely modeled after its popular counterpart in Hollywood, California. Since then, this single, family-oriented theme park, which featured rides, shows, and attractions based on popular and classic movies, has grown dramatically.

Today, Universal Orlando comprises the ever expanding Universal Studios theme park, the Islands of Adventure theme park, CityWalk (a separate 30-acre complex containing shops, restaurants, a 20-screen movie theater, plus several nightclubs), and several on-property and nearby resort hotels. In short, it's been transformed into a complete entertainment and vacation destination suitable for adults and the entire family.

While business travelers will probably want to skip the kid-oriented rides, shows, and attractions, both theme parks offer a great selection of thrill rides and other activities designed for adults. If you're looking for a fun nightspot, check out CityWalk, which offers a handful of nightclubs, midpriced and upscale restaurants, plus a variety of live entertainment options.

In June 2007, Universal Orlando became a permanent new home to Blue Man Group, which presents a unique show combining music, comedy, and multimedia theatrics. The show stars a small cast of talented male performers who are painted blue from head to toe. For years, Blue Man Group has entertained audiences in New York City, Boston, and Las Vegas. Blue Man Group ticket prices are $59 to $69, with matinee and evening shows presented daily.

 MONEY SAVER
To save money and catch Blue Man Group plus experience the thrills offered at Universal Studios and Islands of Adventure, as well as the entertainment options offered at CityWalk, consider purchasing a Blue Man Group Show Ticket Plus 2-Park Unlimited Admission Pass for between $130 and $140. This package offers unlimited seven-day admission to the theme parks and CityWalk, plus a ticket to see Blue Man Group.

The live entertainment offered at Universal Orlando doesn't end with Blue Man Group. Throughout CityWalk and the theme parks, live music and comedy is performed daily and nightly at the restaurants and clubs, including the Hard Rock Café, Jimmy Buffet's Margaritaville, the Latin Quarter, the Red Coconut Club, and CityJazz.

WARNING!
When visiting any theme park in Orlando, dress appropriately! This means wearing comfortable walking shoes, lightweight attire that'll protect you from the sun, sunglasses, a hat, and sunscreen. Even on overcast days, the Florida sun can quickly cause severe sunburn. It's also important to stay hydrated. Throughout the day, drink plenty of water. You might also consider bringing a change of clothing (including extra socks), since some of the rides will cause you to get wet. Lockers are available at each of the theme parks for a small fee.

Both Universal Studios and Islands of Adventure are jam-packed with fun and exciting rides, shows, and attractions. Seeing and doing everything would take several days per park, but if you're a business traveler looking to experience the best of what each park offers (based on what's suitable for adults), this section will help you plan your time accordingly. For each popular ride, show, and attraction, you can quickly see what age group(s) it'll most appeal to, and whether it's a must-see ride, show, or attraction for its appropriate age group(s).

TIP
To save a lot of time when visiting Universal Studios and/or Islands of Adventure, consider purchasing an Express Plus ticket upgrade. This allows you to automatically step to the front of the line for most of popular rides and attractions within the theme parks.

UNIVERSAL STUDIOS ATTRACTIONS

What sets all of the rides, shows, and attractions apart at Universal Studios is that they're all based on classic and recent major motion pictures and television shows. Throughout both Universal theme parks, you'll find a variety of places to dine (mostly fast food) plus a variety of gift and souvenir shops. The following chart lists the various attractions and their ratings.

The rides, shows, and attractions at Universal Studios are all based on popular movies and television shows. (Photo courtesy of Universal Orlando.)

ATTRACTIONS AT UNIVERSAL STUDIOS

Attraction Name	Attraction Type	Must See?	Adults	Teens	Kids (Under 10)	All Ages
Universal 360: A Cinesphere Spectacular	Show	✓	✓	✓		
Fear Factor Live	Show	✓	✓	✓		
Revenge of the Mummy: The Ride	Thrill ride	✓	✓	✓		
Shrek 4-D	Interactive movie					✓
Jimmy Neutron's Nicktoon Blast	Ride				✓	
Men In Black Alien Attack	Ride			✓	✓	
Terminator 2: 3-D	3-D movie	✓	✓	✓		
Twister . . . Ride It Out	Movie/show		✓	✓		
The Simpsons	Ride	✓	✓	✓		
Jaws	Ride		✓	✓		
Earthquake: The Big One	Ride		✓	✓		
Woody Woodpecker's KidZone	Interactive playground				✓	

ATTRACTIONS AT UNIVERSAL STUDIOS

Attraction Name	Attraction Type	Must See?	Adults	Teens	Kids (Under 10)	All Ages
E.T. Adventure	Ride	✓				✓
A Day in the Park with Barney	Show				✓	
Beetlejuice's Graveyard Revue	Show	✓				✓
The Lucy and Ricky Show	Show		✓			
The Blues Brothers	Show		✓	✓		
Animal Actors on Location	Show					✓
Horror Make-Up Show	Show		✓	✓		

ISLANDS OF ADVENTURE ATTRACTIONS

As the name of the park implies, Islands of Adventure is divided up into five uniquely themed areas, each of which offers its own selection of rides, shows, and attractions. When you visit this theme park, you'll discover the islands are arranged in a circle, making them easy to find and navigate through.

TIP
The Toon Lagoon and Seuss landing areas of Islands of Adventure are definitely more suitable for kids and preteens than adults.

ATTRACTIONS AT ISLANDS OF ADVENTURE

Attraction Name	Attraction Type	Must See?	Adults	Teens	Kids (Under 10)	All Ages
Doctor Doom's Fearfall (Marvel Super Hero Island)	Thrill ride	✓	✓	✓		
The Amazing Adventures of Spider-Man (Marvel Super Hero Island)	Ride	✓	✓	✓		

ATTRACTIONS AT ISLANDS OF ADVENTURE

Attraction Name	Attraction Type	Must See?	Adults	Teens	Kids (Under 10)	All Ages
Incredible Hulk Coaster (Marvel Super Hero Island)	Thrill ride	✓	✓	✓		
Storm Force Acceleration (Marvel Super Hero Island)	Thrill ride	✓	✓	✓		
Dudley Do-Right's Ripsaw Falls (Toon Lagoon)	Thrill ride		✓	✓		
Popeye & Bluto's Bilge-Rat Barges (Toon Lagoon)	Ride	✓	✓	✓		
Me Ship, the Olive (Toon Lagoon)	Interactive play area				✓	
Jurassic Park River Adventure (Jurassic Park)	Thrill ride	✓	✓	✓		
Pteranodon Flyers (Jurassic Park)	Ride			✓	✓	
Camp Jurassic (Jurassic Park)	Interactive playground			✓	✓	
Jurassic Park Discovery Center (Jurassic Park)	Interactive area					✓
Dueling Dragons Coaster (The Lost Continent)	Thrill ride	✓	✓	✓		
Poseidon's Fury (The Lost Continent)	Interactive show/attraction	✓	✓	✓		
The Eighth Voyage of Sinbad Stunt Show (The Lost Continent)	Show					✓
The Flying Unicorn (The Lost Continent)	Ride		✓	✓		
High in the Sky Suess Trolley Train Ride (Suess Landing)	Ride	✓			✓	

ATTRACTIONS AT ISLANDS OF ADVENTURE

Attraction Name	Attraction Type	Must See?	Adults	Teens	Kids (Under 10)	All Ages
The Cat in the Hat (Seuss Landing)	Ride	✓			✓	
Caro-Seuss-el	Ride				✓	
One Fish Two Fish Red Fish Blue Fish	Ride	✓			✓	
If I Ran the Zoo	Interactive play area				✓	

The Incredible Hulk Coaster within Islands of Adventure is one of this theme park's high-speed roller coasters. It's an extremely popular thrill ride. (Photo courtesy of Universal Orlando.)

MONEY SAVER

The Go Orlando Card (800-887-9103, www.goorlando-card.com) offers unlimited, discounted admission to more than 50 Orlando-area attractions for a period of between one and seven days. Priced at $59 for one day, $99 for two days, $126 for three days, $169 for five days, and $211 for seven days, this card allows holders to experience any participating attractions or tours they'd like, at their own pace. You'll also receive discounts at dozens of participating restaurants and at many of the gifts shops within the various museums and attractions. One nice feature is that the cards that are valid for multiple days do not have to be used consecutively. Plus, with a bit of planning, you can fit multiple attractions and tours into a single day to maximize the value you receive from the Go Orlando Card. While this card doesn't apply to major theme parks, it does offer admission to most of the smaller attractions and popular tours found along International Drive, as well as surrounding areas. It also includes admission to Kennedy Space Center, Cypress Gardens Adventure Park, *Titanic*: The Exhibition, Boggy Creek Airport Rides, the Orlando Museum of Art, plus other attractions and museums featured in this guide.

EXCLUSIVE TOURS AND ACTIVITIES FOR UPSCALE BUSINESS TRAVELERS

Many business travelers are on a tight schedule, but during what little free time they have, they want to experience tours, attractions, or other aspects of Orlando in the most exciting and time-efficient ways possible. Other business travelers are seeking out innovative and memorable ways to impress clients and customers while in Orlando. No matter what your motivation, one company has put together a menu of innovative and truly memorable tour experiences that most everyday tourists never get to experience.

To learn about the many different tours available, from private limousine, helicopter, and yacht tours, to innovative and unusual walking tours, contact Viator (866-648 5873, www.viator.com).

By working closely with a wide range of highly reputable, competitively priced, independent tour operators and service providers, Viator is able to help business travelers choose from more than 62 different tours offered in the Orlando area and handles all scheduling and booking details on their behalf.

Visit Viator.com to research the various tours available in Orlando that meet your interests, schedule, and budget, and then book them all before you travel. The company fully understands the unique needs of business travelers and specializes in memorable helicopter tours, dinner cruises, show and sporting event packages, luxury motor coach tours, and private limousine tours.

Viator offers a low-price guarantee for all tours booked through the service, plus it allows participants to earn frequent flier miles (on American Airlines, Delta, United, and U.S. Airways) for their purchases. Viator specializes in booking tours for individuals and groups.

MONEY SAVER
If you plan on spending several days visiting a handful of Orlando's top theme parks and attractions, consider purchasing a multiday Orlando FlexTicket to save money on admissions. The four-park FlexTicket is priced at $207.62 and is good for 14 consecutive days of unlimited access to Universal Studios, Islands of Adventure, SeaWorld, and Wet 'n Wild. The five-park FlexTicket offers 14 consecutive days of unlimited admission to Universal Studios, Islands of Adventure, SeaWorld, Wet 'n Wild, and Busch Gardens. For more information, call (407) 396-9020 or (877) 406-4836. Tickets can be purchased at any participating theme park, or from the Official Ticket Center (3148 Vineland Road, SR 535, Kissimmee).

PROFESSIONAL SPORTING EVENTS

If you're interested in being a spectator at a professional sporting event while in Orlando, read on for information about the various pro teams and venues.

Disney's Wide World of Sports

Address: I-4 Exit 26, Lake Buena Vista
Main number: (407) 828-3267
Web site: www.disneyworldsports.com

Throughout the year, a variety of sporting events take place at this multifaceted venue. The 220-acre facility hosts more than 170 amateur and professional events each year, the majority of which are open to spectators and fans. This complex also serves as the spring training facility for the Atlanta Braves baseball team and the Tampa Bay Buccaneers football team. Visit the web site for a listing of events taking place during the dates of your visit.

Amway Arena/Orlando Centroplex

Address: 600 West Amelia Street, Orlando
Box office: (407) 849-2020
Event information: (407) 849-2001
Orlando Magic info: (407) 89-MAGIC
Administrative offices: (407) 849-2000
Web site: www.orlandocentroplex.com

The Orlando Centroplex includes several major venues in the downtown Orlando area. The Amway Arena (formally known as the TD Waterhouse Center), for example, is home to the Orlando Magic basketball team and the American Football League's Orlando Predators. This arena is also where the new Orlando Sharks Major Indoor League Soccer team plays. To find the location of your seat using an interactive, 3-D web site that offers a layout of the venue, visit www.seats3d.com/nba/orlando_magic. A variety of other types of events are held here throughout the year. For a complete event listing, visit www.orlandocentroplex.com/calendar/calendar.php or call (407) 849-2001.

TIP
To hear Orlando Magic games on the radio while in Orlando, tune your radio to the Team (740 AM on the dial).

Florida Citrus Bowl Stadium

Address: 600 West Amelia Street, Orlando
Main number: (407) 849-2000
Box office: (407) 849-2020
Web site: www.orlandocentroplex.com

Originally built in 1936 (it has since been modernized and expanded), this stadium is the home of the annual New Year's Day football classic the Capital One Bowl, as well as the University of Central Florida and Jones High School football teams. It was also the site of five 1994 World Cup soccer games and 1996 Olympic soccer (first and second rounds). The annual American Motorcyclist Association's Supercross series is also held at this stadium, which contains 70,000 seats and 30 luxury skyboxes.

As a concert venue, the stadium has hosted artists including the Rolling Stones, the Who, Genesis, Pink Floyd, George Michael, Paul McCartney, Guns n' Roses, Billy Joel, Elton John, and the Eagles.

Daytona International Speedway

Address: 1801 West International Speedway Boulevard, Daytona Beach
Main number: (386) 254-2700
Ticket office: (800) PIT-SHOP
Web site: www.daytonaspeedway.com

The Daytona International Speedway is one of the most famous tracks in the world. An ongoing series of events is held here throughout the year, including the Daytona 500 and the Pepsi 400.

For a 3-D, interactive seating chart of this venue, visit www.seats3d.com/international_speedway_corporation/daytona_international_speedway.

To drive to Daytona International Speedway from Orlando, follow these directions: Take the I-4 East to SR 44 (exit 118). Take SR 44 East to US 1. Take US 1 North to SR 400/Beville Road. Follow SR 400 West to Clyde Morris Boulevard. Follow Clyde Morris Boulevard north to access Parking Lot 7 at the speedway. Depending on traffic, the drive will take between 90 minutes and two hours.

TIP
The Florida Gators (college football) play at the Ben Griffin Stadium in Gainesville, Florida. For ticket and schedule information, call (800) 279-4444.

HOW TO SEE SOLD-OUT SHOWS, CONCERTS, AND SPORTING EVENTS

The fastest, safest, and easiest way to get your hands on tickets to any sold-out show, concert, or sporting event is to work with your hotel's concierge, who will have a pre-existing relationship with a reputable and licensed ticket broker. Be prepared, however, to pay a hefty premium for the tickets. Tickets purchased through a broker often go for double, triple, or even quadruple the original ticket price, depending on demand. Some ticket brokers will purchase tickets from private sellers unable to use them.

Another, less reliable option is to purchase tickets from scalpers (often found outside of theaters or venues) or from private sellers using an online service, such as eBay.com. When utilizing one of these two methods, however, you don't know if the tickets you're buying are authentic until you try to enter the theater or venue.

The following is a partial listing of independent ticket brokers you can contact yourself to obtain tickets for sporting events, shows, concerts, and other events happening in the Orlando area:

- *FrontRowUSA.com*—www.frontrowusa.com/city_596/Orlando.htm, (800) 277-TIXX
- *GoTickets*—www.gotickets.com/broker/fl/orlando.php, (800) 775-1617
- *OnlineSeats.com*—www.onlineseats.com/orlando/orlando-brokers.htm, (800) 288-7710

- *TickCo*—www.tickco.com/cities/orlando_ticket_brokers.htm, (800) 279-4444
- *Ticket Retriever*—www.ticketretriever.com, (877) 22-FETCH
- *Ticketmaster*—www.ticketmaster.com, (407) 839-3900

GOLF COURSES

Orlando and the surrounding area has become a premier destination for golfers, both amateur (all skill levels) and professional. The WDW Resort has multiple championship golf courses on its property (including the Eagle Pines, Magnolia, Oak Trail, Palm, and Osprey Ridge courses); however, dozens of other courses are located a short drive away.

Grand Cypress, Omni Orlando at Champions Gate, Bay Hill Club, and the Ritz-Carlton Golf Club at Grand Lakes are among the top-rated courses in the area. However, Celebration Golf Club, Rosen Shingle Creek Golf Club, and the three courses at Ginn Reunion Resort all offer championship courses and the first-class amenities golfers appreciate.

The following is a partial description of golf courses in the Orlando area. Tee times can be reserved online for most of these courses by visiting their respective web sites. It's important to make your reservations in advance, especially during peak travel times or when you're seeking popular tee times. If you don't travel with your own clubs and equipment, you can rent clubs, carts, and/or caddy services at each golf club and course.

For a complete listing of public and private golf courses in the Orlando area, as well as a detailed schedule of tournaments, visit www.golfholes.com. Information about local courses and available tee times can also be found at www.golflink.com/golf-courses/city.asp?dest=Orlando+FL.

Bay Hill Club and Lodge

Address: 9000 Bay Hill Boulevard, Orlando
Phone number: (888) 422-9445
Web site: www.bayhill.com

DESCRIPTION
Although, the Bay Hill Club and Lodge has been open since 1961, it was in 1976 that golf legend Arnold Palmer purchased the facility. Today, this 270-acre resort offers a 70-room lodge, day spa, salon, fitness center, pool, tennis courts, and, of course, a championship golf course. Visiting and playing at this course offer golfers the sense of being a member of a private club. It includes 27 holes

of championship golf, a pro shop, caddy service, as well as the Arnold Palmer Golf Academy.

Celebration Golf Club

Address: 701 Golf Park Drive, Celebration

Phone number: (407) 566-GOLF (566-4653)

Web site: www.celebrationgolf.com

DESCRIPTION

Located in the Disney-created town of Celebration, this par-72, 6,786-yard championship course was designed by Robert Trent Jones Sr. and his son, Robert Trent Jones Jr. Greens fees are between $85 and $139. This is the site of the 2002 U.S. Senior Open Qualifier, 2003 Florida State Public Links Championship, 2004–2006 Robert Gamez Celebration Invitational, and the 2004 and 2005 Buick Scramble National Championships.

Eagle Creek Golf Club

Address: 10350 Emerson Lake Boulevard, Orlando

Phone number: (407) 273-4653

Web site: www.eaglecreekgolf.info

DESCRIPTION

This is a par-73, 7,198-yard, 18-hole championship course designed by Ron Garl and Howard Swan. Greens fees are between $55 and $129. This club also offers a golf academy and pro shop.

Ginn Reunion Resort

Address: 1000 Reunion Way, Reunion

Phone number: (407) 396-3180

Web site: www.reunionresort.com/golf/golf.asp

DESCRIPTION

Located on the 2,300-acre Ginn Reunion Resort is a trio of signature, 18-hole, championship courses created by Arnold Palmer, Tom Watson, and Jack Nicklaus. This is an extremely upscale resort (see Section III, "Where to Stay While in Orlando), that offers top-notch accommodations overlooking the courses. The resort is located less than 15 minutes from the Orange County Convention Center and six miles from the WDW Resort. It is an ideal place for business travelers to stay, play, dine, and/or host a corporate event. After an afternoon of golf, Forte is the perfect fine-dining restaurant for enjoying a superb dinner. This golf club also features a golf academy, a golf shop, and a driving range.

Grand Cypress Resort

Address: One North Jacaranda, Orlando

Phone number: (407) 239-1909

Web site: www.grandcypress.com

DESCRIPTION

This resort offers 45 holes of Jack Nicklaus-designed golf with four unique course combinations. Greens fees are between $120 and $250.

Omni Orlando at Champions Gate

Address: 1500 Masters Boulevard, Kissimmee

Phone number: (407) 390-6664

Web site: www.omnihotels.com/FindAHotel/OrlandoChampionsGate/Golf.aspx

DESCRIPTION

This is one of the area's newest luxury resorts, which offers two separate 18-hole, Greg Norman-designed championship courses. The Omni Resort overlooks these courses and offers packages, complete with accommodations and greens fees, starting at $198 per person. Private lessons are available through the David Leadbetter Golf Academy. There's also an on-site pro shop. The resort is located about 15 minutes from the Orange County Convention Center.

TIP

Need to purchase golf equipment or accessories? In addition to the pro shops located at many of the Orlando-area golf clubs and courses, Edwin Watts Golf Shops offer everything from top-of-the-line equipment to hard-to-find items. Hours: Monday through Friday, 9:30 A.M. to 8 P.M.; Saturday, 9:30 A.M. to 6 P.M.; and Sunday, 11 A.M. to 4 P.M. Locations include 7501 Turkey Lake Road, Orlando (407-345-8451); 8330 South International Drive, Orlando (407-351-1444); and 7024 International Drive, Orlando (407-352-2535).

Ritz-Carlton Golf Club

Address: Grande Lakes, 4048 Central Florida Parkway, Orlando

Phone number: (407) 393-4906

Web site: www.ritzcarlton.com/en/Properties/Orlando/Golf/Default.htm

DESCRIPTION

Part of the Ritz-Carlton and JW Marriott Resort, this 18-hole course was designed by Greg Norman. Greens fees are between

$120 and $215. In addition to hosting group events, this course offers a golf caddy concierge service.

Rosen Shingle Creek Golf Club

Address: 9939 Universal Boulevard, Orlando
Phone number: (407) 996-9933
Web site: http://shinglecreekgolf.com

DESCRIPTION

Consistently ranked one of the top courses in Florida, this is a David Harman-designed, par-72, 18-hole course (7,228 yards). It's also home to the Brad Brewer Golf Academy and the Golf Shop. Greens fees range from $49 to $139.

MONEY SAVER
For details about all of the Orlando-area golf courses, plus discounted tee times, visit www.orlando-golftrips.com.

Walt Disney World Golf

Address: Walt Disney World Resort, Lake Buena Vista
Phone number: (407) 938-GOLF (938-4653)
Web site: http://disneyworld.disney.go.com/wdw/moreMagic/golf/golfHome

DESCRIPTION

In addition to over 30 resort hotels, four theme parks, more than 100 restaurants, and countless other activities, the WDW Resort is also where you'll find over 99 holes of championship golf. Courses include Eagle Pines, Osprey Ridge, Lake Buena Vista, Palm, Magnolia, and Oak Trail. Each course offers its own unique experience. Golf carts are equipped with the latest global positioning system (GPS) technologies. Lessons and equipment rentals are available. Greens fees vary by season and are different for each course, ranging from $55 to $165. Disney resort guests receive discounted greens fees, plus preferred tee times.

TIP
Enjoy Las Vegas-style gambling plus a lovely cruise aboard Sterling Casino Lines (321-784-8558, www.sterlingcasinolines.com). This luxurious cruise ship departs Cape Canaveral, Florida, twice daily (11 A.M. to 4 P.M. and 7 P.M. to midnight). It provides an exciting five-hour cruise

aboard a 75,000-square-foot ship. Once aboard, you'll discover more than 1,000 slot machines, Las Vegas-style entertainment, five cocktail lounges, plus 50 casino table games. Private parties and small groups can be accommodated.

SHOPPING OPPORTUNITIES FOR BUSY BUSINESS TRAVELERS

The Orlando area is home to several upscale malls and premium outlet malls, plus dozens of department stores and countless stand-alone shops, boutiques, and other shopping opportunities. No matter what you're looking for, the shopping offered in the Orlando area will meet your tastes and budget.

The following is a summary of the best shopping experiences that a true shopaholic won't want to miss.

Downtown Disney

Address: Walt Disney World Resort, Lake Buena Vista
Phone number: (407) 939-6244
Web site: www.downtowndisney.com

DESCRIPTION

Part of the WDW Resort, the Downtown Disney area includes dining, shopping, and entertainment. Here you'll find the World of Disney and several other Disney-themed stores, selling everything from souvenirs to clothing, plus toy stores, a Virgin Megastore, contemporary art galleries, candy shops, and other fun boutiques. The Downtown Disney area also features several midpriced and fine-dining restaurants, a 24-screen AMC movie theater, the DisneyQuest indoor interactive theme park, and the custom-built theater where Cirque du Soleil's La Nouba is presented. Connected to the Downtown Disney area is Pleasure Island, which offers a handful of dance clubs, bars, and other nighttime activities (an admission fee applies after dark).

Florida Mall

Address: 800 South Orange Blossom Trail, Orlando
Phone number: (407) 851-6255
Web site: www.simon.com/mall/default.aspx?ID=139

DESCRIPTION

Featuring more than 250 specialty stores, plus Macy's, Dillard's, Lord and Taylor, JCPenney, Nordstrom, Sears, and Saks Fifth Avenue, this is definitely the largest indoor mall in the area. In addition to a food court, you'll also find several full-service restaurants here. This mall features boutiques from top designers, plus plenty of staple stores you'd typically find in malls across the country. Hours: Monday through Saturday, between 10 A.M. and 9 P.M.; Sunday, between noon and 6 P.M. The mall is located about five minutes from the Orlando International Airport and about 20 minutes from the International Drive, Walt Disney World, Universal Orlando, and downtown Orlando areas.

Lake Buena Vista Factory Stores

Address: 15591 State Road 535, Lake Buena Vista
Phone number: (407) 238-9301
Web site: www.lbvfs.com

DESCRIPTION

This outdoor outlet mall features dozens of name-brand designer stores, such as Aeropostale, Bass, Converse, Dressbarn, Eddie Bauer, Gap, Izod, Jockey, Nike, Liz Claiborne, Old Navy, Nine West, Reebok, Sony, and Van Heusen, offering up to 75 percent off suggested retail prices. Hours: Monday through Saturday, 9 A.M. to 9 P.M.; Sunday, 9 A.M. to 6 P.M. (Hours may vary by season.) This shopping complex is located about one mile from the WDW Resort.

Mall at Millenia

Address: 4200 Conroy Road, Orlando
Phone number: (407) 363-3555
Web site: www.mallatmillenia.com

DESCRIPTION

This large upscale mall contains more than 80 stores, including Apple, Banana Republic, Coach, Dior, Chanel, Burberry, Louis Vuitton, Nine West, Rockport, Tiffany and Company, the Body Shop, Cartier, Lenscrafters, MAC Cosmetics, L'Occitane, Brookstone, the Sharper Image, Express, Gucci, Juicy Couture, Kenneth Cole, Lacoste, Talbots, Victoria's Secret, and Zara. The three anchor department stores are Bloomingdale's, Macy's, and Neiman Marcus. In addition to a large food court, there are several full-service restaurants to choose from, such as California Pizza Kitchen, McCormick and Schmick's Seafood Restaurant, P. F. Chang's China Bistro, and the Cheesecake Factory. Hours: Monday through Saturday, 10 A.M. to 9 P.M.; Sunday, noon to 7 P.M. The mall is conveniently located off the I-4, about ten minutes from the

Orange County Convention Center, 15 minutes from the WDW Resort, and 5 minutes from the Universal Orlando area.

Orlando Premium Outlets

Address: 8200 Vineland Avenue, Orlando
Phone number: (407) 238-7787
Web site: www.premiumoutlets.com

DESCRIPTION

Here you'll find more than 110 outlet stores, from top-name companies like Versace, Coach, Fendi, Burberry, Kenneth Cole, Nike, Ralph Lauren, and Tommy Hilfiger. Discounts of 25 to 65 percent off suggested retail are offered. Hours: Monday through Saturday, 10 A.M. to 10 P.M.; Sunday, 10 A.M. to 9 P.M. If you're staying along International Drive, you can reach this shopping area via the I-Ride Trolley.

Pointe Orlando

Address: 9101 International Drive, Orlando
Phone number: (407) 248-2838
Web site: www.pointeorlando.com

DESCRIPTION

Located across the street from the Orange County Convention Center (about a five-minute walk), this outdoor shopping complex has a nice selection of shops, restaurants, and bars as well as a 21-screen movie theater. The stores here include Armani Exchange, Bimini Shoes, Foot Locker, Image Leather, Tommy Bahama Tropical Emporium, and Victoria's Secret. After spending a day at the convention center, you can relax and enjoy a good meal at Hooters, Maggiano's Little Italy, the Grape Wine Bar, or the Capital Grille (which is ideal for a business lunch or dinner). Hours: Monday through Saturday, 10 A.M. to 10 P.M.; Sunday, 11 A.M. to 9 P.M. Many of the bars and restaurants are open later.

Prime Outlets Orlando

Address: 5401 West Oak Ridge Road, Orlando
Phone number: (407) 352-9600
Web site: www.primeoutlets.com/cntrdefault.asp?cntrid=1077

DESCRIPTION

Boasting in excess of 180 stores, this is the nation's largest outlet shopping center. Hours: Monday through Saturday, 10 A.M. to 9 P.M.; Sunday, 10 A.M. to 7 P.M. (Hours may vary by season.) Here you'll find everything from top-designer-label clothing to household items and consumer electronics offered at a significant savings off suggested retail prices.

TIP
Located along International Drive are literally hundreds of shops, selling everything from Florida- and Orlando-themed souvenirs to consumer electronics and designer clothing. Within all of the area theme parks and attractions, you'll also find countless shops that sell souvenirs, gifts, and apparel.

MEDIA LISTINGS FOR ORLANDO

To stay up-to-date on the latest news events and local happenings, become familiar with the local media in the Orlando area.

Major Newspapers and Regional Magazines

The following resources are available at newsstands throughout the city.

- *Orlando Business Journal* (http://orlando.bizjournals.com/orlando)—A weekly newspaper of interest to people doing any type of business in the Orlando area. Available through newsstands or by subscription. An online edition (updated daily) is also available.
- *Orlando CEO* (www.orlandoleisure.com)—A quarterly, full-color magazine of interest to business leaders in the Orlando area.
- *Orlando Leisure* (www.orlandoleisure.com)—A monthly, full-color magazine covering local arts, entertainment, tourism, fashion, and dining.
- *Orlando Sentinel* (www.orlandosentinel.com)—Orlando's largest and most-read daily newspaper. Covers news, sports, weather, local events, and a wide range of other topics. Available at newsstands.
- *Orlando Weekly* (www.orlandoweekly.com)—A weekly newspaper covering local arts, entertainment, and dining. This publication promotes itself as "Central Florida's alternative source for news, views, arts and entertainment." Available at newsstands and distributed through hotels and attractions.
- *USA Today* (www.usatoday.com)—A nationwide, full-color newspaper covering news, travel, money, sports,

lifestyles, national weather, and technology. Published Monday through Friday.
- *Wall Street Journal* (www.wsj.com)—A national daily newspaper covering Wall Street and finance. Published Monday through Friday.
- *Where Orlando* (www.wheremagazine.com)—A monthly, full-color magazine for tourists, visitors, and vacationers. Offers up-to-date event listings, restaurant recommendations, plus details about area attractions and activities. This publication is distributed free of charge through many hotels and resorts.

TIP
Channel numbers will vary based on the cable programming service offered at your hotel or resort. Many hotels offer a full lineup of cable TV channels, including CNN, Showtime, HBO, the Weather Channel, and ESPN.

Local TV Stations

- WFTV Channel 9 (ABC Affiliate)
- WKMG Channel 6 (CBS Affiliate)
- WRBW Channel 65 (CW Affiliate)
- WSWB Channel 35 (Fox Affiliate)
- WESH Channel 2 (NBC Affiliate)
- WMFE Channel 24 (PBS Affiliate)
- WACX Channel 55 (Independent)
- WNTO Channel 26 (Independent)
- WTGL Channel 52 (Independent)

TIP
For Orlando-area television listings, visit the *TV Guide* web site at (www.tvguide.com/Listings/default.aspx).

Radio Stations

The following are some of the popular AM and FM radio stations in the Orlando area. Many rental cars are also now equipped with XM or Sirius satellite radio (the two companies will be merging in late 2007), which offers several hundred additional radio stations.

- Adult contemporary music (Star 94.5)—WCFB-FM 94.5

- Classic rock music—WHTQ-FM 96.5
- Country music—WPCV-FM 97.5
- Country music—WWKA-FM 92.3
- Gospel—WLVF-FM 90.3
- Hip-Hop and R&B music (Power 95.3)—WPYO-FM 95.3
- Music from the '80s, '90s, and today—WOMX-FM 105.1
- News/weather and traffic radio—WDBO-AM 580
- News/radio radio—WAMT-AM 1190
- News/talk radio—WFLF-AM 540
- Radio disney—WDYZ-AM 990
- Smooth jazz music—WLOQ-FM 103.1
- Soft rock music—WMMO-FM 98.9
- Sports radio (ESPN)—WIXC-AM 1060 and WHOO-AM 1080
- Sports radio (The Fan)—WORL-AM 660
- Sports radio (The Team)—WQTM-AM 740
- Today's hit music—WXXL-FM 106.7

TIP

For a more complete radio station listing, visit www.ontheradio.net.

TRAVEL NOTES

SECTION VII

Cinderella Castle (at night with fireworks) © Disney

VISITING THE WALT DISNEY WORLD RESORT

Covering more than 47 square miles, the WDW Resort has become a premier vacation and business travel destination for a multitude of reasons. In addition to offering world-class service, every aspect of the resort allows guests to experience a touch of memorable "Disney magic" that only the Walt Disney Company can provide.

The WDW Resort includes:

- Four major theme parks—the Magic Kingdom, Epcot, Disney's Hollywood Studios, and Disney's Animal Kingdom
- More than 32 separate resort hotels (with more currently being built)
- More than 100 fast food, casual, and fine-dining restaurants
- Multiple championship golf courses
- Several timeshare resorts
- Disney's Wide World of Sports, a massive sports complex
- Two major water parks—Disney's Blizzard Beach and Disney's Typhoon Lagoon
- Downtown Disney and Pleasure Island (a nightclub and shopping area)
- Its own public transportation system, including buses, water taxis, and the monorail
- Countless on-property recreational activities
- Several world-class day spas
- Multiple conference, convention, and banquet facilities

While families and people of all ages visit the Walt Disney World Resort to experience an ultimate dream vacation, more and more companies are hosting conferences, trade shows, seminars, workshops, and other corporate and business events here. So, if you're visiting the WDW Resort for business, hopefully you'll also have a chance to enjoy at least some of the fun, excitement, and leisure activities offered at this unique and massive destination.

CITY FACTOID
As of January 2008, the popular Disney-MGM Studios Theme Park was given a new name and some new rides, shows, and attractions. The new name of the theme park is Disney's Hollywood Studios. Some of the new things to experience include: *Toy Story Mania!* (an interactive play area for kids, opening in summer 2008), the *Block Party Bash* (which replaces the *Disney Stars* and *Motor Cars* parade in spring 2008), a newly revamped *Playhouse Disney-Live On Stage!* show (opening February 2008), and the *High School Musical 2: School's Out!* show, which replaced the *High School Musical Pep Rally* in fall 2007.

This chapter will help you make the most of your free time, enjoying all that the WDW Resort has to offer, plus provide useful information if you're planning to conduct any type of business here.

TIP
For help planning your time at the Walt Disney World Resort, whether you're staying at one of the on-property resort hotels or just visiting the theme parks, be sure to visit the official Walt Disney World web site at www.disneyworld.com.

CITY FACTOID
Since opening back in 1971, the Walt Disney World theme parks have closed their doors just once. They're typically open 365 days a year. The only exception was when Hurricane Floyd (a category four storm) swept through Orlando in September 1999. The park closed the afternoon of September 14th and remained closed until September 16th.

WARNING!
When visiting any theme park in Orlando, dress appropriately! This means wearing comfortable walking shoes, lightweight attire that'll protect you from the sun, sunglasses, a hat, and sunscreen. Even on overcast days, the Florida sun can quickly cause severe sunburn. It's also important to stay hydrated. Throughout the day, drink plenty of water. You might also consider bringing a change of clothing (including extra socks), since some of the rides will cause you to get wet. Lockers are available at each of the theme parks for a small fee.

The following is a listing of important direct-dial phone numbers for all on-property resorts (for reaching guests or the resort's front desk), major activities, and dining within the Walt Disney World Resort.

WDW RESORT PHONE NUMBERS

Resort or Service	Phone
All-Star Movies Resort	(407) 939-7000
All-Star Music Resort	(407) 939-6000
All-Star Sports Resort	(407) 939-5000

WDW RESORT PHONE NUMBERS

Resort or Service	Phone
Animal Kingdom Lodge	(407) 938-3000
Babysitting services	(407) 828-0920
Beach Club Villas	(407) 934-2175
Beach Club	(407) 934-8000
BoardWalk Inn & Villas	(407) 939-5100
Car care center	(407) 824-0976
Caribbean Beach Resort	(407) 934-3400
Cirque du Soliel box office	(407) 939-1298
Contemporary Resort	(407) 824-1000
Coronado Springs Resort	(407) 939-1000
Disney fishing expeditions	(407) WDW-FISH
Disney resort reservations	(407) W-DISNEY
Disney switchboard	(407) 824-2222
Disney Vacation Club (timeshare) information	(800) 800-9100
DisneyQuest	(407) 828-4600
Disney's Saratoga Springs Spa	(407) 827-4455
Dolphin Resort	(407) 934-4000
Downtown Disney private event information and reservations	(407) 828-3200
Florist and gift baskets	(407) 827-3505
Fort Wilderness Resort	(407) 824-2900
Golf reservations and information	(407) WDW-GOLF
Grand Floridian Resort	(407) 824-3000
Grand Floridian Spa	(407) 824-2332
Guest information	(407) 939-6244
Lost and found (Lost and found offices are located at each theme park and resort)	(407) 824-4245
Mandara Spa at the Disney World Dolphin	(407) 934-4772
Medical care (emergencies)	911
Medical care (nonemergencies)	(407) 648-9234
Old Key West Resort	(407) 827-7700
Photographic services	(407) 827-5099
Pleasure Island information	(407) WDW-2NITE
Polynesian Resort	(407) 824-2000
Pop Century Resort	(407) 938-4000

WDW RESORT PHONE NUMBERS

Resort or Service	Phone
Port Orleans French Quarter Resort	(407) 934-5000
Port Orleans Riverside Resort	(407) 934-6000
Restaurant reservations	(407) WDW-DINE
Richard Petty Driving Experience	(800) BE-PETTY
Swan Resort	(407) 934-3000
Taxi service (at WDW Resort)	(407) 699-9999
Tennis reservations and instruction	(407) 621-1991
Theme park annual passport information	(407) 560-PASS
Theme park hours of operation	(407) WDW-INFO
Town car and limo service	(407) 299-8696
Transportation information	(407) 824-4321
Vacation package reservations	(407) 939-7675
VIP Disney theme park tours	(407) WDW-TOUR
Weather forecast (for Disney World)	(407) 824-4104
Wide World of Sports box office	(407) WDW-GAME
Wilderness Lodge Resort	(407) 824-3200
Wilderness Lodge Villas	(407) 938-4300
Yacht Club Resort	(407) 934-7000

TIP
For information about getting to and from the WDW Resort and the Orlando International Airport or other nearby locations, such as the Orange County Convention Center, see Section IV, "Getting Around Town."

PLENTY OF PERKS FOR WDW RESORT HOTEL GUESTS

In addition to being able to enjoy the world-class service offered at all of the on-property Disney resort hotels, you'll receive some definite perks by staying at one of Disney's 22 company-owned-and-operated resort properties during your trip to Orlando, especially if you plan to visit the theme parks.

Each day, one of the Disney theme parks (the Magic Kingdom, Epcot, the Disney's Hollywood Studios, or Disney's Animal Kingdom) opens one hour early and remains open for up to three hours after normal closing time exclusively for WDW Resort hotel guests. This greatly reduces the crowds you'll encounter in the parks and allows you to see and experience more of the popular attractions in much less time. When you check in to your Disney resort hotel, you'll be given a schedule listing which parks are open during extended hours and on what days. To take advantage of this Extra Magic Hours perk, you'll need a valid theme park ticket, plus your resort ID.

Getting to and from the airport is also more convenient and totally free, when you utilize Disney's Magical Express transportation, offered to guests at any of the on-property WDW Resort hotels. See Section I, "Welcome to Orlando," for more information about this ground transportation service. If you're under tight time constraints, however, you're better off hiring a taxi, town car or limo to provide transportation from and back to the airport.

TIP
WDW Resort guests are free to utilize the Disney transportation system (which includes a fleet of air-conditioned buses, water taxis, and the monorail) to get around the massive resort property—whether it's between hotels or to get to and from one of the theme parks.

Another perk offered to Disney resort guests is the ability to upgrade to the Disney Dining Plan. This allows guests to save up to 40 percent on their meals while staying at the WDW Resort. The dining plan is honored at more than 100 on-site restaurants. When you upgrade to the Disney Dining Plan, you're entitled to one table-service meal, one quick-service meal, and one snack per day.

When you check into your WDW Resort hotel, your room key also serves as your Key to the World charge card. Using your room key, you can charge souvenirs and other items to your room when you shop at many of the stores located on the property, including within the theme parks. You can also have your purchases delivered directly to your hotel room, so you don't have to carry them around while you're enjoying the theme parks.

These are just some of the reasons that visitors to Orlando opt to stay at one of the on-site hotels at the WDW Resort. More information about accommodations options can be found in Section III, "Where to Stay While in Orlando." If the purpose of your visit is mainly for business, definitely consider staying at one of the more business-friendly resort hotels, like the Walt Disney World

Swan or Dolphin, the Grand Floridian, the Yacht Club, or the Beach Club.

CITY FACTOID
During peak travel times, the WDW Resort employs between 54,000 and 60,000 cast members (employees). Disney is the largest single-site employer in the United States.

DISNEY THEME PARKS

Seeing and doing everything at each Disney theme park could easily take two or three full days (or more) per park, depending on crowds and your own stamina. If you're a business traveler looking to experience the very best of what each park offers in the shortest time possible (based on what's suitable for adults), this section will help you plan your time accordingly.

This guide categorizes each of the popular rides, shows, and attractions based on age appropriateness and gives each a star rating (between one and four stars). If a ride, show, or attraction is absolutely incredible and should not be missed, we've given it four stars (☆☆☆☆), taking into account its entertainment value, overall quality, originality, and whether it's really worth waiting in line for.

For each popular ride, show, and attraction, you can quickly see what age group(s) it'll most appeal to, plus quickly determine whether or not experiencing it is worthy of your valuable time. You can also determine what type of attraction each item is, such as a ride, thrill ride, show, interactive play area, character meeting spot, or parade. You can also determine if the attraction is part of the Fastpass program, which is described later in this section.

CITY FACTOID
The Walt Disney World Resort is about the size of San Francisco, or two Manhattan islands. Of the more than 30,000 acres Disney currently owns, less than one-fourth has been developed. About 25 percent of the property has been designated as a wilderness preserve.

Understanding the Star Ratings

- *One Star* (☆)—An average attraction. It's worth seeing if you have plenty of time or if there's no wait. You're definitely

better off utilizing your time seeing or experiencing the ☆☆☆ and ☆☆☆☆ attractions first.
- *Two Stars* (☆☆)—Average. The ride, show, or attraction is really good and well worth seeing, but it can be skipped if you're under a time crunch or the line for it is too long.
- *Three Stars* (☆☆☆)—Above average. An excellent attraction that's well worth experiencing, even if you have to wait up to 60 minutes in line to experience it. If possible, utilize Fastpass to save time, but if the particular ride, show, or attraction is suitable for your age group, be sure to check it out!
- *Four Stars* (☆☆☆☆)—Best of the best. These are definitely must-see ride, show, or attraction. This rating is given only to the very best of what the WDW theme parks offer. Chances are, you'll enjoy your time at each theme park the most if you first focus on these superior rides, shows, and attractions, understanding that to experience them, you'll probably need to utilize Fastpass and/or wait in line for up to 60 or 90 minutes for each of them.

Disney Theme Park Ticket Prices

As of February 2007, Disney theme park tickets (referred to as "base tickets") were available for between one- and ten-day periods. During each day a ticket is valid, you can visit one Disney theme park (the Magic Kingdom, Epcot, Disney's Hollywood Studios, *or* Disney's Animal Kingdom).

BASE TICKET THEME PARK ADMISSION PRICES										
Number of Days	1	2	3	4	5	6	7	8	9	10
Adult Ticket Price	$71	$139	$203	$212	$215	$217	$219	$221	$223	$225
Child Ticket Price	$60	$117	$171	$178	$179	$181	$182	$185	$186	$187

For an additional fee of $45 per ticket, you can add the Park Hopper option. This allows you to visit multiple Disney theme parks during each single day. Thus, you can travel between theme parks as much as you want during each day your ticket is valid.

MONEY SAVER
By purchasing a five-day pass, adults pay only $43 per day to visit each theme park. When purchasing a ten-day pass, adults pay only $22.50 per day to visit each theme park. This does not include any ticket upgrades.

For yet an additional upgrade fee of $50 per ticket, you can add multiple admissions to the Disney water parks (Typhoon Lagoon and Blizzard Beach), DisneyQuest, Pleasure Island, and Disney's Wide World of Sports complex can be added. This is referred to as the Water Park Fun and More add-on.

TIP
For a seven-day pass, you wind up paying $6.43 per day extra for the Park Hopper privilege. For a ten-day pass, you wind up paying just $4.50 per day extra for the Park Hopper privilege.

For a one- or two-day ticket, the $50 Water Park Fun and More upgrade allows for unlimited access to one or two of the four main theme parks (unless you also purchase the Park Hopper upgrade), plus two separate admissions to your choice of the following additional theme parks or attractions—which include Typhoon Lagoon, Blizzard Beach, DisneyQuest, Pleasure Island, and/or Disney's Wide World of Sports. For each additional day added to your base ticket, one additional visit is offered to either Typhoon Lagoon, Blizzard Beach, DisneyQuest, Pleasure Island, and/or Disney's Wide World of Sports with the Water Park Fun and More upgrade.

Multiday park passes do not need to be used on consecutive days; however, unused days remain valid for only 14 days from the date of first use, unless you purchase the no-expiration option for an additional fee. When this option is purchased, unused days never expire and can be used anytime (during future visits, for example).

MONEY SAVER
The more days you purchase on your Disney theme park ticket, the more you'll save. Additional savings are available for four- to ten-day tickets if you prepurchase them

NO-EXPIRATION ADD-ON PRICES

Number of Days	1	2	3	4	5	6	7	8	9	10
No-expiration option	N/A	$15	$20	$45	$60	$65		$95	$130	$155	$180

outside of Florida prior to your arrival. Purchases can be made at any Disney Store and from the www.disneyworld.com web site.

Unless you purchase a Park Hopper ticket, separate admission is charged for the Disney water parks, DisneyQuest, Pleasure Island, and Disney's Wide World of Sports complex.

MONEY SAVER

For the greatest savings, consider purchasing an Annual Pass or Premium Annual Pass (good for 365 days from the date of first use). An Annual Pass ($448 per adult, $395 per child) allows for unlimited admission to all four Disney theme parks, as well as complimentary parking. A Premium Annual Pass ($579 per adult, $510 per child) offers unlimited admission to all four Disney theme parks, complimentary parking, plus admission to Disney's water parks, DisneyQuest, Pleasure Island, and Disney's Wide World of Sports complex.

NO-EXPIRATION ADD-ON PRICES

Theme Park/ Attraction	Adult One-Day	Adult Annual Pass	Child One-Day	Child Annual Pass
Typhoon Lagoon Water Park	$39.00	$99.95	$33.00	$80.50
Blizzard Beach Water Park	$39.00	$99.95	$33.00	$80.50
DisneyQuest	$37.00	$89.00	$31.00	$71.00
DisneyQuest/ Water Park Combo	N/A	$129.00	N/A	$99.00
Pleasure Island	$21.95	$55.95	N/A	N/A

For convention-goers and small to large (business-oriented or corporate) groups, Disney's special Meeting/Convention theme park tickets are available. The After 2 P.M., After 4 P.M., and Multi-Day Meeting/Convention tickets are designed to fit any business agenda. To learn more about these discounted ticket options, call (407) 566-5600 or visit http://disneymeetings.disney.go.com/dwm/ticketpages/genericTickets.

The following is a list of potential additional costs you'll pay when visiting a Disney theme park.

- Parking—$10 per day
- Stroller rental—$10 to $18 per day
- Locker rental—$5 per day (plus a $2 refundable deposit)
- Wheelchair rental—$10 per day (or $8 per day for length-of-stay rentals)
- Electronic convenience vehicle (ECV) rental—$35 per day (plus a $5 refundable deposit)

MONEY SAVER
Discounted theme park tickets are available to Florida residents (proper ID required).

Park Hours

Each theme park operates during different hours throughout the week, and hours also vary by season. To determine the hours of operation for each park during the dates of your visit, call (407) WDW-INFO (select option 2) or (407) WDW-MAGIC (select option 4, followed by option 2, followed by option 2). This information is also available at the www.disneyworld.com web site.

TIME SAVER
If you're a guest at one of the on-property WDW resorts, you're entitled to take advantage of extended theme park hours offered throughout the week. This allows you to experience the most popular rides, shows, and attractions with significantly shorter lines.

Getting Around the WDW Resort and Parking

The Disney transportation system is available throughout the WDW Resort property. It consists of buses, boats, and the Disney monorail system and is designed to help guests travel between on-site resorts and the various on-property theme parks and attractions. The transportation system is available free of charge to resort and theme park guests.

Bus stops for the Disney bus system are located in front of each on-property resort, attraction, and theme park. Look for the bus headed to your destination. Depending on the route, buses operate between every 5 and 30 minutes. Hours of operation vary by route. For more information, call (407) 824-4321 or see Section IV, "Getting Around Town."

The monorail system connects the Magic Kingdom and Epcot with several on-property resorts (including the Contemporary, Polynesian, and Grand Floridian), as well as the Ticket and Transportation Center.

If you choose to drive yourself around the WDW Resort, you'll find ample parking available at all of the on-property hotels, as well as at the various theme parks. There is a $10 per-day parking fee for cars at each hotel and theme park. Once you pay the daily parking fee, however, you can park at any of the resorts or theme parks that day and come and go as you please.

The most costly way (albeit one of the fastest) to get around the WDW Resort property is via taxi. Taxi stands are located in front of each on-property resort, as well as each of the theme parks and major attraction areas. You can also call Yellow Cab Company at (407) 699-9999. This is the exclusive taxi company for the WDW Resort. The metered rates are $3.50 for the first mile and $2 for each additional mile.

Budgeting Your Time When Visiting the Theme Parks

The best way to see and do everything that's of interest to you while visiting the WDW theme parks is to do some preplanning. Learn about the best age-appropriate rides, shows, parades, and attractions, then choose what you'd most like to see and do based on your available time.

TIP

To get the best seats or viewing spots for all parades and most shows with open seating, be sure to arrive 30 to 60 minutes before the posted show time. Since parade and show times vary each day, be sure to pick up a free copy of the *Times & Information Guide*, which is distributed at the entrance to each theme park, at all gift and souvenir shops, and at the Guest Information Board areas within each park.

When the theme parks are experiencing average to heavy crowds, it will take about 60 to 90 minutes to wait in line and then experience each must-see ride, show, or attraction. Even during peak travel times, however, some rides and attractions will have a much shorter or zero wait. One excellent strategy is to utilize Fastpass for the must-see rides and attractions. While you're waiting for your designated Fastpass time, you can go to several of the no-wait or minimal-wait attractions.

Current wait times for every ride and attraction are posted on the Guest Information Board in each theme park. At the entrance to each ride or attraction, you'll see a sign listing the current wait time for it. This information is updated throughout the day as crowd patterns change.

TIME SAVER
To easily find your way around each theme park, be sure to pick up a free, full-color guide map for each park you visit. The maps are distributed at all ticket counters, the entrance to each theme park, all gift and souvenir shops, and at the Guest Information Board areas within each park.

Understanding the Guest Information Boards and Fastpass

Near the entrance to each of the Disney theme parks, you'll find a Guest Information Board, which is staffed by a Disney cast member (theme park employee). On this board you'll see a list of the park's most popular rides, shows, and attractions, along with the current wait times for them. Using this information, you can better plan your time in the park and strategically work to avoid long lines.

At the Magic Kingdom, the Guest Information Board is located at the Hub, in front of Cinderella's castle at the end of Main Street USA, to the left of the large statue of Walt Disney and Mickey Mouse.

The Guest Information Board at Epcot is located near Innoventions East and West, in front of the large fountain within Future World. At the Disney's Hollywood Studios, the Guest Information Board can be found at the intersection of Hollywood Boulevard and Sunset Boulevard, near the Brown Derby restaurant. When you're visiting Disney's Animal Kingdom, you'll find the Guest Information Board located in front of Discovery Island and the Tree of Life as you enter the park from the Oasis area.

TIME SAVER
During lunch and dinner times, as well as during parade times, you'll notice the crowds within the Disney theme parks thin out considerably. These are the ideal times to experience the most popular rides, shows, and attractions.

Another thing you can do to eliminate the need to wait on long lines for the most popular rides, shows, and attractions is to utilize Fastpass when it's available. Fastpass is like an automated reservations system. Instead of waiting in a line to experience a ride, you simply insert your Disney theme park admission ticket or Park Hopper pass into the attraction's Fastpass machine. A separate printed ticket will be provided that lists a specific one-hour time period during which you should return to the attraction in order to experience it. When you return during the designated time, simply approach the Fastpass entrance to that ride, show, or attraction and you'll have little or no wait.

CITY FACTOID
The lost and found office at the Magic Kingdom is always busy. For example, more than 100 pairs of sunglasses are turned in every day. That translates to 36,500 pairs of lost sunglasses per year and more than 1,277,500 pairs of lost sunglasses since the park first opened in 1972.

For each guest, only one Fastpass can be issued at a time, so choose which attractions you want to experience the most. Once a Fastpass is issued for an attraction, go and enjoy other non-Fastpass rides, shows, and attractions. When your designated time to experience the chosen Fastpass attraction approaches, return to that attraction. After you've experienced it, proceed directly to the next Fastpass attraction to request your new Fastpass.

The Fastpass program is free of charge and is included with all admission tickets to the Disney theme parks. Utilizing this service on three or four popular attractions in a single day could save you between 30 and 90 minutes of waiting time per attraction, thus freeing you up to see and do more while also giving you the chance to experience the very best of what each theme park has to offer.

CITY FACTOID
Just like the real world around us, the Walt Disney World Resort is always expanding and evolving. In January 2007, for example, the *Finding Nemo—The Musical!* show opened in Disney's Animal Kingdom. In April 2007, the *Monsters, Inc. Laugh Floor* show opened in the Magic Kingdom. As for new Disney resort properties, between fall 2007 and spring 2009, Disney's Animal Kingdom Villas will be built and opened in several phases. In 2010, a 900-acre Four Seasons Resort luxury hotel property will open within Disney World. In 2008, Disney's Wide World of Sports complex will undergo a 220-acre expansion. You can also expect a handful of new themed restaurants to open within the WDW Resort in 2007 and 2008, including T-Rex: A Prehistoric Family Adventure: A Place to Eat, Shop, Explore, and Discover.

The Magic Kingdom

The Magic Kingdom is the original theme park at the Walt Disney World Resort. It was modeled after Disneyland in Anaheim, California, and features many classic and famous rides

As you'll discover, the Magic Kingdom is divided into several separate themed areas, including Main Street USA, Adventureland, Frontierland, Liberty Square, Fantasyland, Mickey's Toontown Fair, and Tomorrowland. (Main Street, U.S.A. with Cinderella Castle in background © Disney)

and attractions, many of which Walt Disney himself conceived of or helped develop. The rides, shows, and attractions within the Magic Kingdom are all based on popular Disney characters and movies.

With a few exceptions, the majority of rides, shows, and attractions offered within Fantasyland and Mickey's Toontown Fair are all kid oriented. The rides, shows, and attractions that are more appropriate for adults, including several thrill rides, can be found scattered throughout the park.

Every year or two, Disney revamps the popular afternoon and nighttime parades, so when you visit this park, the parade might be called something different, but it will feature all of the classic and newer Disney characters, plus some of the most popular Disney music from the animated, computer-generated, and live-action movies.

TIP
Because this theme park is primarily kid oriented, you'll find it will be less crowded during lunch and dinner times, plus in the evenings (after young children have gone to bed).

The following is a summary of the most popular rides, shows, parades, and attractions located at the Magic Kingdom. Adults traveling without kids or teens should be able to experience the most popular and age-appropriate rides, shows, parades, and attractions within a half day to a full day, depending on crowds and how well they utilize Fastpass. Families visiting this theme park, especially with kids, should plan on spending a minimum of two to three full days here to see and experience the majority of what's offered.

ATTRACTIONS AT THE MAGIC KINGDOM

Attraction Name	Attraction Type	Location	Star Rating	Fastpass	Adults	Teens	Kids	All Ages
Walt Disney World Railroad	Ride	Stations located throughout Magic Kingdom, including Main Street	☆☆	No				✓

ATTRACTIONS AT THE MAGIC KINGDOM

Attraction Name	Attraction Type	Location	Star Rating	Fastpass	Adults	Teens	Kids	All Ages
Walt Disney World Railroad		USA, Frontierland, and Mickey's Toontown Fair						
Swiss Family Treehouse	Play area	Adventureland	☆☆	No		✓	✓	
The Magic Carpets of Aladdin	Ride	Adventureland	☆☆☆	No			✓	
The Enchanted Tiki Room Under New Management	Show	Adventureland	☆☆☆	No				✓
Jungle Cruise	Ride	Adventureland	☆☆☆	Yes				✓
Pirates of the Caribbean	Ride	Adventureland	☆☆☆☆					✓
Splash Mountain	Thrill ride	Frontierland	☆☆☆☆	Yes	✓	✓		
Big Thunder Mountain Railroad	Thrill ride	Frontierland	☆☆☆☆	Yes	✓	✓		
Tom Sawyer Island	Play area	Frontierland	☆☆	No		✓	✓	
Country Bear Jamboree	Show	Frontierland	☆☆☆	No			✓	
The Hall of Presidents	Show	Liberty Square	☆☆☆	No	✓	✓		
Liberty Square Riverboat	Ride	Liberty Square	☆☆☆	No				✓
The Haunted Mansion	Ride	Liberty Square	☆☆☆☆	No				✓
It's a Small World	Ride	Fantasyland	☆☆☆☆	No				✓
Peter Pan's Flight	Ride	Fantasyland	☆☆☆	Yes			✓	
Mickey's PhilharMagic	Show	Fantasyland	☆☆☆☆	Yes				✓
Dream Along with Mickey	Show	Fantasyland	☆☆☆	No		✓	✓	
Fairytale Garden	Character meeting spot	Fantasyland	N/A	No				✓

ATTRACTIONS AT THE MAGIC KINGDOM

Attraction Name	Attraction Type	Location	Star Rating	Fastpass	Adults	Teens	Kids	All Ages
Snow White's Scary Adventure	Ride	Fantasyland	☆☆☆	No			✓	
Cinderella's Golden Carrousel	Ride	Fantasyland	☆☆☆	No				✓
Dumbo the Flying Elephant	Ride	Fantasyland	☆☆☆	No			✓	
Ariel's Grotto	Character meeting spot	Fantasyland	N/A	No				✓
Pooh's Playful Spot	Play area	Fantasyland	☆☆☆	No			✓	
The Many Adventures of Winnie the Pooh	Ride	Fantasyland	☆☆☆☆	Yes			✓	
Mad Tea Party	Ride	Fantasyland	☆☆☆	No		✓	✓	
Minnie's Country House	Character meeting spot and attraction	Mickey's Toontown Fair	☆☆☆	No				✓
Mickey's Country House	Character meeting spot and attraction	Mickey's Toontown Fair	☆☆☆	No				✓
Toontown Hall of Fame Tent	Character meeting spot	Mickey's Toontown Fair	N/A	No				✓
Judge's Tent	Character meeting spot	Mickey's Toontown Fair	N/A	No				✓
Donald's Boat	Play area	Mickey's Toontown Fair	☆☆☆	No			✓	
The Barnstormer at Goofy's Wiseacre	Thrill ride	Mickey's Toontown Fair	☆☆☆☆	No			✓	
Indy Speedway	Ride	Tomorrowland	☆☆☆	No			✓	
Space Mountain	Thrill ride	Tomorrowland	☆☆☆☆	Yes	✓	✓		

ATTRACTIONS AT THE MAGIC KINGDOM

Attraction Name	Attraction Type	Location	Star Rating	Fastpass	Adults	Teens	Kids	All Ages
Astro Orbiter	Ride	Tomorrowland	☆☆☆	No		✓	✓	
Tomorrowland Transit Authority	Ride	Tomorrowland	☆☆☆	No				✓
Walt Disney's Carousel of Progress	Ride and Show	Tomorrowland	☆☆☆	No				✓
Buzz Lightyear's Space Ranger Spin	Ride	Tomorrowland	☆☆☆☆	Yes		✓	✓	
Stitch's Great Escape!	Thrill ride	Tomorrowland	☆☆☆☆	Yes		✓	✓	
Disney Dreams Come True Parade (Afternoon Character Parade)	Parade	Parade route is along Main Street USA and surrounding areas	☆☆☆☆	No				✓
SpectroMagic Parade (Nighttime Character Parade)	Parade	Parade route is along Main Street USA and surrounding areas	☆☆☆☆	No				✓
Wishes Fireworks	Show	Above Cinderella's Castle, viewable from along Main Street USA and surrounding areas	☆☆☆☆	No				✓

Epcot

Epcot is really two theme parks in one. Future World contains eight separate pavilions, each of which houses one or more rides and attractions. Each pavilion has a unique theme and offers a special look at our present and future.

The World Showcase features 11 separate pavilions, each hosted by a different country from around the world. Each pavilion features

features its own rides and/or attractions, show(s), restaurants, shops, and other activities. The World Showcase is situated around a large lake (where the nightly *IllumiNations* fireworks, laser, and special effects show is presented.)

TIP
Each of the pavilions within the World Showcase features at least one fine-dining restaurant that serves authentically prepared, native cuisine from that country. Many of these restaurants offer a business-friendly environment and are open for lunch and dinner. Reservations are typically required.

The following is a summary of the most popular rides, shows, parades, and attractions located at Epcot. Adults traveling without kids or teens should be able to experience the most popular and age-appropriate rides, shows, parades, and attractions within two full days depending on crowds. This includes one day exploring Future World and one day experiencing the World Showcase. You can save time and avoid waiting in lines for popular attractions by utilizing Fastpass. Families visiting this theme park, especially with kids, should plan on spending a minimum of one full day here to

Unlike the attractions at the Magic Kingdom, the variety of rides and attractions within Future World are suitable for people of all ages and will be of interest to adults. Most of the rides, shows, and attractions within the World Showcase are geared toward adults. (Spaceship Earth © Disney)

see and experience the majority of what's offered that's of interest to young guests.

> **TIP**
> As you explore Epcot, you'll see musical performances and other live entertainment in various areas of the park, including in front of many of the World Showcase pavilions. Each show or concert lasts between 10 and 20 minutes.

ATTRACTIONS AT EPCOT

Attraction Name	Attraction Type	Location	Star Rating	Fastpass	Adults	Teens	Kids	All Ages
Leave a Legacy	Monument	Entrance of Epcot's Future World	☆☆	No				✓
Spaceship Earth	Ride	Future World	☆☆☆	No				✓
Ellen's Energy Adventure	45-minute ride and attraction	Universe of Energy in Future World	☆☆☆	No				✓
Mission: Space	Thrill ride	Mission: Space in Future World	☆☆☆☆	Yes	✓	✓		
Test Track	Thrill ride	Test Track in Future World	☆☆☆☆	Yes	✓	✓		
Innoventions East and West	Interactive attractions	Innoventions Pavilion	☆☆☆	No	✓	✓		
The Seas with Nemo and Friends	Ride	The Seas Pavilion	☆☆☆	No			✓	
Turtle Talk with Crush	Show	The Seas Pavilion	☆☆	No			✓	
Soarin'	Ride	The Land Pavilion	☆☆☆☆	Yes	✓	✓		
Living with the Land	Ride	The Land Pavilion	☆☆☆	Yes				✓
The Circle of Life	Movie	The Land Pavilion	☆☆☆☆	No			✓	
Journey Into Imagination with Figment	Ride and interactive attraction	Imagination Pavillion	☆☆☆	No			✓	

ATTRACTIONS AT EPCOT

Attraction Name	Attraction Type	Location	Star Rating	Fastpass	Adults	Teens	Kids	All Ages
Honey, I Shrunk the Audience	3-D movie	Imagination Pavilion	☆☆☆	Yes				✓
El Rio del Tiempo	Ride	Mexico Pavilion (World Showcase)	☆☆☆	No				✓
Maelstrom	Ride and short film	Norway Pavilion (World Showcase)	☆☆☆	Yes				✓
Reflections of China	Circle-Vision 360 film (14 minutes)	China Pavilion (World Showcase)	☆☆☆	No	✓	✓		
The American Adventure	Show (30 minutes)	The American Adventure Pavilion (World Showcase)	☆☆☆	No				✓
Impressions de France	Movie (20 minutes)	France Pavilion (World Showcase)	☆☆☆	No	✓	✓		
O Canada!	Circle-Vision 360 film (22 minutes)	Canada Pavilion (World Showcase)	☆☆☆	No	✓	✓		
IllumiNations	Fireworks, laser, and special effects	World Showcase Lagoon	☆☆☆☆	No				✓

The Disney's Hollywood Studios

This popular Disney theme park offers a variety of rides, shows, parades, and attractions based on movies and television shows. Here, you'll find a nice combination of thrill rides (more suitable for teen and adult guests) and a variety of rides, shows, and attractions that cater more to kids and entire families. Depending on crowds, plan on spending at least one full day and evening at the Disney's

Hollywood Studios to be able to see and experience the majority of the age-appropriate rides, shows, and attractions offered.

As with all of the Disney theme parks, within The Disney's Hollywood Studios you'll find a large selection of fast-food dining options, plus a few upscale, full-service restaurants. For lunch and dinner, for example, one of the very best fine-dining experiences you can have at any Disney theme park is at the Brown Derby (located at the intersection of Hollywood Boulevard and Sunset Boulevard within the Disney's Hollywood Studios).

In addition to all of the rides and attractions, the Disney's Hollywood Studios also puts on several excellent parades and shows that are well worth seeing. *Fantasmic!* for example, is presented nightly and stars your favorite Disney characters in a live-action show that combines fireworks, lasers, special effects, and fire. This show is ideal for adults and teens, but may be a bit scary for kids. People of all ages will enjoy the Disney Stars and Motor Cars parade that proceeds along Hollywood Boulevard almost every afternoon.

The following is a summary of the most popular rides, shows, parades, and attractions available at the Disney's Hollywood Studios.

ATTRACTIONS AT DISNEY'S HOLLYWOOD STUDIOS

Attraction Name	Attraction Type	Location	Star Rating	Fastpass	Adults	Teens	Kids	All Ages
The Great Movie Ride	Ride (22 minutes)	Hollywood Boulevard	☆☆☆	No				✓
Sounds Dangerous— starring Drew Carey	Show (12 minutes)	Echo Lake	☆☆☆	No				✓
Indiana Jones Epic Stunt Spectacular!	Show (30 minutes)	Echo Lake	☆☆☆☆	Yes	✓	✓		
Star Tours	Thrill ride	Echo Lake	☆☆☆☆	Yes	✓	✓		
Muppet-Vision 3-D	3-D movie (25 minutes)	Streets of America	☆☆☆☆	No				✓
Honey, I Shrunk the Kids Movie Set Adventure	Interactive play area	Streets of America	☆☆☆☆	No				✓

ATTRACTIONS AT DISNEY'S HOLLYWOOD STUDIOS

Attraction Name	Attraction Type	Location	Star Rating	Fastpass	Adults	Teens	Kids	All Ages
Lights, Motors, Action Extreme Stunt Show	Show (33 minutes)	Streets of America	☆☆☆	No	✓	✓		
The Disney's Hollywood Studios Backlot Tour	Tram ride and walking tour (35 minutes)	Mickey Avenue	☆☆☆	No				✓
Journey into Narnia: Creating the Lion, the Witch, and the Wardrobe	Exhibit (walking tour—15 minutes)	Mickey Avenue	☆☆	No				✓
Walt Disney: One Man's Dream	Exhibit (walking tour—15 minutes)	Mickey Avenue	☆☆	No	✓	✓		
Voyage of the Little Mermaid	Show (17 minutes)	Animation Courtyard	☆☆☆☆	Yes				✓
The Magic of Disney Animation	Exhibit and tour (15 minutes)	Animation Courtyard	☆☆☆	No	✓	✓		
Playhouse Disney—Live On Stage!	Show (22 minutes)	Animation Courtyard	☆☆☆☆	No			✓	
Beauty and the Beast—Live On Stage!	Show (30 minutes)	Sunset Boulevard	☆☆☆☆☆	No				✓
Rock 'n' Roller Coaster starring Aerosmith	Thrill ride	Sunset Boulevard	☆☆☆☆	Yes	✓	✓		
The Twilight Zone Tower of Terror	Thrill ride	Sunset Boulevard	☆☆☆☆	Yes	✓	✓		
Fantasmic!	Show (25 minutes)	Sunset Boulevard	☆☆☆☆	No				✓
Disney Stars and Motor Cars Parade	Afternoon character parade	Hollywood Boulevard	☆☆☆	No				✓

ATTRACTIONS AT DISNEY'S HOLLYWOOD STUDIOS

Attraction Name	Attraction Type	Location	Star Rating	Fastpass	Adults	Teens	Kids	All Ages
High School Musical Pep Rally	Interactive show	Various locations, see *Times & Information Guide*	☆☆☆☆	No		✓	✓	

The Tower of Terror is one of the Disney Hollywood Studio's most popular thrill ride attractions. (The Twilight Zone Tower of Terror™ © Disney The Twilight Zone™ is a registered trademark of CBS, Inc. and is used pursuant to a license from CBS, Inc.)

Disney's Animal Kingdom

Disney's newest theme park is all about animals and wildlife conservation. Here, you'll find a wide range of rides, shows, parades, and attractions suitable for people of all ages.

To see and experience all of the age-appropriate attractions this theme park offers, it will take at least one full day and evening (possibly longer, depending on crowds). Show and parade times vary each day. See the *Times & Information Guide* or the Guest Information Board at the theme park for exact show and parade times during your visit.

While visually, the centerpiece of this theme park is the Tree of Life (located on Discovery Island in the center of the park), one of the most popular attractions here is the Kilimanjaro Safaris ride, which takes you up close to see a wide range of wild animals roaming freely in their natural habitats, including lions, giraffes, gazelles, and elephants. (Tree of Life® Attraction © Disney)

TIP

The best time to experience the Kilimanjaro Safaris or any attraction featuring live animals (outdoors) is early morning, late afternoon, or in the evening, when it's not too hot. The animals tend to hide under shelter in the midafternoon when the sun is at its peak. You're apt to see more animals on overcast or cooler days.

ATTRACTIONS AT DISNEY'S ANIMAL KINGDOM

Attraction Name	Attraction Type	Location	Star Rating	Fastpass	Adults	Teens	Kids	All Ages
The Oasis Exhibits	Wildlife exhibit (self-paced)	Oasis	☆☆	No				✓
It's Tough to be a Bug!	3-D movie	Discovery Island	☆☆☆☆	Yes				✓

ATTRACTIONS AT DISNEY'S ANIMAL KINGDOM

Attraction Name	Attraction Type	Location	Star Rating	Fastpass	Adults	Teens	Kids	All Ages
Discovery Island Trails	Wildlife exhibit (self-paced)	Discovery Island	☆☆☆	No				✓
Festival of the Lion King	Show	Camp Minnie-Mickey	☆☆☆☆	No				✓
Pocahontas and her Forest Friends	Show	Camp Minnie-Mickey	☆☆☆	No				✓
Greeting Trails	Character meeting spot	Camp Minnie-Mickey	N/A	No				✓
Kilimanjaro Safaris	Ride	Africa	☆☆☆☆	Yes				✓
Pangani Forest Exploration Trail	Walking tour (self-paced)	Africa	☆☆☆	No				✓
Wildlife Express Train	Ride (Departs every 5 to 7 minutes)	Rafiki's Planet Watch	☆☆☆	No				✓
Habitat Habit!	Exhibit	Rafiki's Planet Watch	☆☆☆	No		✓	✓	
Conservation Station	Interactive exhibits with live animals	Rafiki's Planet Watch	☆☆☆	No		✓	✓	
Affection Section	Petting zoo	Rafiki's Planet Watch	☆☆☆	No			✓	
Flights of Wonder	Show	Asia	☆☆☆	No				✓
Maharajah Jungle Trek	Exhibit	Asia	☆☆☆	No				✓
Kali River Rapids	Thrill ride (you will get wet)	Asia	☆☆☆☆	Yes	✓	✓		
Expedition Everest—Legend of the Forbidden Mountain	Thrill ride	Asia	☆☆☆☆	Yes	✓	✓		

ATTRACTIONS AT DISNEY'S ANIMAL KINGDOM

Attraction Name	Attraction Type	Location	Star Rating	Fastpass	Adults	Teens	Kids	All Ages
The Boneyard	Interactive play area	DinoLand USA	☆☆☆	No			✓	
Fossil Fun Games	Carnival-style games	DinoLand USA	☆☆	No		✓	✓	
Finding Nemo—The Musical	Show	DinoLand USA	☆☆☆☆	No				✓
Primeval Whirl	Ride	DinoLand USA	☆☆☆	Yes		✓	✓	
TriceraTop Spin	Ride	DinoLand USA	☆☆☆	No		✓	✓	
Dinosaur	Thrill ride	DinoLand USA	☆☆☆☆	Yes	✓	✓		
Mickey's Jammin' Jungle (Afternoon Parade)	Parade	Around Discovery Island	☆☆☆☆	No				✓

DOWNTOWN DISNEY AND PLEASURE ISLAND

The Downtown Disney area is divided into three sections—the Marketplace, Pleasure Island, and West Side. The Marketplace is primarily a shopping and dining area, where you'll find a nice selection of fast-food, midpriced, and fine-dining restaurants, plus many Disney-themed souvenir and gift shops, like World of Disney, Bibbidi Bobbidi Boutique, Team Mickey, Disney Pin Traders, Once Upon a Toy, Disney's Days of Christmas, Disney's Wonderful World of Memories, the Art of Disney, Pooh Corner, Disney Tails, Mickey's Mart, and Mickey's Pantry. All of the shops and restaurants in the Downtown Disney area are open 365 days a year, typically until 11 P.M. (or later), depending on the season.

Disney's West Side offers additional shops and restaurants, plus this is where you'll find DisneyQuest and Cirque du Soliel's *La Nouba*. DisneyQuest is a high-tech, multifloor, indoor theme park that offers some of the most technologically advanced video games, simulators, and virtual-reality experiences in the world. You can easily spend several hours at DisneyQuest experiencing all that this one-of-a-kind theme park/arcade has to offer. A separate admission is charged if you do not have a Park Hopper theme park pass.

TIP

For information about Cirque du Soliel's *La Nouba*, see Section VI, "Entertainment in Orlando." This is truly a must-see live show featuring the French-Canadian circus troupe. For tickets, call (407) 939-1298.

Also within Disney's West Side area, you'll find House of Blues, which is a midpriced restaurant plus a live concert venue. In addition, there's a 24-screen AMC movie theater, a Planet Hollywood restaurant, a Virgin Megastore, plus more than a dozen other unique shops.

TIP

A variety of other restaurants can be found throughout the Downtown Disney area, including McDonald's, Raglan Road Irish Pub and Restaurant, Bongos Cuban Café, Wolfgang Puck Café, Fulton's Crab House (fine dining), Portobello Yacht Club (fine dining), Rainforest Café, Earl of Sandwich, Wetzel's Pretzels, and Cap'n Jack's Restaurant (fine dining).

After dark, Pleasure Island is a popular nightspot designed mainly for adults. This area (which requires a separate admission unless you have a Park Hopper theme park ticket) features seven different nightclubs, each with a different theme. For one price, you're granted unlimited admission to all of the clubs for the night. Many of the clubs within Pleasure Island are open to guests age 21 and older and remain open at least until 1 A.M. or 2 A.M.

For information about special concerts and events happening at Pleasure Island during your stay, or to book private events, call (407) 828-3200.

The nightclubs in Pleasure Island include:

- *BET Soundstage.* This dance club plays hip-hop and R&B music.
- *Adventurers Club.* A lounge featuring a full bar plus improvisational actors.

- *Comedy Warehouse.* A comedy club featuring multiple improvisational comedy shows every night.
- *8Trax.* A dance club featuring music from the '70s and '80s. The club is equipped with a state-of-the-art sound and light system, plus a lit-up dance floor.
- *Mannequins Dance Palace.* This is the premier nightclub at Pleasure Island. It features a large, revolving dance floor, multiple bars, and a state-of-the-art sound and light system. Current music is played nightly, and a troupe of talented club dancers performs.
- *Rock 'n' Roll Beach Club.* Live bands and disc jockeys perform lightly at this beach-themed dance club.
- *Motion.* This dance club features a full bar and a large dance floor. Top 40 music is played nightly.

DISNEY'S BOARDWALK

For more Disney nightlife, be sure to visit Disney's BoardWalk, which offers a variety of additional fine-dining restaurants, nightclubs, bars, lounges, shops, and activities. The theme of this area is a 1930s Atlantic coastal village, but with modern entertainment attractions. For example, here you'll find Jellyrolls (a dueling-piano bar), Atlantic Dance Hall (nightclub), and the ESPN Club (sports bar). Big River Grille and Brewing Works is also a great place for adults to enjoy a casual evening of drinks, food, and entertainment.

One of the handful of shops you'll find at Disney's BoardWalk is the Wyland Galleries, which features the beautiful oceanographic art of internationally known environmental artist Wyland, the world's most influential marine painter, sculptor, and muralist. His work depicts marine animals in their beautiful, natural settings. Disney's BoardWalk is located about five minutes from Pleasure Island and can be reached by car, water taxi, or bus. It's easily accessible from all Disney resort hotels and surrounding areas. Like the venues of Pleasure Island, the clubs, bars, restaurants, and shops at Disney's BoardWalk remain open late (until 11 P.M. or much later, depending on the season).

RELAXING AT A DISNEY DAY SPA

After a long day of meetings, trade shows, or other work-related events, or once you've had your fill of theme park rides, shows, and attractions, one of the very best ways to pamper yourself and relax is to visit one of the world-class day spas located within the WDW

Resort. These spas offer a full menu of massages, body treatments, and facials, plus they provide luxurious amenities (such as saunas, hot tubs, locker rooms, and relaxation lounges).

The day spas at the WDW Resort are open daily to adults only. All spas also offer full workout and exercise facilities. Private personal trainers are available by appointment for an additional fee. Spa reservations should be booked in advance. Be sure to arrive for your appointment 20 to 30 minutes early so you have time to check in and get changed.

The following is contact information for three of the most popular spas you'll find at the WDW Resort:

- Grand Floridian Spa and Health Club—(407) 824-2332
- Disney's Saratoga Springs Resort and Spa—(407) 827-4455
- Mandara Spa at the Walt Disney World Dolphin—(407) 934-4772

TIP
While full-service spa facilities are not available at all on-property resort hotels within the WDW Resort, many of the hotels offer fitness facilities and massage services by appointment. Call the concierge or front desk for details.

HOSTING PRIVATE CORPORATE EVENTS AT THE WDW RESORT

With a bit of creativity and the support of the Walt Disney World Company, you can host a private party, gathering, or meeting of any size within the WDW Resort. Specific restaurants, and potentially specific rides and/or attractions in the theme parks, can be utilized for private functions, and special VIP behind-the-scenes tours can be coordinated. For more information, call (321) 939-7128 or visit www.disneyparkevents.com.

TIP
When hosting a private event anywhere in the WDW Resort, you can arrange to have world-class performers, improvisational actors, variety artists, musical performers, or even Disney characters attend your event to entertain participants and guests. Variety acts include disc jockeys, emcees, face painters, caricature artists, jugglers, stilt walkers, fortune tellers, hair braiders, and tattoo artists.

The Disney Institute also offers seminars and educational programs (taught Disney style) that are designed to teach businesspeople leadership excellence, loyalty, organizational skills, creativity, people management, quality service, and a variety of other valuable business-oriented skills. These programs showcase the time-tested and proven strategies utilized by the Walt Disney Company, many of which stem from the philosophies of Walt Disney himself. To learn more about the Disney Institute, call (407) 566-2665.

TIP
To view an interactive map of the entire WDW Resort property and see all of the venues capable of hosting private events and functions, visit http://disneymeetings.disney.go.com/dwm/resorts/resortMediaPopup?name=DPEMapsMainSWFPage&CMP=ILC-DWMMAPVanity or call (321) 939-7128.

SECTION VIII

© Jim Lopes

ATTENDING A BUSINESS MEETING OR CONVENTION

Every year, the Orlando area hosts thousands of trade shows, conventions, conferences, symposiums, seminars, expos, and other large gatherings of business professionals from countless industries and from around the world. While small to midsize meetings are typically held at the various Orlando-area resorts (many of which offer large function, banquet, and meeting rooms), the majority of the large conventions and trade shows are held at the Orange County Convention Center, located on International Drive in Orlando.

For information about the Gaylord Palms Resort and Convention Center, as well as The Rosen Centre, plus other resorts that possess large meeting, banquet, and convention facilities, see Section III, "Where to Stay While in Orlando." For more information about hosting a meeting or event at the Walt Disney World Resort, see Section VII, "Visiting the Walt Disney World Resort."

THE ORANGE COUNTY CONVENTION CENTER (OCCC)

Addresses: North Concourse: 9400 Universal Boulevard, Orlando
South Concourse: 9899 International Drive, Orlando
West Concourse: 9800 International Drive, Orlando
Main phone numbers: (800) 345-9845, (407) 685-1061
Guest services: (407) 685-1202
Automated events hotline: (407) 685-9800
Web site: www.occc.net

The Orange County Convention Center (OCCC) is the largest meeting and convention center in the Orlando area, with more than seven million square feet of space, which includes exhibit space, meeting rooms, breakout rooms, a grand ballroom (which can hold 6,000 people), a 200-seat lecture hall, and a 2,643-seat

The Orange County Convention Center. (Photo courtesy of Orange County Convention Center.)

The exhibit space alone within the convention center's North/South Concourse occupies about 22 acres. If Chicago's Sears Tower (which is 1,454 feet tall) were to be placed on its side, it would fit lengthwise inside the West Concourse's exhibition space (which is 2,500 feet in length). All eight halls within this concourse are contiguous.

theater. The complex is also equipped with 6,227 parking spaces, eight food courts, three restaurants, and three full-service FedExKinko's business centers.

The OCCC opened in 1983 and has since expanded considerably. As of April 2006, the convention center had more than 967 events scheduled through the year 2028, and it expected over 13 million attendees during this period. In 2005, the convention center hosted 259 events and was visited by more than 1.4 million attendees.

Located along International Drive, the convention center is divided into two main buildings—the North/South Concourse (which contains more than three million square feet of space) and the West Concourse (which contains an additional four million square feet of space).

ORANGE COUNTY CONVENTION CENTER LAYOUT

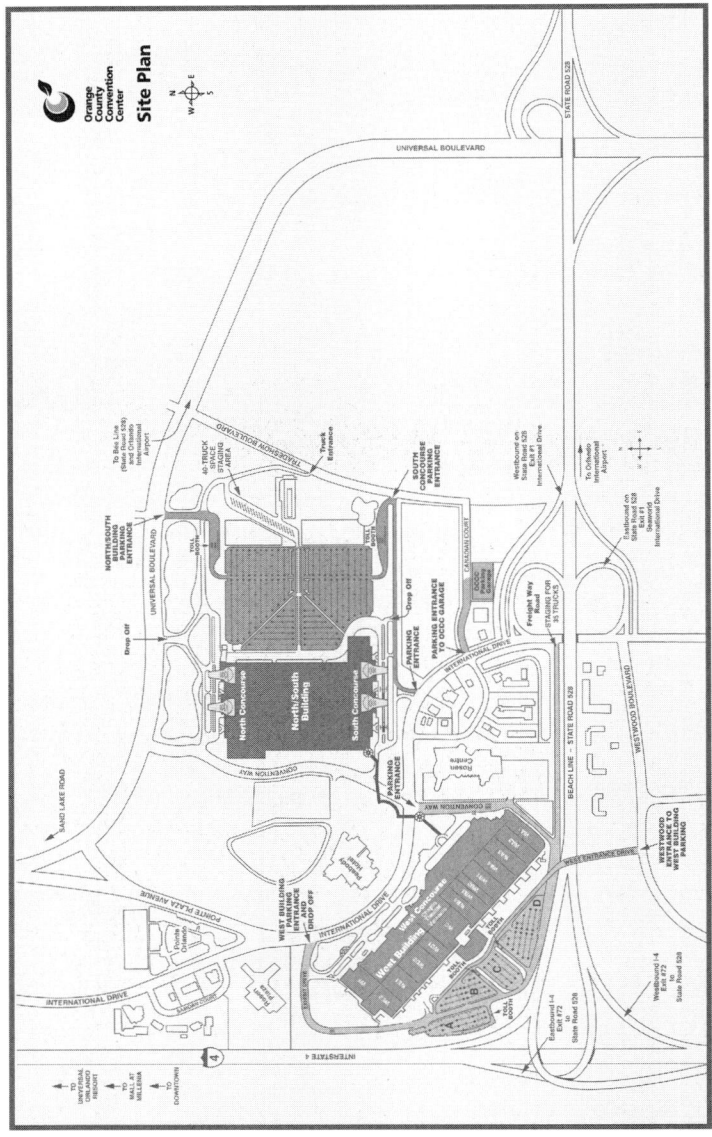

Map courtesy of Orange County Convention Center.

Surrounding the complex are several self-parking lots, plus valet parking. Directly across the street from the West Concourse are the popular Peabody Hotel and Rosen Centre (see Section III, "Where to Stay While in Orlando," for details about these conveniently located, business-friendly hotels).

TIP
For a comprehensive list of events scheduled to be held at the convention center, visit www.occc.net/global/Calendar/default.asp.

Directions to the Convention Center

The OCCC is located along International Drive, which is one of the most populated areas in Orlando, in terms of hotels, resorts, motels, restaurants, and attractions. Several major roads, including State Road 528 and Interstate 4, surround the convention center, making it easy to reach by car from anywhere in the area.

FROM ORLANDO INTERNATIONAL AIRPORT

Travel west on SR 528 to Exit 1 (International Drive). Exit right, onto International Drive, and travel north for approximately one mile to the convention center. Follow the signs as you approach the convention center for the most convenient parking, based on which building your event is being held in. The ride should take about 25 minutes by car or taxi.

FROM THE DOWNTOWN ORLANDO AREA

Take Interstate 4 West to SR 528. Take Exit 72 off SR 528. Travel east on SR 528 to Exit 1 (International Drive). Make a right onto International Drive and travel north for approximately one mile to reach the convention center. Follow the signs as you approach the convention center for the most convenient parking, based on which building your event is being held in. The ride should take 20 to 30 minutes.

FROM THE WALT DISNEY WORLD RESORT (LAKE BUENA VISTA) AREA

From the WDW Resort, follow signs to SR 535 South. Take SR 535 South to I-4 East (toward Orlando). Take the SR 528 East exit (Exit 72) toward Orlando International Airport/Cape Canaveral/International Drive/Convention Center. Merge onto SR 528 East. Get off SR 528 at Exit 1 (International Drive). From the exit ramp, take a right onto International Drive and follow it until you reach the convention center in approximately .5 mile. The ride should take about 14 minutes.

Nearby Public Parking Lots

The OCCC operates three large parking structures surrounding the complex. As you approach the convention center, look for dynamic message system signs along International Drive, State Road 528, Universal Boulevard, and Westwood Boulevard, which will direct you to the appropriate lot for the event you're attending.

The self-parking rate at the OCCC is $10 per car, per entry. Cash, traveler's checks, American Express, Visa, and MasterCard are accepted for parking. Depending on the event, valet parking may also be available (for an additional fee).

TIP

If the main parking structures fill up at the OCCC, the nearby Canadian Court Parking Garage will be opened to the public. A free shuttle bus to the convention center is provided when this lot becomes operational. It's located about two blocks west of the OCCC, on International Drive (follow the signs, if applicable).

Taxi Service to and from the OCCC

Located outside the OCCC's main entrances are three separate taxi stands where you can hail a private taxi to get from the convention center back to your hotel (or to any location in the Orlando area). From the convention center, the approximate taxi fares to popular destinations are as follows:

- Downtown Orlando—$29 each way
- International Drive/Sand Lake Road area (aka "Restaurant Row")—$8 each way
- Lake Buena Vista area—$21 each way
- North International Drive area—$11 each way
- Orlando International Airport—$32 each way
- SeaWorld area—$8 each way
- South International Drive area—$8 each way
- Universal Studios resort area—$15 each way
- WDW Resort—$34 each way

MONEY SAVER

An inexpensive alternative to taking a taxi or driving to the OCCC, if you're staying at a hotel or motel along International Drive (or you want to visit a nearby restaurant or attraction), is taking the I-Ride Trolley.

The trolley has a pickup/drop-off location near the West Concourse of the convention center, outside of Hall C, as well as Halls E and F. See Section IV, "Getting Around Town," for details about the I-Ride Trolley, or visit www.iridetrolley.com. The trolley departs every 20 minutes.

Navigating Around the Convention Center

Most trade shows, conventions, and meetings held at the OCCC do not utilize the entire facility. Refer to the program or trade show guide created for your specific event to more easily navigate around the appropriate areas of the convention center, keeping in mind that it's common for multiple, unrelated events, trade shows, and conventions to be held at the convention center simultaneously.

WARNING
This convention center is large, so be prepared to do a significant amount of walking when you attend a trade show or convention here. Be sure to wear comfortable shoes.

The following maps (on pages 216–217) are overall floor plans and maps of the entire Orange County Convention Center complex. To view interactive floor plans online, visit www.occc.net/Planner/OverviewFloorPlans.asp.

Dining Options at and near the Convention Center

Within the convention center, you'll find three full-service restaurants. The Northside and Southside restaurants offer a diverse menu and full bar service, while the Osprey Café serves freshly prepared panini sandwiches and other entrees. Several fast-food restaurants, including McDonald's, plus several convenience stores are located across the street from the OCCC (within a three- to five-minute walk).

For a quick bite to eat without leaving the OCCC, each of the on-premises food courts offers pizza, deli sandwiches, grilled burgers, and fresh salads. A handful of refreshment stands and food carts located throughout the complex offer sodas, snacks, and sandwiches, plus to-go food selections from around the world.

NORTH/SOUTH CONCOURSE OF THE OCCC

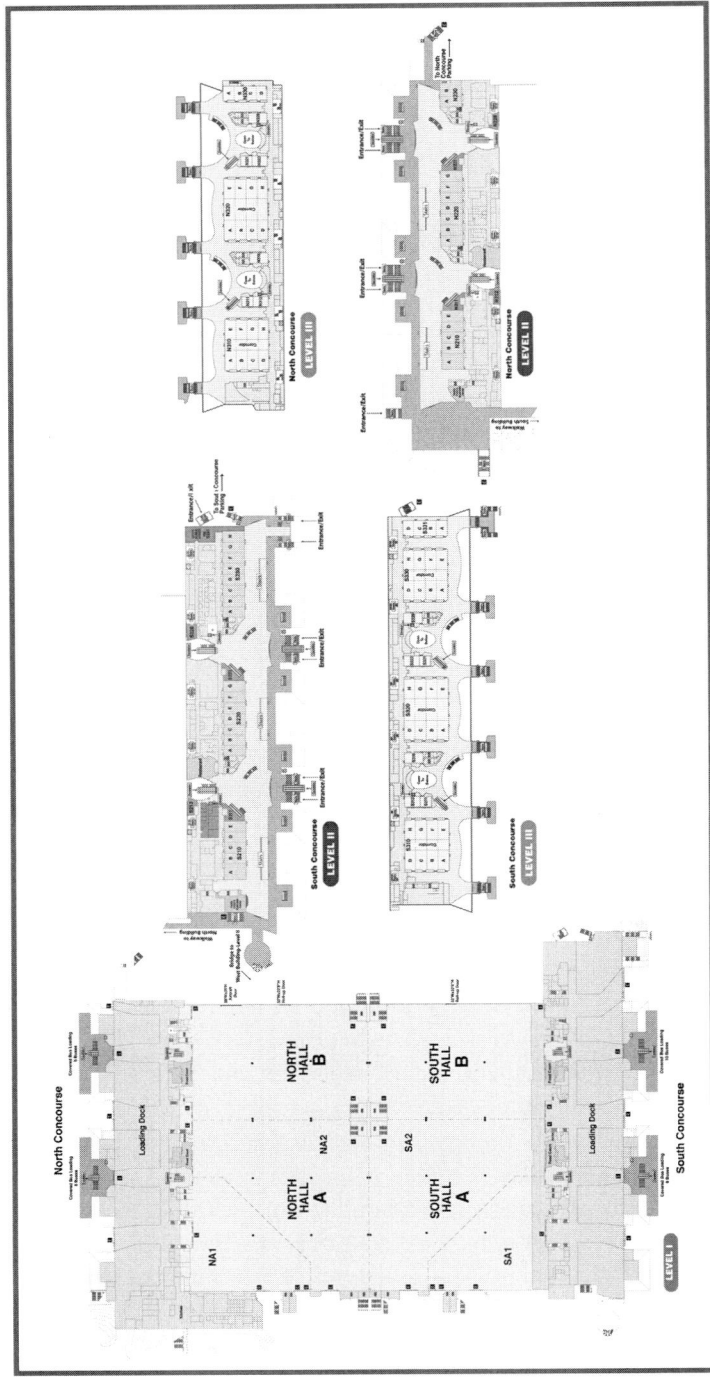

Map courtesy of Orange County Convention Center.

WEST CONCOURSE OF THE OCCC

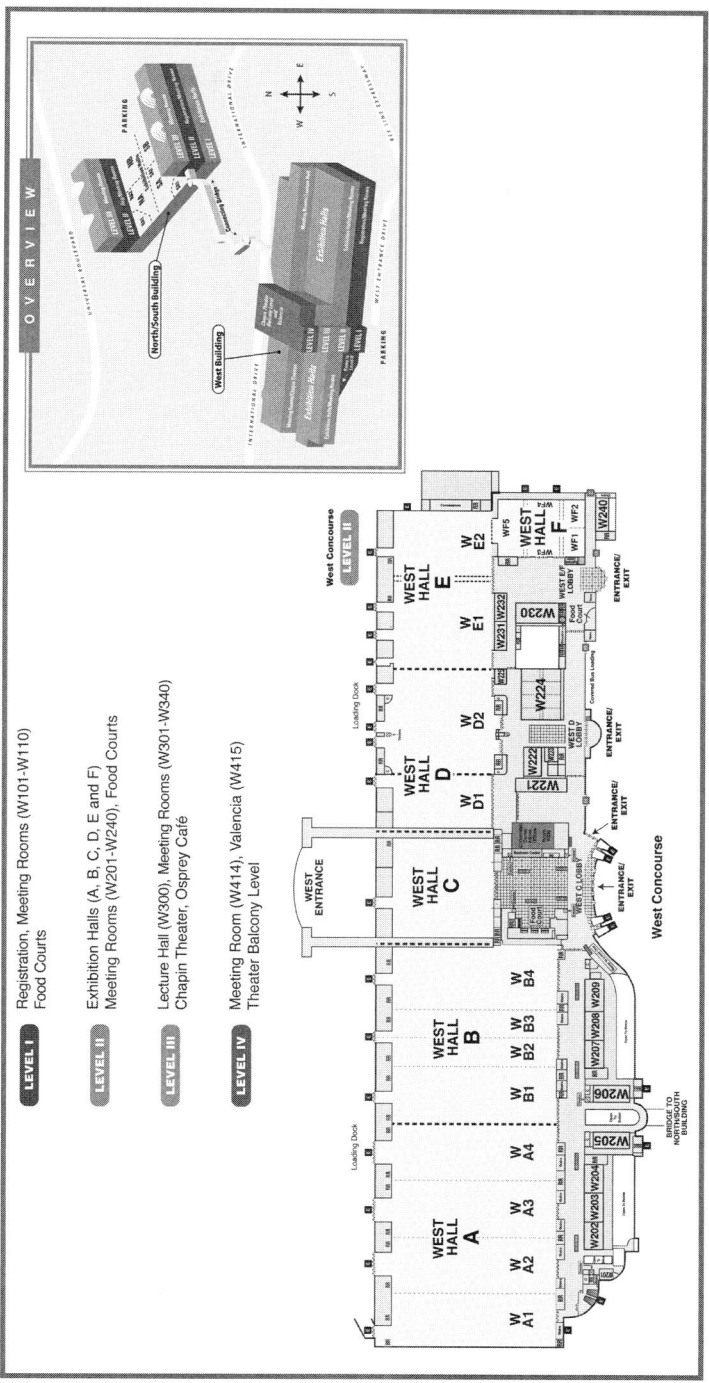

Map courtesy of Orange County Convention Center.

TIP

In addition to the multiple food courts located within the convention center, within a short walk or drive, there are dozens of restaurants, ranging from fast-food options to fine-dining establishments, such as the Capital Grille. The Peabody Hotel, the Rosen Plaza Hotel, the Rosen Centre Hotel, and the Pointe Orlando complex also offer multiple fine-dining options within a five-minute walk from the convention center.

Services and Amenities at the Convention Center

Whether you're attending a trade show or convention, or exhibiting at one, you may want to utilize the following services and amenities located within the convention center:

- *ATMs.* Multiple ATMs are located in the lobby of every building within the convention center complex.
- *Coat and luggage check.* Several coat and luggage check locations are available within the convention center complex. Follow signs for the appropriate location being utilized by the event you're attending. A fee will apply to store your coat and/or luggage.

TIP

The three FedEx Kinko's locations in the OCCC are open from 8 A.M. to 5 P.M. daily. FedEx packages slated for overnight delivery must be dropped off no later than 4 P.M. (Monday through Saturday). Packages slated for FedEx ground service must be dropped off by 5 P.M. (Monday through Friday). This location offers a full complement of office, printing, and business services, including self-service and full-service black-and-white and color copying, along with printing, binding, and finishing services, computer rentals, sign and graphic printing, packing, and FedEx Express and FedEx Ground shipping services. Locations: outside the West Concourse Hall C; in the North Concourse; and within the South Concourse. Call (407) 363-2831 for information. For after-hours commercial production work, call (407) 240-6610. To submit a printing order online (24 hours per day), visit http://conventions.kinkos.com/sites/orlando.php.

There are three FedEx Kinko's printing and shipping centers located at the convention center.

MONEY SAVER

When you preorder your printing and business services needs, the FedEx Kinko's locations at the OCCC offer a 20 percent discount. Call (407) 363-2831 for details.

- *Information desk.* Several information counters are available throughout the convention center.
- *Meeting rooms.* Private, fully equipped meeting rooms in a variety of sizes are available for rent within the convention center, as well as at the Peabody Hotel and the Rosen Centre (located across the street). Within these meeting rooms, a full complement of audiovisual equipment is available, as is a wide range of catering options. See "Exhibitor Services at the Convention Center" later in this section.
- *Remote skycap service.* Check-in and baggage check-in services are available at the OCCC for travelers on some domestic airlines (traveling out of Orlando International Airport) during some events held at the convention center.
- *Restrooms.* Public restrooms are located throughout the convention center complex.
- *Scooter rentals.* Scootaround offers a selection of electronic scooters, manual and electric wheelchairs, as well as oxygen

rentals on the OCCC's premises. Half-day, full-day, and weekly rentals are available, seven days a week. The scooters or wheelchairs can be picked up at the business centers (located within the OCCC) or can be delivered to any hotel in the Orlando area. For information and rates, call (888) 441-7575 or visit www.scootaround.com.

TIP
For assistance while at the convention center, call Guest Services at (407) 685-1202. The Guest Services desk can assist you with acquiring discount local-area attraction tickets, arrange for airport transfers, coordinate scooter rentals, provide driving directions, make restaurant recommendations and reservations on your behalf, and sell you sundries (such as aspirin, batteries, and other commonly requested items).

Tips for Attending a Convention or Trade Show

The following tips will help you maximize your time and efficiency when attending a trade show or convention:

- *Preregister for the event you'll be attending.* This will allow you to avoid long registration lines at the start of the event. Don't forget to bring your registration papers and/or ID badge to the event. Make your hotel accommodations early to get the best rates and ensure you're able to get the room configuration and hotel you desire.
- *Preschedule your meetings and appointments.* Use the Trade Show Meeting Planner (found in the Appendix of this guide). For each meeting, write down the scheduled time and date, the location (booth or meeting room number), the name of the person you're meeting, his or her company, and the purpose of the meeting. Allow ample time (at least five to ten minutes) between meetings to walk between exhibit booths or meeting rooms. You can obtain an advance listing of trade show exhibitors by visiting the web site operated by the company coordinating or hosting your event.
- *Bring a durable backpack, shoulder bag, or wheeled suitcase* to store and carry around brochures, catalogs, swag, freebees, and trade show materials you collect.
- *Wear comfortable shoes* (be prepared for a lot of walking and standing around), plus a comfortable, business casual outfit that's appropriate for the event you'll be attending.

- *Bring a stack of business cards and/or company literature to distribute at the event.*
- *Bring a pad and pen* to take notes during seminars and meetings.
- *Utilize the coat check at the convention center* to store heavy items that you don't want to lug around on the convention show floor.

TIP
It's often easier to ship home the catalogs, brochures, press kits, freebees, and other materials you collect at a trade show than it is to pack them in your luggage. If these items cause your suitcase to weigh more than 50 pounds, you'll need to pay an overweight-bag charge to your airline when you check in at the airport.

Exhibitor Services at the Convention Center

If you're exhibiting or hosting a meeting at the convention center, the following are services that will be useful. For additional information, call the OCCC's Exhibitor Services office at (407) 685-9824 or (800) 345-9898. The majority of these trade show exhibitor services must be pre-ordered. For details or to place an order for an exhibitor service online, visit www.occc.net/Exhibitor/ Orders.

- *Audio or video equipment, production, and lighting.* To coordinate all of your audio, video, and lighting equipment rental, setup, and production needs within the convention center, call LMG Inc. at (888) 226-3100 or visit www.lmg.net. To receive a 30 percent discount on your equipment rentals, reserve your equipment at least 21 days prior to the start of your event or trade show. LCD projectors and screens, LCD and plasma monitors, microphones and audio systems, lighting systems, and computer rentals are among LMG's offerings to OCCC exhibitors.
- *Baggage and valet services for exhibitors.* To arrange for valet parking, bag and coat check, or remote skycap services for your employees or VIP guests, call Baggage Airline Guest Services at (407) 447-5547 and ask for the OCCC coordinator. You can also visit www.airportbags.com.
- *Disney concierge service.* For exhibitors, Disney offers a special concierge service that provides assistance for planning any type of meeting or gathering at the Walt Disney World Resort (including the theme parks). Disney's exhibitor

concierge is a complimentary service available for groups at the Orange County Convention Center. To learn more, call (407) 685-1610 or visit www.disneyparkevents.com/occc. Similar event planning services are offered at SeaWorld (407-685-1630, www.seaworldgroupevents.com) and Universal Orlando (407-224-6222, www.universalevents.com).

- *Electrical and plumbing service.* All orders for electrical, plumbing, or gas service at trade show booths or for meeting rooms must be ordered by calling (800) 345-9898. Installation and labor are included.
- *Food and beverages (catering).* Levy Restaurants, which operates the three full-service restaurants as well as the food courts at the OCCC, also handles private catering needs for exhibitors. Whether you need specialty coffee service, box lunches, or multicourse sit-down meals, Levy Restaurants' fully customizable catering menus will fit the bill. The company can also arrange for shoeshine services and in-booth massage services. Call (407) 685-5712 or visit www.levyrestaurants.com.
- *Internet and telephone service.* To order internet and/or telephone service at your booth or within your meeting room, contact Smart City at (407) 685-2000 or visit www.smartcity.com. High-speed internet access, Wi-Fi, T-1 and other special data circuits, voice networking and telecommunications, web casting, temporary LAN/WAN/VPN construction, point-to-point networking, video conferencing, and DNS services are offered.
- *Meeting room rental.* To inquire about private meeting room rentals, rates, and availability at the convention center, call (800) 345-9898.
- *Press release electronic distribution services.*
  - PR Newswire—(888) 776-0942, www.prenewswire.com
  - Businesswire.com—(800) 221-2462, www.businesswire.com

TIP
For additional business services of interest to trade show exhibitors and attendees alike, see Section IX, "Business Services."

- *Printing and photocopying.* The FedExKinko's locations on the OCCC's premises can handle a wide range of

printing (including signs and banners), binding, volume photocopying, packing, and shipping needs. Hours: 8 A.M. to 5 P.M.; some services are available 24 hours per day. Call (407) 363-2831.
- *Rigging services.* To order rigging services, call (407) 685-5555.
- *Security and police.* For any security-related issues pertaining to the OCCC, call (407) 685-9828 or (407) 685-7102. The Orange County Sheriff's Office also has a presence at the OCCC. Call (407) 351-9368.

TIP
For assistance with planning a meeting or business-related event in the Orlando area, contact the Orlando/Orange County Convention and Visitors Bureau at www.orlandoinfo.com/b2b/meet or call (800) 662-2825. The CVB will help you find the ideal meeting or convention space, coordinate travel, line up catering, and assist with every aspect of the meeting or event planning process, whether your meeting will be attended by a handful of people or several thousand.

TRAVEL NOTES

SECTION IX

© Feng Yu

BUSINESS SERVICES

If you're hosting or attending business meetings; participating in a convention, trade show, seminar, or workshop; or visiting Orlando to entertain important clients, you may require various business services during your trip. Many of the larger hotels and resorts offer nicely equipped business centers capable of handling the majority of your business-related needs, including:

- Black-and-white or color copies
- Cell phone rentals
- Computer and printer rentals
- Fax machines
- High-speed internet access
- Meeting room rentals (with catering)
- Messenger services
- Packing and shipping of packages (via FedEx, UPS, or DHL)
- Secretarial, typing, and translation services
- On-site rental cars and chauffeured town car and/or limo service

You typically pay a premium to utilize the services offered through a hotel or resort at these business centers; however, they do provide convenience. This section focuses on your needs beyond what the on-site business centers within the resorts and hotels usually offer.

TIP
Your hotel's concierge or business center can help you track down and utilize a wide range of business-related services that are not offered inhouse. Also see Section VIII, "Attending a Business Meeting or Convention."

Keep in mind, the companies and services listed here are for reference or referral purposes only, and are just a sampling of the many companies offering similar products and services within the Orlando area. Inclusion in this section does not constitute an endorsement. Additional referrals can be obtained from your hotel's concierge or the local Yellow Pages. All addresses are in Orlando, unless otherwise noted.

AUDIOVISUAL EQUIPMENT RENTALS, PHOTOGRAPHY, AND PRODUCTION COMPANIES

For your trade show or meeting audiovisual needs, contact your hotel or resort, the Orange County Convention Center (LMG Inc., 888-226-3100, www.lmg.net), or any of the following companies.

ORLANDO AUDIOVISUAL EQUIPMENT RENTALS

Audio Excellence Recording, Inc.   (727) 360-6726
www.audioexcellencerecording.com

ORLANDO AUDIOVISUAL EQUIPMENT RENTALS	
Audio Visual Innovations	(888) 251-9651
	www.creativeshowservices.com
Cross Video Productions	(407) 805-0505
	www.crossvideo.com
J&R Productions Group	(407) 772-9000
	www.jrpartys.com
LMG, Inc.	(888) 226-3100
	www.lmg.net
Megapixel Productions	(407) 277-7568
	www.megapixelpro.com
ProShots Event Photography	(407) 857-0862
	www.proshotsevent.com
Universal Convention Photography	(407) 352-5302
	www.universalphoto.com
Z Audio Visual Productions	(407) 370-3000
	www.zavproductions.com

BALLOONS

The following companies can provide balloons for events, parties, or trade shows, or have balloons sent anywhere as a gift suitable for almost any occasion.

ORLANDO BALLOON SERVICES	
Balloon Bouquets	(407) 894-4800
Balloon Magic Inc.	(407) 592-3702
Balloon World	(407) 898-8500
Balloons by Renee	(407) 275-2232
Frank Torres' Balloons	(407) 348-4502

TIP

A unique and fun alternative to sending flowers or balloons as a gift is to send a fruit bouquet created by Edible Arrangements. These lavish arrangements look like colorful floral bouquets, but they're made from edible fruits and vegetables. They can be delivered or shipped anywhere in the country. These bouquets also make a great centerpiece for catered events and parties. Edible Arrangements has three Orlando-area locations: 4104 Millenia Boulevard, Orlando (407-903-0900), 12720 South Orange Blossom Trail, Orlando (407-812-1585), and 7307 West Colonial Drive, Orlando (407-296-7430). Web site: www.ediblearrangements.com.

BANKING AND FINANCIAL SERVICES

There are ATMs located within most of the hotels, resorts, shopping areas, convenience stores, and airports and within the Orange County Convention Center. You'll also find full-service banks and ATMs throughout Orlando. The hotel or resort where you're staying probably also offers check-cashing services.

WARNING
The ATMs located in the hotels, resorts, and airports often charge a hefty fee for withdrawals (up to $3 or more). You can save money by utilizing an ATM owned and operated by your own bank or one that's affiliated with your bank's ATM network.

Full-Service Banks in Orlando

The following are customer service phone numbers for popular banks with branches and ATMs located throughout the Orlando area. Call to determine where the closest branch to where you're staying is, or ask your hotel's concierge. While the following customer service centers are typically open 24 hours per day, the hours of operation of each local branch will vary.

ORLANDO FULL-SERVICE BANKS	
AM South Bank	(800) 267-6884
	www.amsouthbank.com
Bank of America	(800) 841-4000
	www.bankofamerica.com
Chevy Chase Bank	(407) 380-7855
	www.chevychasebank.com
Citibank (Offers ATM machines throughout Orlando, including at all 7-Eleven stores)	www.citibank.com
First Commercial Bank Florida	(407) 835-1835
	www.fcbflorida.com
Sun Trust Bank	(800) 786-8787
	www.suntrust.com

ORLANDO FULL-SERVICE BANKS	
Wachovia Bank	(800) 922-4684
	www.wachovia.com
Washington Mutual	(800) 788-7000
	www.wamu.com
Wells Fargo Bank	(800) 869-3557
	www.wellsfargo.com

TIP
To locate an ATM that's close to you and that's affiliated with your bank's ATM network, check the back of your ATM, debit, or credit card and look for the "Cirrus" or "PLUS" logo, then call the appropriate network: Cirrus (800-424-7787) or PLUS (800-843-7587).

BOXES AND SHIPPING SUPPLIES

For small quantities of boxes and shipping supplies, also see "FedExKinko's Locations," "UPS Shipping Locations," and "Office Supply Superstores" in this section.

ORLANDO BOX AND SHIPPING SUPPLY COMPANIES	
Central Florida Box Corp.	(407) 841-0147
	www.cfbdisplaygroup.com
K&G Box Company	(800) 741-2699
Mr. Mover	(407) 830-6683
	www.mr-mover.com
Redd Paper Co.	(407) 299-6656
	www.reddpaper.com
U-Boxes	(877) 826-9371
	www.uboxes.com
U-Line Shipping Supplies	(800) 958-5463
	www.uline.com

BUS CHARTERS

For small groups or large ones, when your transportation needs exceed the capacity of a stretch limousine and you want a well-qualified, highly professional and friendly driver, contact one of the following companies to charter anything from a minivan to a full-size, air-conditioned luxury bus.

SELECT ORLANDO BUS CHARTER COMPANIES	
BTM Charters Orlando	(407) 855-6321
	www.btmtravel.com
Bus Bank	(866) 428-7226
	www.busbank.com
Crestline Coach Charter Buses	(407) 423-0222
	www.crestlinecoachtours.com
Empire Coach Line	(407) 888-2624
	www.empirecoachline.com
Mears Transportation	(407) 422-2222
	www.mearstransportation.com

CAR AND TRUCK RENTALS

See Section IV, "Getting Around Town," for a listing of rental car companies in the Orlando area. For one-way or round-trip truck rentals, call U-Haul at (407) 857-7867 or visit www.uhaul.com.

TIP
For emergency roadside assistance, if you're a AAA member, call (800) AAA-HELP. The AAA office in Orlando is located at 4300 East Colonial Drive, Orlando (407-894-3333). Hours: Monday through Friday, 8:30 A.M. to 5:30 P.M.; Saturday, 9 A.M. to 1 P.M.

CATERERS

All of the mid- to large-size hotels, resorts, banquet halls, theme parks, and meeting room facilities, as well as the Orange County Convention Center (407-685-5712, www.levyrestaurants.com), offer inhouse catering services. Many of the business-friendly restaurants featured in Section V, "Where to Dine in Orlando," also have banquet rooms and private dining rooms available.

CELL PHONE SERVICES AND ACCESSORIES

Authorized service agents for AT&T/Cingular, Sprint/Nextel, T-Mobile, and Verizon Wireless are located throughout Orlando, including with The Mall at Millenia in the Florida Mall. Cellular phone accessories (chargers, headsets, etc.) can also be purchased at Radio Shack stores and from hundreds of other consumer electronics dealers citywide.

Electronics Plus, located in the Pointe Orlando shopping center (across from the Orange County Convention Center, 9101

At the Orlando International Airport, the Airport Wireless store (407-582-0500, www.airportwireless.com) offers a vast selection of accessories, chargers, cables, and related items for all popular cell phones, MP3 players, digital cameras, laptop computers, PDAs, and other consumer electronics items.

International Drive, Orlando, 407-447-4979), offers a wide selection of cell phone, camera, MP3 player, and laptop computer accessories, chargers, cables, and related items.

ORLANDO CELL PHONE SERVICES	
AT&T Wireless/Cingular	(800) 888-7600 (AT&T), (800) 331-0500 (Cingular)
	www.wireless.att.com/home
Sprint PCS/Nextel	(866) 438-1371
	www.sprint.com
T-Mobile	(800) 866-2453
	www.t-mobile.com
Verizon Wireless	(800) 922-0204
	www.verizonwireless.com

MONEY SAVER
If you need a temporary cell phone while in Orlando, you can rent one for a high per-day fee (plus high airtime charges, up to $2 per minute), or you could purchase a prepaid cellular phone for under $50, along with prepaid airtime for as low as $.12 per minute. Companies like

Tracefone (800-867-7183, www.tracefone.com), Virgin Mobile (888-322-1122, www.virginmobileusa.com), AT&T/Cingular, and T-Mobile all offer inexpensive but full-featured prepaid phones and service plans with no long-term contracts. This is an ideal option for international travelers visiting Orlando, anyone who needs a replacement phone, or anyone who quickly needs to establish temporary cell phone service.

COMPUTER RENTALS, REPAIRS, SALES, DATA RECOVERY, AND TECHNICAL SUPPORT

If your computer breaks and needs emergency repair, your system crashes and you lose important data, you require technical support, or you need to rent a computer or peripherals while in the Orlando area, contact any of the companies in the following chart.

ORLANDO COMPUTER SERVICES

Apple Store	(407) 352-5551
Mall at the Millenia, 4200 Conroy Road, Orlando	www.apple.com
	Apple sales and service
Apple Store	(407) 858-1310
Florida Mall, 8001 South Orange Blossom Trail, Orlando	www.apple.com
	Apple sales and service
Best Buy	(407) 855-6114
8350 South Orange Blossom Trail, Orlando	www.bestbuy.com
	Computer sales and service
Best Buy	(407) 894-5003
4601 E Colonial Dr, Orlando	www.bestbuy.com
	Computer sales and service
CompUSA	(407) 438-1270
7802 South Orange Blossom Trail, Orlando	www.compusa.com
	Computer sales, service, and support
ESS Data Recovery	(800) 237-4200
N/A	www.essdatarecovery.com
	Data recovery
Firewall Computer Services	(407) 647-3430
N/A	www.firewall-cs.com
	Repair, support, and networking
Geek Squad (Best Buy)	(800) 433-5778
N/A	www.geeksquad.com
	Repair, networking, and tech support
Laptop A Plus	(407) 629-4233
N/A	http://laptopaplus.net
	Laptop sales, service, and rentals

SECTION IX / **BUSINESS SERVICES** ·· **233**

ORLANDO COMPUTER SERVICES	
Laptop Direct	(407) 629-4296
1841 West Fairbanks Avenue, #200, Winter Park	www.laptopdi.com
	Laptop repair
MyOnSiteTech.com	(877) 696-6748
3640 North Federal Highway, #922, Lighthouse Point	http://myonsitetech.com
	Networking, virus removal, repairs, and support
OrLAN tech	(407) 228-7290
1510 East Colonial Drive, Suite 103, Orlando	www.orlantech.com
	Networking, repairs, and IT support
Tech Geeks	(321) 251-6948
709 Forester Avenue, Orlando	www.tech-geeks.com
PC and laptop repair, virus removal, data recovery, tech support, and networking	
Titan Information Technology Solutions	(407) 888-9441
N/A	www.titanits.com
	Computer repair and support

TIP

For major laptop computer repairs, for example, determine if your unit is still covered under the manufacturer's warranty. If so, you can typically ship it back to the manufacturer, have it repaired, and have it returned to you via overnight courier. The process takes just a few days, especially if you pay extra for expedited services. If the unit is not covered under warranty, the manufacturer will typically charge a fortune to conduct diagnostic and repair work.

CREDIT CARD COMPANIES

Listed in the following chart are the 24-hour emergency phone numbers for the major credit card companies. For customer service issues pertaining specifically to your account, call the phone number displayed on the back of your credit card or on your monthly statement. Use the phone numbers in the chart to report a lost or stolen credit card, request an emergency replacement card, obtain an emergency cash advance, access account balances, or to find an ATM near you.

ORLANDO CREDIT CARD COMPANIES	
American Express	(800) 528-4800, (800) 528-2122
	www.americanexpress.com

ORLANDO CREDIT CARD COMPANIES	
Diners Club	(800) 234-6377
	www.dinersclub.com
Discover	(800) 347-2683
	www.discovercard.com
MasterCard	(800) 622-7747
	www.mastercard.com
Visa	(800) 847-2911
	www.usa.visa.com

FEDEX KINKO'S LOCATIONS

Phone number: (800) 463-3339

Web site: www.fedex.com/us/officeprint/main

There are three full-service FedEx Kinko's locations within the Orange County Convention Center. There are also more than a dozen other full-service FedEx locations, several dozen authorized ShipCenters, and hundreds of FedEx drop boxes throughout the Orlando area.

Each FedEx Kinko's location offers FedEx supplies and package drop-off service, plus copying, collating, printing, sign making, internet access, on-site computer rentals, and a wide range of other services. Rates are typically considerably less than at the business centers located in the hotels. There isn't a surcharge added to packages shipped using your FedEx account.

TIP

FedEx's rush delivery service (800-399-5999) offers *same-day*, door-to-door delivery of packages up to 70 pounds. This service is available 365 days per year to and from all 50 states. Other services include overnight delivery (between 8 A.M. and 10 A.M.), overnight delivery by 10:30 A.M., overnight delivery by 3 P.M., and second-day, third-day, and ground delivery for letters and packages.

SELECT FEDEX KINKO'S LOCATIONS IN THE ORLANDO AREA	
12181 S. Apopka Vineland Road, Orlando	Open 24 hours
	Latest package drop-off: 6 P.M. (12 P.M. Saturday)
9800 International Drive, Orlando	8 A.M.–5 P.M. (Monday–Friday)
	Latest package drop-off: 4 P.M. (12 P.M. Saturday)

SELECT FEDEX KINKO'S LOCATIONS IN THE ORLANDO AREA	
6900 Presidents Drive, Orlando	8 A.M.–7:30 P.M. (Monday-Friday)
	9 A.M.–4:00pm (Saturday)
	Latest package drop-off: 7:30 P.M. (4 P.M. Saturday)
7200 South Orange Blossom Trail, Orlando	Open 24 hours
	6:45 P.M. (2 P.M. Saturday)
3120 South Kirkman Road, Orlando	7:30 A.M.–9 P.M. (Monday-Friday)
	10 A.M.–6 P.M. (Saturday)
	12 P.M.–6 P.M. (Sunday)
	Latest package drop-off: 6:30 P.M. (12 P.M. Saturday)
10445 Tradeport Drive, Orlando	12 P.M.–8:30 P.M. (Monday-Friday)
	Latest package drop-off: 8:30 P.M. (no Saturday drop offs)
7828 West Colonial Drive, Orlando	Open 24 hours
	Latest package drop-off: 6:40 P.M. (12 P.M. Saturday)
47 East Robinson Street, Orlando	6 A.M.–10 P.M. (Monday-Friday)
	9 A.M.–6 P.M. (Saturday)
	7 A.M.–10 P.M. (Sunday)
	Latest package drop-off: 7:15 P.M. (12:30 P.M. Saturday)
950 Bennett Road, Orlando	8 A.M.–7:30 P.M. (Monday-Friday)
	Latest package drop-off: 7:30 P.M. (5 P.M. Saturdays)
350 W. Fairbanks Avenue, Winter Park	7:30 A.M.–9 P.M. (Monday-Friday)
	10 A.M.–6 P.M. (Saturday)
	12 P.M.–6 P.M. (Sunday)
	Latest package drop-off: 6:30 P.M. (12 P.M. Saturday)

FLORISTS

Some of the larger and more upscale Orlando-area hotels and resorts offer full-service florists inhouse. All the florists listed in the following chart can have flower arrangements, plants, balloons, and other gift items shipped anywhere. They can also provide flower arrangements for trade shows, banquets, and other functions.

SELECT ORLANDO FLORISTS	
Blooms Today	(800) 521-4085
	www.bloomstoday.com
Flourish Floral Productions	(407) 644-7474
	www.flourishproductions.com
FTD	(800) SEND-FTD
	www.ftd.com
Lowe and Behold Event Accents	(407) 852-0069
	www.loweandbehold.net
1-(800) FLOWERS	(800) FLOWERS
	www.1800flowers.com

SELECT ORLANDO FLORISTS	
Orlando Florist	(407) 894-4320
	www.orlandoflorist.com
Special Event Floral	(407) 872-0099
	www.specialeventfloral.com

FOREIGN CURRENCY EXCHANGE SERVICES

Many full-service banks in Orlando (and surrounding areas) offer currency exchange services.

You'll find several Travelex (407-825-4988, www.travelex.com) currency exchange kiosks within the Orlando International Airport.

GOLF COURSES

See Section VI, "Entertainment in Orlando."

JET CHARTERS

If your travel plans cannot be accommodated by a major commercial airline, consider utilizing a charter jet. The cost is, of course, higher, but the added luxury and convenience may be worthwhile to you and your company.

ORLANDO JET CHARTER COMPANIES	
Air Royale	(800) 7-ROYALE
	www.airroyale.com
Blue Star Jets	(866) 471-2856
	www.bluestarjets.com
Executive Charter Service	(888) 522-0883
	www.executivecharterservice.com
I Fly Jet Set	(877) 301-9609
	www.iflyjetset.com
Imperial Jets	(888) 599-5387
	www.imperialjets.com
Jet Charter	(212) 856-5747
Luxury Air Jets	(866) 420-5060
	www.luxuryairjets.com
Skyline Jets	(888) 898-5387
	www.skylinejets.com

LAWYERS

For a lawyer referral in Orlando, call the Florida Bar Association's referral line at (850) 561-5832 or visit www.floridabar.org and select the "Find a Lawyer" option.

LIMOUSINE AND TOWN CAR SERVICES

For listings, see Section IV, "Getting Around Town."

LOCKSMITHS

These companies offer 24-hour emergency service. Be sure the locksmith you hire is fully licensed and insured.

ORLANDO LOCKSMITH SERVICES	
AAAA Action Locksmiths	(407) 841-4422
Advanced Auto Locksmith	(407) 260-0261
All Florida Locks and Safes	(407) 931-1555
Locksmith Orlando	(866) 522-9815
Vic's Locksmith Services	(407) 897-3636

MALLS AND SHOPPING

See Section VI, "Entertainment in Orlando."

MEETING AND BANQUET ROOM RENTALS

To rent a meeting room of any size at the hotel where you're staying, contact the concierge, sales office or business center (see Section III, "Where to Stay While in Orlando" for a partial listing of area hotels). Meeting rooms can also be rented at the Orange County Convention Center (800-972-3304, www.OCCC.net), as well as within most upscale restaurants.

TIP

To rent a conference room or corporate office space by the half day or full day, contact Regus (800-633-4237, www.regus.com/easy). This company rents fully equipped offices and meeting rooms in 400 cities throughout the world, including at several corporate locations in and around Orlando.

Many available meeting rooms offer high-speed internet access; conference room, theater-style, or classroom seating; video conferencing; teleconferencing; television and DVD player; projectors; whiteboards; photocopying services; flipcharts with easel; and catering services. Meeting rooms can often be rented by the hour, half day, or full day.

MESSENGER SERVICES

The following services can transport documents and packages within the Orlando area. Same-day and immediate rush service are typically available. Some of these services operate 24 hours per day.

ORLANDO MESSENGER SERVICES	
Ace Expediters	(407) 423-4223
	www.aceexpediters.com
A1 Express Delivery Service	(877) 219-7737
	www.a1express.com
Avis Couriers	(877) 683-8080
	www.aviscouriers.com

OFFICE SUPPLY SUPERSTORES

In addition to stocking a vast selection of office supply products, these retail stores offer copying and printing services, as well as same-day or next-day delivery of office supplies and related products. You can also shop at the retail stores for all of your office supply needs. Most of these retail stores are open until 9 P.M. (or later).

Staples

Phone number: (800) 333-3330

Web site: www.staples.com

Operates four retail locations within the Orlando area:

- 8421 South John Young Parkway, Orlando—(407) 345-1006
- 101 West Vine Street, Kissimmee—(407) 944-4405
- 867 Hood Homes Road, Orlando—(407) 295-4684
- 2774 East Colonial Drive, Orlando—(407) 894-7226

Office Depot

Phone number: (800) GO-DEPOT

Web site: www.officedepot.com

Offers ten retail locations within the Orlando area:

- 7600 Dr. Phillips Boulevard, Orlando—(407) 248-1163
- 4161 Town Center Boulevard, Orlando—(407) 812-5855
- 6855 South Kirkman Road, Orlando—(407) 370-2624
- 7687 South Orange Blossom Trail, Orlando—(407) 855-9405
- 7174 West Colonial Drive, Orlando—(407) 298-6465
- 2847 South Orange Avenue, Orlando—(407) 423-9907
- 2112 East Colonial Drive, Orlando—(407) 893-5225
- 989 North Semoran Boulevard, Orlando—(407) 281-9075
- 501 North Orlando Avenue, Winter Park—(407) 644-1218
- 2559 East Highway 50, Clermont—(352) 241-7052

Office Max

Phone number: (800-283-7674)

Web site: www.officemax.com

Offers five retail locations within the Orlando area:

- 3107 West Vine Street, Kissimmee—(407) 870-2041
- 1649 Florida Mall Avenue, Orlando—(407) 858-9777
- 7401 West Colonial Drive, Orlando—(407) 296-7255

- 3001 Colonial Market Place, Orlando—(407) 895-2400
- 1989 South Semoran Boulevard, Orlando—(407) 737-6440

SECRETARIAL AND TEMPORARY EMPLOYMENT SERVICES

Whether you need temporary personnel to help staff or facilitate a meeting, or require the use of a secretary, bookkeeper, or other specialist while in the Orlando area, any of these temporary employment agencies will be able to help you meet your short-term, last-minute staffing needs.

ORLANDO STAFFING SERVICES	
AppleOne	(877) 221-5171
Beloved Staffing	(407) 574-2186
Convention Connection	(866) 333-2228
Hospitality Staff	(407) 855-8586
Labor Finders	(800) 864-7749
Manpower	(888) 222-6495
Office Team	(800) 804-8367
Personnel One	(407) 422-5800
United Temps	(800) 248-8558

SHIPPING AND FREIGHT SERVICES

Packages can be dropped off at the business center of any hotel; however, you will be charged an additional service fee. To find a courier or shipping company-owned drop box or to schedule a package pickup yourself, contact the company you want to use directly.

ORLANDO SHIPPING AND FREIGHT SERVICES	
DHL	(800) CALL-DHL
	www.dhl.com
FedEx	(800) GO-FEDEX
	www.fedex.com
UPS	(800) PICK-UPS
	www.ups.com

TICKET BROKERS

See Section VI, "Entertainment in Orlando."

TRADE SHOW EXHIBIT SALES, INSTALLATION, REPAIR, AND DISMANTLING

For trade show exhibit sales, installation, emergency repairs, or dismantling, contact any of the following companies. The trade show coordinator or hosting venue where your event is being held will also be able to offer referrals.

For information relating to exhibiting at the Orange County Convention Center, call (407) 685-9824 or (800) 345-9898, or visit www.occc.net/Exhibitor.

ORLANDO TRADE SHOW SERVICES	
Advantage Expo South	(407) 852-9920
	www.advantageexpo.com
GES Exposition Services	(800) 418-4744
	www.ges.com
Goben Convention Services	(407) 240-3348
	www.gobencs.com
PDMG Nimlok Orlando	(407) 648-5171
	www.nimlok-orlando.com
Signs Now	(800) 356-3373
	www.signsnow.com
Tradeshow Decorators International	(407) 877-1340
	www.tradeshow-decorators.com
US Tradeshows	(407) 812-8223
	www.ustshows.com
XeroGraphic Digital Printing	(407) 236-0616
	www.xerocopy.com

TRADE SHOW AND PRIVATE SECURITY SERVICES

For your private security needs within a hotel, contact the hotel's management or concierge. For private security services within the Orange County Convention Center, call (407) 685-9828 or (407) 685-7102. Additional private security firms include the following.

ORLANDO SECURITY SERVICES	
Century Security and Event Staffing	(407) 226-7076
	www.centurytradeshow.com
Guards To Go	(800) 970-3437
	www.guardstogo.com
Watchman Protective Services	(866) 608-8000
	www.watchmanprotection.com

TRANSLATORS AND INTERPRETERS

To find a translator or interpreter to meet your specific needs, contact one of the following companies.

ORLANDO TRANSLATION SERVICES	
Alisa International Spanish Translations	(407) 381-2962
Berlitz	(407) 248-8222
German Translations	(407) 898-2290
International Translators & Interpreters	(407) 426-7396
Japan Orlando Connection	(407) 856-8999
Language Bank	(407) 894-3300
Languages Unlimited	(407) 292-3911
Milagros Montiel Translations	(407) 293-6874
Tsuruko Moenchmeier Japanese Interpreter-Translator	(407) 855-7600
Ultra Translate	(800) 59-ULTRA
United Nations Translators & Interpreters	(407) 894-6020

TRAVELER'S CHECKS

Traveler's checks are widely accepted and can be used at most locations just like cash. They typically come in a variety of different denominations, including $20, $50, $100, and $500. If you need to acquire traveler's checks or need to report that your traveler's checks have been lost or stolen, contact one of the following companies:

- American Express: (800) 807-6233
- MasterCard Traveler's Checks: (800) 223-9920
- Visa Traveler's Checks: (800) 732-1322

You can acquire traveler's checks at most banks. They are an excellent alternative to carrying large sums of cash when traveling, because if they're lost or stolen, they are replaceable. When you first purchase the checks, be sure to sign them in the appropriate location, and keep the receipt for the checks (listing the check numbers) in a separate location from the traveler's checks themselves.

MONEY SAVER

If you're a member of AAA, you can obtain traveler's checks with no processing fee at any AAA travel office. In other words, you pay only the face value of the traveler's check(s) you acquire.

UPS SHIPPING LOCATIONS

While UPS drop boxes can be found throughout the Orlando area (call 800-PICK-UPS, or visit www.ups.com for locations), the following is a list of UPS stores, where you can purchase shipping supplies, drop off packages, make copies, and handle a wide range of work-related tasks. You do not need a pre-existing UPS account to ship packages or overnight letters from any of the UPS stores.

Select UPS Store Locations

- 8131 Vineland Avenue, Orlando—(407) 465-1700
- 52 Riley Road, Celebration—(407) 939-7678
- 3956 Town Center Blvd., Orlando—(407) 855-8766
- 7862 West Irlo Bronson Highway, Kissimmee—(407) 390-1899
- 127 West Fairbanks Avenue, Winter Park—(407) 643-9150
- 4630 South Kirkman Road, Orlando—(407) 851-5772
- 7226 West Colonial Drive, Orlando—(407) 294-5777
- 5415 Lake Howell Road, Winter Park—(407) 678-0816

U.S. POST OFFICE LOCATIONS

Phone number: (800) ASK-USPS

Web site: www.usps.com

The following are just some of the full-service post offices located in the Orlando area. For additional locations, call (800) ASK-USPS.

TIP
You'll find a FedEx drop box located outside of most U.S. Post Office locations.

Select full-service U.S. Post Offices in Orlando

- Mall at Millenia, 4200 Conroy Road, Orlando
- 440 South Orange Blossom Trail, Orlando
- 51 East Jefferson Street, Orlando
- 10401 Post Office Boulevard, Orlando
- 601 Market Street, Kissimmee
- 2600 Michigan Avenue, Kissimmee
- 15155 West Colonial Drive, Winter Garden
- 821 Herndon Avenue, Orlando
- 5087 Edgewater Drive, Orlando
- 503 Florida Parkway, Kissimmee

- 12133 South Apopka Vineland Road, Orlando
- 10450 Turkey Lake Road, Orlando
- 3152 Vineland Road, Kissimmee

WESTERN UNION ELECTRONIC MONEY-TRANSFER SERVICES (WORLDWIDE)

Customer service: (800) 325-6000

Web site: www.westernunion.com

Money can be sent from the Western Union web site, but it must be picked up in person at a Western Union location. Call (800) 325-6000 for the location closest to you. Throughout Florida, locations can be found within most 7-Eleven, Winn Dixie, Publix, and Circle K convenience stores and supermarkets.

SECTION X

© Robert Pitman

PERSONAL
SERVICES

Whether you're looking for a tailor, fitness center, hairstylist, hospital, dentist, or massage therapist, you'll be able to find these all-important personal products and services throughout Orlando and the surrounding areas.

Keep in mind, the companies and services listed here are for reference or referral purposes only, and are just a sampling of the many companies offering similar products and services within the Orlando area. Inclusion in this section does not constitute an endorsement. Additional referrals can be obtained from your hotel's concierge or the local Yellow Pages. All addresses are in Orlando unless otherwise noted.

AIRLINE DIRECTORY
See Section I, "Welcome to Orlando."

ALCOHOLICS ANONYMOUS
To find an Alcoholics Anonymous meeting in Orlando, call (407) 260-5408 (24-hour hotline) or visit www.aaorlandointergroup.org.

CHIROPRACTORS
For a referral to a chiropractor close to where you're staying, visit www.chirodirectory.com. When setting up an appointment, determine if your out-of-state medical insurance will cover the cost of the visit and treatment. The following chiropractors offer same-day appointments for emergencies.

ORLANDO-AREA CHIROPRACTORS	
Graham Chiropractic 7532 West Sand Lake Road, Orlando	(407) 363-0052
Lake Buena Vista Chiropractic 11953 South Apopka Vineland Road, Orlando	(407) 238-2306
Pain Specialist of Orlando 6005 Silver Star Road, Orlando	(407) 299-5003
Rose Healthcare Center 6638 Old Winter Garden Road, Orlando	(407) 298-9211
Spargo Medical & Rehabilitation Center 12554 South John Young Parkway, Orlando	(407) 888-5995
Winter Park Chiropractic & Acupuncture Center 606 North Wymnore Road, Winter Park	(407) 622-2251
World Health Chiropractic 9464 South Orange Blossom Trail, Orlando	(407) 857-8453

DENTISTS
The following dentists offer same-day appointments for emergencies. There are hundreds of dentists in the Orlando area. For additional referrals, contact your hotel's concierge, or call 1-(800) DENTIST or visit www.1800dentist.com. You can also visit www.dentists.com and select "Orlando."

ORLANDO-AREA DENTISTS

Dental Emergency Service of Greater Orlando 1100 Symonds Avenue, Winter Park	(407) 629-6955
Dental Excellence 7932 Sand Lake Road, #300, Orlando	(407) 351-4229
Florida Dentist 5724 Hansel Avenue, Orlando	(407) 812-7499
Greenberg Dental & Orthodontics 4780 South Kirkman Road, Orlando	(407) 292-9557
24-Hour Dentist 7259 International Drive, Orlando	(407) 903-0320

DEPARTMENT STORES

When it comes to shopping, Orlando is home to several upscale malls, multiple outlet malls, plus countless shopping centers and stand-alone shops. Here's a list of where you'll find the major department stores. For more information about the malls in Orlando, see Section VI, "Entertainment in Orlando."

ORLANDO DEPARTMENT STORES

Bloomingdale's 4200 Conroy Road, Orlando	(407) 363-3555 Located at the Mall at Millenia
Dillard's 8001 South Orange Blossom Trail, Orlando	(407) 830-1211 Located at the Florida Mall
Macy's 4200 Conroy Road, Orlando	(407) 363-3555 Located at the Mall at Millenia
Macy's 8001 South Orange Blossom Trail, Orlando	(407) 851-6255 Located at the Florida Mall
Neiman Marcus 4200 Conroy Road, Orlando	(407) 264-5900 Located at the Mall at Millenia
Nordstrom 8001 South Orange Blossom Trail, Orlando	(407) 851-6255 Located at the Florida Mall
Saks Fifth Avenue 8001 South Orange Blossom Trail, Orlando	(407) 812-4500 Located at the Florida Mall

TIP
For all of your golf equipment needs, visit Edwin Watts Golf Shop. There are three locations in the Orlando area, including 7501 Turkey Lake Road (407-345-8451),

83330 South International Drive (407-351-1444), and 7024 International Drive (407-352-2535).

DOCTORS

Doctors-on-Call (407-399-3627) is available 24 hours per day and will arrange to have a doctor visit you at your hotel room. You can also call Main Street Physicians (407-370-4881), Resort Physicians (407-465-0000) or Doc at Your Door (407-970-3138) to consult with a doctor 24 hours per day. These doctors will also make house calls to your hotel room.

For a doctor referral, call any of the Orlando-area hospitals listed in Section XI, "Help for Travel-Related Problems and Emergencies," or visit www.flhosp.org. In-room medical services are also available from Florida Hospital Centra Care (407-238-2000).

DRY CLEANERS

Most hotels offer a dry cleaning service for a fee (and will send out your garments to a professional dry cleaner on your behalf). Contact your hotel's front desk or concierge for details. For same-day service, garments typically need to be picked up from your hotel room by 10 A.M. (at the latest).

If you choose to deliver your garments to a dry cleaner yourself, for same-day service, you'll typically need to drop off your items before 1 P.M. Your hotel will be able to direct you to the closest dry cleaning service.

MONEY SAVER
It's much cheaper to drop off your garments yourself at a local dry cleaner than to utilize a hotel's dry cleaning service, although the services offered at your hotel will be much more convenient, since garments will be picked up at and delivered to your hotel room.

ORLANDO-AREA DRY CLEANERS	
Broadway Dry Cleaners 417 Broadway, Kissimmee	(407) 847-2292
Contemporary Cleaners 4882 South Kirkman Road, Orlando	(407) 295-1414
Conway Cleaners 4450 Curry Ford Road, Orlando	(407) 275-0397

ORLANDO-AREA DRY CLEANERS	
Custom Shoe Repair & Dry Cleaners 752 South Bluford Avenue, Ocoee	(407) 877-8889
Hangers Cleaners 161 West Fairbanks Avenue, Winter Garden	(407) 478-0020
Hangers Cleaners 7589 West Sand Lake Road, Orlando	(407) 264-0264
Jon's Dry Cleaner & Laundry 329 East Michigan Street, Orlando	(407) 540-1030

EYEWEAR STORES AND OPTOMETRISTS

For replacement prescription eyeglasses and contact lenses, there are many optometrists and eyewear stores throughout the Orlando area. Many are open seven days a week for eye exams and can create or repair prescription eyewear within hours.

LensCrafters

Web site: www.lenscrafters.com

Operates nine locations in the Orlando area, including:

- 4319 East Colonial Drive, Orlando—(407) 894-4552
- 1415 State Road 436, Casselberry—(407) 679-8080
- 520 West Highway 436, Altamonte Springs—(407) 788-2929
- Mall at Millenia, 4200 Conroy Road, Orlando—(407) 903-1066
- Florida Mall, 8001 South Orange Blossom Trail, Orlando—(407) 438-0202
- 8074 South Orange Blossom Trail, Orlando—(407) 851-2020

Pearl Vision

Web site: www.pearlevision.com

Operates two locations in the Orlando area, including:

- 3461-A East Colonial Drive, Orlando—(407) 898-7744
- 600 East Altamonte Drive, #100, Altamonte Springs—(407) 834-6554

Wal-Mart Vision Centers

Operates six locations in the Orlando area:

- 2500 South Kirkman Road, Orlando—(407) 290-6977
- 1239 State Road 436, Casselberry—(407) 679-0377
- 1700 South Orange Blossom Trail, Apopka—(407) 889-8668
- 10500 West Colonial Drive, Ocoee—(407) 877-6900
- 8101 South John Young Parkway, Orlando—(407) 354-5665
- 11250 East Colonial Drive, Orlando—(407) 281-8941

1-800-CONTACTS

Phone number: (800) 266-8228
Web site: www.1800contacts.com

Order prescription contact lenses and have them delivered overnight to your hotel.

FITNESS CENTERS AND GYMS

Virtually every midpriced and upscale hotel in the Orlando area offers a nicely equipped fitness center. Some are open 24 hours per day and are available to hotel guests for free. Others have more limited hours and/or charge a per-visit fee.

There are also dozens of fitness centers and gyms that are not affiliated with hotels in the Orlando area. These tend to be membership based, but they are often open to anyone willing to pay for a visitor's pass. If you are already a member of a club that is part of a nationwide chain, you can probably visit that gym's Orlando-area location for free, or for a reduced fee.

TIP
Some of these fitness centers and health clubs also feature full-service day spas and offer massages, facials, and a wide range of body treatments.

ORLANDO GYMS, HEALTH CLUBS, AND FITNESS CENTERS

Bally Total Fitness	(407) 277-1144
4650 South Semoran Boulevard, Orlando	
Bally Total Fitness	(407) 297-8400
4850 Lawing Lane, Orlando	
Bally Total Fitness	(407) 296-4231
6385 West Colonial Drive, Orlando	
Citrus Athletic Club	(407) 423-4070
255 South Orange Avenue, Orlando	

ORLANDO GYMS, HEALTH CLUBS, AND FITNESS CENTERS

Curves 1706 Woolco Way, Orlando	(407) 384-2694
Curves 3334 Edgewater Drive, Orlando	(407) 244-3999
Curves 4401 Hoffner Avenue, Orlando	(407) 812-8454
Gold's Gym 7733 Turkey Lake Road, Orlando	(407) 226-9996
LA Fitness Sports Club 815 North Alafaya Trail, Orlando	(407) 380-1526
Orlando Fitness & Racquet Club 825 Courtland Street, Orlando	(407) 645-3550
Orlando Sport & Social Club 4043 Bobolink Lane, Orlando	(407) 265-8280
Ozone 133 East Robinson Street, Orlando	(407) 481-0507
Paramount Health Club 491 West Silver Star Road, Orlando	(407) 275-8200
RDV Sports Plex 8701 Maitland Summit Boulevard, Orlando	(407) 916-2442
Your Health Center 511 Virginia Drive, Orlando	(407) 898-1059

FLORISTS AND BALLOON DELIVERY

See Section IX, "Business Services."

HAIRSTYLISTS, HAIR SALONS, AND BARBERS

Some of the upscale hotels offer a full-service salon inhouse, or can arrange to have a hairstylist come to your hotel room (contact your hotel's concierge for details). In the Orlando area, visiting a hairstylist or barber can cost anywhere from $20 to $100 (or more), depending on the salon and stylist.

To ensure you find exactly the services you're looking for, seek out a reliable referral from your hotel's concierge, since there are literally hundreds of hairstylists, salons, barbers, and manicurists working in the Orlando area.

HOSPITALS AND WALK-IN MEDICAL CENTERS

In case of a medical emergency, call 9-1-1 from any telephone. For a listing of hospitals and walk-in medical centers in the Orlando area, see Section XI, "Help for Travel-Related Problems and Emergencies."

In the Orlando area, Florida Hospital operates 15 Centra Care walk-in medical centers. Call (407) 200-2300 or visit www.centracare.org to find the closest location. The following are contact numbers for additional medical-related services and resources:

- Mental Health Crisis Hotline—(800) 627-5906
- Poison Control Hotline—(800) 222-1222
- Rape Crisis Hotline—(407) 843-4357
- Red Cross—(407) 894-4141
- Suicide Prevention Hotline (Lifeline of Central Florida)—(407) 425-2624

LIMOUSINES AND TOWN CARS

The most popular and largest taxi, town car, and limousine service in Orlando is Mears Transportation (407-422-2222, www.mearstransportation.com). See Section IV, "Getting Around Town," for more information.

JEWELRY STORES

Need a memorable gift for someone special? There are multiple jewelry stores located in the Orlando area, including:

- Blue Nile—www.bluenile.com
- Park Promenade Jewelers—(407) 903-1001, The Mall at Millenia
- Tharoo & Company—(407) 264-0200, Pointe Orlando
- Tiffany & Company—(407) 351-3133, The Mall at Millenia
- Zales Outlet—(407) 239-0554, Orlando Premium Outlets

MASSAGE THERAPISTS AND DAY SPAS

Many of the upscale hotels and resorts have a full-service day spa inhouse. To schedule an in-room massage or treatment at almost any hotel, contact the concierge. Throughout Orlando, you'll also find dozens of independent world-class day spas, some affiliated with fitness centers.

For information about the four upscale days spas located at the WDW Resort, see Section VII, "Visiting the Walt Disney World Resort."

TIP
For help finding a spa that offers the facilities and treatments you're looking for, visit the SpaFinder web site at www.spafinder.com.

The following is a sampling of the Orlando area's day spas:

ORLANDO-AREA DAY SPAS	
Canyon Ranch Spa at Gaylord 6000 West Osceola Parkway, Kissimmee	(866) 794-9402
Faces Skin Care 2120 Edgewater Drive, Orlando	(407) 426-7690
Faces Skin Care 7524 West Sand Lake Road, Orlando	(407) 345-5690
Grand Floridian Spa & Health Club 4401 Grand Floridian Way, Lake Buena Vista (WDW Resort)	(407) 824-2332
Mandara Spa at the Portofino Bay Hotel 5601 Universal Boulevard, Orlando	(407) 503-1244
Mandara Spa at the Walt Disney World Dolphin 1500 Epcot Resorts Boulevard, Lake Buena Vista (WDW Resort)	(407) 934-4772
Ritz-Carlton Spa 4024 Central Florida Parkway, Orlando	(407) 393-4200
Spa at Buena Vista Palace 1900 Buena Vista Drive, Lake Buena Vista	(407) 827-3200
Spa at Omni Orlando Resort 1500 Masters Boulevard, Champions Gate	(407) 390-6664
Spa at Saratoga Springs Resort 1920 Magnolia Way, Lake Buena Vista (WDW Resort)	(407) 827-4455
Spa at the Wyndham Palace Resort 1900 Buena Vista Drive, Lake Buena Vista (WDW Resort)	(407) 827-2727

FOR THE ULTIMATE FACIAL, VISIT FACES SKIN CARE

Most day spas offer a large selection of massage treatments, facials, and full-body wraps and treatments, plus a variety of other services designed to calm the mind and pamper the body. Faces Skin Care, as the name suggests, takes a very different approach.

Faces Skin Care provides the same top-notch service you'd find at the best day spas in the country; utilizes the most state-of-the-art equipment available, as well as the best-quality skin care products on the market; plus hires only the most skilled and qualified skin care professionals available. The difference between Faces Skin Care and your typical day spa is that this company offers only a wide range of extraordinary facial treatments.

FOR THE ULTIMATE FACIAL, VISIT FACES SKIN CARE, continued

Faces Skin Care has two convenient locations (within 15 minutes of the International Drive and WDW Resort areas). Both locations offer more than a dozen different types of facials (which last about 55 minutes each). Each facial includes a detailed skin analysis, cleansing, steaming, exfoliation, mask, facial massage, moisturizer, sunscreen, and gentle hand treatment.

Prices for facials range from $75 for the signature Faces Facial, to $130 for the Galvanic Rejuvenation Facial. For men, a luxurious Gentleman's Facial is offered ($85). If you're in a hurry, there's also a wonderful Express Facial, which lasts about 25 minutes ($55). A variety of advanced treatments and corrective facial peels are also available.

All facials are performed in an upscale spa environment using one of more than 14 different, premium-quality skin care product lines, many of which are imported from overseas. The experience offered at Faces Skin Care is extremely relaxing and rejuvenating. A facial is a wonderful and convenient way to pamper yourself, and the service you'll receive at Faces Skin Care is exceptional. All of the employees are well trained, are extremely friendly, and cater to the needs of clients by providing a truly personalized experience.

Faces Skin Care is located at 2120 Edgewater Drive, Orlando (407-426-7690) and 6524 West Sand Lake Road, Orlando (407-345-5690). Hours: Monday through Friday, 10 A.M. to 8 P.M.; Saturday, 10 A.M. to 6 P.M.; and Sunday, 10 A.M. to 4 P.M. (or by appointment at the 2120 Edgewater Drive location). Appointments should be scheduled in advance, however, same-day appointments are often available. For more information, visit www.MyFaceCare.com.

For both male and female business travelers, Marlene Waganheim, general manager of Faces Skin Care, offers the following six tips to properly manage your skin, especially when traveling to warm and sunny places like Orlando:

- *Tip 1*. Make sure there's sunscreen in your daily moisturizer (15-30 SPF) for protection from the sun.
- *Tip 2*. Drink plenty of water to stay hydrated. Also, utilize a portable hydration spritz to provide the skin on your face with refreshment and to prevent overheating.

FOR THE ULTIMATE FACIAL, VISIT FACES SKIN CARE, continued

- *Tip 3.* Consider using an oxygen serum or stimulating moisturizer on your face to increase circulation and maintain a healthy skin tone. Changes in altitude from flying cause oxygen loss in skin cells and makes skin more dehydrated.
- *Tip 4.* Practice proper hand sanitation. This will help to kill bacteria and prevent it from spreading to your face. Acne can result from touching your face with dirty hands.
- *Tip 5.* Use a lip treatment with SPF to prevent chapping from the rapid temperature changes or wind resistance if partaking in outdoor recreation.
- *Tip 6.* When outdoors, wear sunglasses to protect your eyes and prevent squinting. This helps to reduce crow's feet and fine lines around eyes as your skin matures. A good eye cream will prevent this, too, and help reduce tired or puffy eyes.

With two locations in the Orlando area, Faces Skin Care is an upscale spa facility that focuses exclusively on offering premium-quality facials performed by skin care professionals using state-of-the-art equipment in a luxurious and relaxing setting.

NAIL SALONS

Need a manicure or pedicure? Most day spas and hair salons offer manicure and pedicure services. The following are just some of the more than 200 nail salons within the Orlando area.

ORLANDO NAIL SALONS	
All Star Unisex Beauty Salon 11320 South Orange Blossom Trail, Orlando	(407) 251-1112
Beauty Corner 12427 South Orange Blossom Trail, Orlando	(407) 251-2210
Creation Nails 11025 International Drive, Orlando	(407) 465-1555
Elegant Nails 11973 South Apopka Vineland Road, Orlando	(407) 477-0323
Fantasy Nails 7235 International Drive, Orlando	(407) 370-9023
Fountain Salon & Spa 7541 West Sand Lake Road, Orlando	(407) 351-9300
Happy Nail & Spa 4807 West Irlo Bronson Memorial, Kissimmee	(407) 390-8181
Luxury Nail & Spa 12221 University Boulevard, Orlando	(407) 281-7665
Magic Nails & Spa 47 Blake Boulevard, Kissimmee	(321) 939-2020
Modern Nail 4658 South Kirkman Road, Orlando	(407) 541-3192
Nail Place 8125 Vineland Avenue, Orlando	(407) 239-1799
Nails 4 U 11570 South Orange Blossom Trail, Orlando	(407) 447-1414
Natural Nails 3160 Vineland Road, Kissimmee	(407) 397-7388
Oscar Nail Salon 8687 West Irlo Bronson Memorial, Kissimmee	(407) 238-4445
Professional Nails 5250 International Drive, Orlando	(407) 248-2246
Salon Victoria 7844 West Irlo Bronson Memorial, Kissimmee	(407) 396-8333

PHARMACIES

For prescription medication refills and over-the-counter remedies, many Orlando-area pharmacies are open 24 hours per day. If your doctor is out of state, be sure to have a copy of your written prescription and your health insurance card with you. Otherwise, your doctor will have to make contact with the pharmacy directly to call in or verify your prescription.

TIP
Ask your hotel's concierge for a referral to the pharmacy that's closest to where you're staying.

CVS Pharmacy

Phone number: (888) 607-4287

Web site: www.cvs.com

Offers more than 40 locations around the Orlando area:

- 5308 West Irlo Bronson Memorial Highway, Kissimmee—(407) 390-9431
- 7599 West Sand Lake Road, Orlando—(407) 352-1177
- 5402 Central Florida Parkway, Orlando—(407) 239-6065
- 3250 North John Young Parkway, Kissimmee—(407) 933-0947
- 12339 South Orange Blossom Trail, Orlando—(407) 240-2474
- 13454 South Orange Blossom Trail, Orlando—(407) 240-3191
- 5300 South John Young Parkway, Orlando—(407) 370-2522

Walgreen's

Phone number: (800) 289-2273

Web site: www.walgreens.com

Offers more than 25 locations around the Orlando area:

- 4502 South Orange Blossom Trail, Orlando—(407) 851-6040
- 3301 Edgewater, Orlando—(407) 649-7859
- 920 South Kirkman Road, Orlando—(407) 253-6288
- 4774 South Semoran Boulevard, Orlando—(407) 273-9399
- 4578 Kirkman Road, Orlando—(407) 293-8458
- 7669 South Orange Blossom Trail, Orlando—(407) 856-1809
- 12100 South Apopka Vineland Road, Lake Buena Vista—(407) 238-0600
- 13502 South Apopka Vineland Road, Orlando—(407) 827-1004
- 12650 International Drive, Orlando—(407) 238-4677
- 5935 West Irlo Bronson Highway, Kissimmee—(407) 396-1006
- 7650 Sand Lake Road, Orlando—(407) 370-6742

Wal-Mart Pharmacy

Web site: www.walmart.com

Offers 20 locations around the Orlando area:

- 2500 South Kirkman Road, Orlando—(407) 290-6977
- 1239 State Road 436, Casselberry—(407) 679-0377
- 1700 South Orange Blossom Trail, Apopka—(407) 889-8668
- 10500 West Colonial Drive, Ocoee—(407) 877-6900
- 8101 South John Young Parkway, Orlando—(407) 354-5665
- 11250 East Colonial Drive, Orlando—(407) 281-8941
- 444 West Vine, Kissimmee—(407) 397-7000
- 3250 Vineland Road, Kissimmee—(407) 397-1125
- 1471 East Osceola Parkway, Kissimmee—(407) 870-2277

TIP

Need a prescription filled and delivered to your hotel room? Call Centra Care at (407) 239-7777.

RENTAL CARS

See Section IV, "Getting Around Town," for more information about rental cars.

ORLANDO RENTAL CAR COMPANIES	
Alamo	(800) 462-5266 www.alamo.com
Avis	(800) 331-1212 www.avis.com
Budget	(800) 527-0700 www.budget.com
Dollar	(800) 800-3665 www.dollar.com
Enterprise	(800) 261-7331 www.enterprise.com
Hertz	(800) 654-3131 www.hertz.com
National	(800) 227-7368 www.nationalcar.com
Thrifty	(800) THRIFTY www.thrifty.com

> **TIP**
> For emergency roadside assistance, if you're a AAA member, call (800) AAA-HELP. For AAA membership information, call (800) 222-1134. For AAA maps, tour books, and TripTiks, call (800) 222-1134. The AAA office in Orlando is located at 4300 East Colonial Drive, Orlando (407-894-3333). Hours: Monday through Friday, 8:30 A.M. to 5:30 P.M.; Saturday, 9 A.M. to 1 P.M.

SHOE AND LUGGAGE REPAIR AND LUGGAGE SALES

There are dozens of shoe and luggage repair shops located throughout the Orlando area. Some offer immediate or while-you-wait service.

ORLANDO SHOE AND LUGGAGE REPAIR SERVICES	
American Alterations 616 North Bumby Avenue, Orlando	(407) 898-7165
Heel Sew Quik 8001 South Orange Blossom Trail, Orlando	(407) 856-7726
Hendrick's Shoe Repair 141 Lincoln Avenue, Winter Park	(407) 644-7565
Orlando Shoe Repair 325 South Orlando Avenue, Winter Park	(407) 629-5837
Pine Hills Shoe Repair 5139 West Colonial Drive, Orlando	(407) 299-8680
Shoe Repair USA 5410 Edgewater Drive, Orlando	(407) 296-7550
Ted's Shoe Repair 2601 Curry Ford Road, Orlando	(407) 898-9511
Ultimate Shoe Repair 341 East Michigan Street, Orlando	(407) 423-8893

TAILORS AND CLOTHING ALTERATIONS

All of the major department stores in the Orlando area, as well as the upscale clothing stores and boutiques, offer inhouse tailoring services for their customers. Same-day or next-day service is often available. Many of the upscale hotels also have inhouse tailoring and alteration services available to guests. Contact your hotel's concierge for details. Also see "Dry Cleaners" earlier in this section.

THEME PARKS

Here are the main phone numbers for the popular Orlando-area theme parks and tourist attractions:

- Busch Gardens Tampa Bay—(888) 800-5447
- Cypress Gardens Adventure Park—(863) 324-2111
- Daytona International Speedway—(800) PIT-SHOP
- Kennedy Space Center Visitor's Complex—(321) 449-4444
- SeaWorld and Discovery Cove—(407) 351-3600
- Universal Orlando—(407) 363-8000
- Walt Disney World Resort—(407) 824-4321
- Wet 'n Wild—(407) 351-1800

TUXEDO RENTALS

Formalwear for men and women can be purchased at many of the designer clothing shops, boutiques, and department stores in the Orlando area. The following are tuxedo rental locations, virtually all of which have tailors on the premises.

ORLANDO TUXEDO RENTAL COMPANIES	
After Hours Formalwear 3457 East Colonial Drive, Orlando	(407) 896-0851
After Hours Formalwear Florida Mall, 8001 South Orange Blossom Trail, Orlando	(407) 857-5761
Any Tux 45 Bucks 3800 Edgewater Drive, Orlando	(407) 521-7678
Black Tie Formal 10707 East Colonial Drive, Orlando	(407) 380-5218
Carolyn Allen's Bridals and Tuxedos 5410 Central Florida Parkway, Orlando	(407) 238-2722
Ever After Formal Wear 9484 South Orange Blossom Trail, Orlando	(407) 854-0259
Formal Penguin 697 North Semoran Blvd., Orlando	(407) 823-9933
Men's Warehouse 1355 Sand Lake Road, Orlando	(407) 851-5204
Men's Warehouse 2606 East Colonial Drive, Orlando	(407) 895-8408
Men's Warehouse 7332 West Colonial Drive, Orlando	(407) 523-7400
Sears Tuxedo Services 451 East Altamonte Drive, Altamonte Springs	(407) 767-6116

ORLANDO TUXEDO RENTAL COMPANIES	
T&A Formal Wear 9480 South Orange Blossom Trail, Orlando	(407) 251-6900
Tuxedo King 3800 Edgewater Drive, Orlando	(407) 521-7699

WHEELCHAIR AND SCOOTER (ECV) RENTALS

Within all of the major theme parks (at the guest services desk near the main entrance of each park), you can rent either a manually operated or electronic wheelchair by the day. At any of the Disney theme parks, for example, a manual wheelchair can be rented for $10 per day, while an electronic convenience vehicle (ECV) can be rented for $35 per day. A refundable deposit is required. Wheelchairs and ECVs can also be rented from any on-property WDW Resort hotel.

TIP

Be sure to ask for the free *Guests with Disabilities* guidebook when visiting any of the theme parks at the Walt Disney World Resort. This brochure and wheelchair rentals are available at City Hall within the Magic Kingdom, at the guest relations desk within Spaceship Earth at Epcot, at the guest relations desk at the Disney-MGM Studios, and at Garden Gate Gifts at Disney's Animal Kingdom.

The Scootaround Mobility Solutions wheelchair rental service is located within the Orange County Convention Center (call 888-441-7575 or visit www.scootaround.com). For a multiday (length-of-stay rental), Scootaround will deliver a wheelchair or scooter (ECV) to your hotel room. For a detailed description of the wheelchair models available, visit www.scootaround.com/rentals_vehicles.htm. Rates vary based on model and rental duration.

Another company that rents electronic wheelchairs and scooters in the Orlando area is Scooter Vacations (866-77-VISIT, www.scootorlando.com). Rates for an ECV start at $25 per day.

TRAVEL NOTES

SECTION XI

© Wolfgang Shaller

HELP FOR TRAVEL-RELATED PROBLEMS AND EMERGENCIES

Let's face it, no matter how much preplanning you do for a trip, sometimes things go wrong. As a business traveler, you always run the risk of losing your wallet, having your luggage lost or delayed by the airline, having to deal with unexpected travel delays, or running into a situation where you must change your travel itinerary at the last minute. This section will help you deal with some of the more common problems business travelers encounter.

MAKING LAST-MINUTE CHANGES TO YOUR TRAVEL ITINERARY

If you decide to save money and purchase a deeply discounted airfare from one of the popular travel-related web sites, such as Hotwire.com or Priceline.com, your airline ticket, rental car, and/or hotel accommodations must be prepaid and typically cannot be changed or refunded. In other words, unless you experience a medical emergency (and can get a letter from a doctor), you lose the money you paid if you don't take advantage of exactly what you purchased.

By paying a full coach, business, or first-class fare with one of the major airlines (by calling the airline's toll-free phone number, booking from the airline's own web site, or utilizing the services of a travel agent), you generally have the option to change your ticket for a fee. Depending on the airline, the change fee can be anywhere from $50 to $150, plus any change in price of the ticket based on the new travel itinerary you request. One of the most flexible airlines in terms of last-minute itinerary changes is JetBlue, available at (800) JET-BLUE or www.jetblue.com.

WARNING
If you plan to change your airline ticket, you must do it before the scheduled flight's departure. Otherwise, the value of your existing ticket will be lost.

In some situations if you want to change your flight, the airline allows you to fly standby. When flying standby, there generally isn't a change fee; however, you are not guaranteed a seat on the aircraft until the very last minute. If you're traveling with checked baggage, many airlines won't allow you to fly standby.

Purchasing travel insurance (for an additional fee) allows you to be refunded for your airline ticket, hotel accommodations, rental car, and so on, as long as the reason for the claim is covered by the insurance. While medical emergencies are covered, a change in your personal or business schedule generally is not covered.

WARNING
If you make a change to your travel itinerary, don't forget to call the hotel and/or rental car company to change or

cancel your reservation as far in advance as possible to avoid being charged. Attempting to cancel a hotel reservation within 24 hours before your scheduled check-in often results in a fee, unless extenuating circumstances apply.

If you think you may need to change your travel itinerary, consider purchasing a full-fare airline ticket directly from the airline, but ask in advance what the policy is for last-minute changes. One of the most flexible options is to book your airline ticket using frequent flier miles. Many airlines allow these reward tickets to be changed without extra fees.

Many corporate travel agents are able to make changes to travel itineraries, even on a last-minute basis, and eliminate or greatly reduce the fees charged by the airline. Depending on the circumstances, the airline ticket agents at the airport, the airline gate attendants, or the airline customer service representatives (available by calling the airline's toll-free number) all have varying degrees of discretion when it comes to helping a passenger make changes to a nonchangeable travel itinerary.

If you need to make any change to your travel itinerary, the first step should be to contact the airline, travel agency, or online travel service through which the travel reservations were made.

TIP
The customer service desks operated by the airlines (located within each airline's terminal at the airport) are always staffed by airline representatives who are trained to help passengers experiencing travel-related problems. If your flight is canceled or you need to be rerouted, these tend to be the most helpful people to consult.

DEALING WITH TRAVEL AND WEATHER DELAYS

If you experience bad weather in Orlando, or you're traveling from or returning to a city experiencing bad weather, travel delays or even flight cancellations are always a possibility. By calling the airline, you can sometimes determine if your flight is delayed or canceled before leaving for the airport. If your flight is canceled or delayed because of bad weather, the airline is not responsible for putting you up in a hotel or paying for meals.

When your flight gets canceled, the airline must rebook you on the next available flight to your destination. If, however, a flight is canceled because of mechanical problems with the aircraft or for a reason caused by the airline itself, the airline is responsible for rebooking you on another flight (possibly another airline), putting you up in a hotel, and/or paying for meals during the time your travel is delayed.

Depending on the situation, you may find yourself stuck at an airport waiting for the delayed flight to take off. If you're able to remain in the airport terminal (as opposed to on the aircraft), consider using the time to shop, eat, read, catch up on phone calls, or check your e-mail. (Most airports offer wireless internet access, so you can use your laptop to access your e-mail account via the web.)

For a fee, you can pay for a one-day pass to utilize an airline's VIP club or private lounge. In these lounges you likely can find comfortable couches, TVs, newspapers, magazines, telephones, business services, and full bar service, all in a quiet, living room-like atmosphere. The airline VIP lounges are also staffed by competent customer service representatives. These people can assist you with booking alternative flights, if necessary.

MONEY SAVER
It's common for the airlines to oversell seats on flights leaving Orlando, especially on a Friday or Sunday. To ensure all ticketed passengers get to their destinations, the airlines sometimes ask for passengers to voluntarily give up their seat on an aircraft and take a later flight. In exchange for the inconvenience, an airline will sometimes offer a travel voucher good for one free round-trip airline ticket within the continental United States, along with a meal voucher and possibly a voucher for a free night of hotel accommodations. This is a great way to earn free travel if you have flexibility in your schedule. The award vouchers can be transferred to friends, co-workers, or relatives, but they must be used within one year of receipt. Listen at the gate for announcements asking for volunteers to give up their seats. If you're interested, approach the ticket counter and submit your name.

LOST LUGGAGE
Airlines sometimes temporarily (or permanently) lose luggage. There are several things you can do to avoid this. Always check your bags with the airline at least 60 minutes before your flight's departure time. Make sure each of your bags is clearly marked with a luggage tag containing your name, address, and phone number.

In addition, when the ticket agent attaches the airline's baggage tags to each of your bags, make sure the tags list your correct name and destination. If an airline's ticketing agent accidentally attaches the wrong tags to your bags, they'll be put on the wrong aircraft and ultimately could wind up at the wrong destination.

Even if the bags are tagged correctly, things can still go wrong that will result in your luggage being delayed or lost. Always make sure you retain the baggage claim tags or tag numbers supplied by the airline when you check your bags. If you arrive at your destination and your bags don't appear in the baggage claim area (with the other passengers' luggage from your flight), go directly to the airline's baggage counter, which is located near the baggage claim area. Report your missing bag(s) immediately. You will be required to describe your luggage and fill out a form; the more information you can provide about your bags, the better.

TIP

For domestic flights, the airline baggage liability is capped at $2,800 per person for checked baggage and $400 per person for carry-ons. To file a claim and recover your losses, you will need to produce receipts for lost or damaged items. For an additional fee, you can purchase excess valuation protection for your luggage when you check in at the airport. Keep in mind that there is a long list of items that an airline will not take responsibility for or be willing to replace. Most airlines require that you file a claim within 21 to 45 days.

Once your lost bags are found, they generally get delivered (free of charge) to the destination of your choice (such as your hotel); however, this can take anywhere from several hours to several days. If your bags are delayed by more than six to eight hours (depending on the airline), you are entitled to be refunded for certain expenses, such as the replacement of toiletries or certain clothing items.

If you have a meeting within the first few hours of your arrival, it's an excellent strategy to bring everything you need for that meeting with you in your carry-on. Thus, if your checked luggage is lost or delayed, it does not affect your ability to attend the meeting.

When you report a lost bag to the airline, make sure you ask the attendant for a special local phone number for lost-luggage tracking. You should also receive a tracking number or case number specifically for your claim. This information will allow you to obtain progress reports from the airline relating to the location and status of your luggage. In some cases, you may need to contact the airline multiple times in order to receive your bags in a timely manner.

When you receive your luggage, do a detailed inventory to ensure than none of the contents was lost or stolen. If a problem exists, contact the airline immediately. Likewise, if the airline has damaged your bags or their contents, it's important to report this immediately, preferably in person at the airport. If necessary, you can report a theft or damage by calling the airline directly.

WARNING
There are a variety of items—such as electronics, computers, antiques, jewelry, and business documents—that none of the airlines will take responsibility for, even if the items are in your checked luggage. Never pack any of these items in your checked luggage.

For coverage above and beyond what the airline or your homeowner's insurance policy offers for lost, stolen, or delayed luggage, consider purchasing independent travel insurance. You can buy this insurance with a major credit card through any travel agent or by contacting an insurance provider on the phone or online. Travel insurance must be purchased before your trip begins.

TIP
One way to minimize the risk that your important luggage will get lost or stolen is to hire a luggage-forwarding service. This type of service picks up your luggage from your home or office two to seven days prior to your departure and arranges to have it delivered to your hotel (or any location) on the date of your arrival. All details are handled on your behalf, and you don't have to worry about airport security or the airline misplacing your bags. Utilizing a luggage-forwarding service isn't cheap, but it can take some of the stress and hassle out of business travel. These services also handle oversize luggage items, such as golf clubs, skis, trade show displays, and wheelchairs. The Luggage Club (877-231-5131, www.theluggageclub.com), Luggage Concierge (800-288-9818 www.luggageconcierge.com), and Luggage Free (800-361-6871,

www.luggagefree.com), are a few of companies that offer this service. Fees are based on the size and weight of your luggage, desired delivery time, and the pickup and drop-off fees charged by the service provider.

You can learn more about travel insurance and what it covers, or purchase an insurance policy, by contacting any of these companies:

- CSA Travel Protection—(800) 348-9505 or www.csatravelprotection.com
- Insure My Trip.com—(800) 487-4722 or www.insuremytrip.com
- Travel Guard International—(800) 826-4919 or www.travelguard.com
- Travel Insurance Center—(866) 979-6753 or www.travelinsurancecenter.com
- Travelex Insurance Services—(800) 228-9792 or www.travelex-insurance.com

The cost of travel insurance varies, based on the amount of coverage, the duration of your trip, and the value of the travel and your belongings. Make sure you understand what coverage you're purchasing and be sure to file any claims immediately by calling the insurance company's toll-free phone number and following the directions. If your claim involves a theft, it is often necessary to obtain a police report relating to the incident, so contact the local police department. Expect to wait four to six weeks for your claim to be processed and to be reimbursed for your covered losses.

WARNING
All of the major airlines (especially United Airlines) now strictly adhere to their luggage weight guidelines. If a bag weighs more than 50 pounds (for domestic flights), expect to pay an overweight fee of between $25 and $75, depending on the airline. When you pack, be sure your luggage adheres to airline guidelines to avoid extra charges.

LOST OR STOLEN CREDIT CARD, DRIVER'S LICENSE, AND/OR PASSPORT

If your wallet is lost or stolen, immediately call your bank or financial institution; the phone number is listed on your statement and on the back of your ATM card(s).

TIP

If you suspect the theft of your credit cards or personal identification, call the local police department and file a police report immediately. Also, contact the three major credit bureaus—Equifax, (800) 525-6285; Experian, (888) 397-3742; and TransUnion, (800) 860-7289—to report possible identify theft. You should also call the Identity Theft Data Clearing House at (877) ID-THEFT.

Immediately call the toll-free phone numbers for all your credit, ATM, and debit cards individually to report the situation. This can be done 24 hours a day. Following is the contact information for major credit card companies:

- American Express—(800) 528-4800, (800) 528-2122, www.americanexpress.com
- Diners Club—(800) 234-6377, www.dinersclub.com
- Discover—(800) 347-2683, www.discovercard.com
- MasterCard—(800) 622-7747, www.mastercard.com
- Visa—(800) 847-2911, www.usa.visa.com

If your driver's license is lost or stolen, contact the department of motor vehicles in your home city to arrange for a replacement license.

For a lost or stolen passport, if you're an American citizen, contact the U.S. Department of State, Passport Services, at (202) 955-0430 or visit http://travel.state.gov/passport/lost/us/us_848.html. You need to complete and file a Statement Regarding Lost or Stolen Passport Form (Form DS-64). For additional information, call (877) 487-2778.

WARNING

Without a valid government-issued form of identification, you cannot travel on any airline. Some airlines also require that you present a credit or debit card as a secondary form of identification when checking in at the airport using an automated kiosk.

LOST, STOLEN, OR DAMAGED LAPTOP COMPUTER

If your laptop is stolen, file a report with the local police and your insurance company immediately. You can purchase or rent a new computer while in Orlando, or you can utilize the computers available at the business centers found in the various hotels.

For emergency laptop repair or data recovery, see the companies listed in Section IX, "Business Services."

TIP
Before leaving your home or office, be sure to back up all your important computer data. Also, be sure to keep current records pertaining to your computer, including the sales receipt from when it was purchased, as well as its serial, make, and model numbers. If you purchased the extended warranty for your computer, bring the necessary information with you so you can contact the manufacturer if an emergency repair or replacement is required.

BUYING A NEW OUTFIT FAST OR REMOVING A STAIN

If you accidentally stain or damage your outfit, or if you need to purchase a new business outfit fast, the malls in Orlando, including the Florida Mall (8001 South Orange Blossom Trail, Orlando, 407-851-6255) and the Mall at Millenia (4200 Conroy Road, Orlando, 407-363-3555), offer a wide range of upscale department stores and clothing boutiques, many of which offer same-day alterations.

Section X, "Personal Services," lists local tailors and dry cleaners offering while-you-wait or same-day service. Some tailors even come to your hotel room for on-the-spot fittings or alterations. If you need help finding a tailor or seamstress who will come to your hotel, contact your hotel's concierge.

Many of the popular hotels have inhouse, same-day laundering and dry cleaning services that will pick up garments from your guestroom, which is helpful when you need to have a stain removed.

TIP
To clean up or remove clothing stains yourself, consider packing a travel-size container of Oxi-Clean, Tide-to-Go, or another popular stain remover. For tips on removing specific types of stains, visit the Tide web site (www.tide.com). Also consider traveling with a portable clothing steamer or travel steam iron, plus a small sewing kit. The Buttoneer ($19.95, www.buybuttoneer.com) is a handy and portable device that allows you to reattach buttons to almost any garment in seconds, with no sewing required.

PRESCRIPTION REFILLS

There are many pharmacies located in and around Orlando, many of which are open 24 hours. If you need to have a prescription filled, refilled, or replaced, you'll need a copy of your original prescription or your doctor will have to contact the pharmacy directly. Be sure to travel with your doctor's contact information and your medical insurance card (if applicable). If you already have your prescription on file with your hometown Walgreen's (800-289-2273), for example, go to the Orlando-area location of that same pharmacy to save time and hassle.

TIP
Centra Care can arrange to have your prescription(s) filled and delivered to your hotel room. Call (407) 239-7777.

REPLACING PRESCRIPTION EYEWEAR

Thanks to companies such as LensCrafters (www.lenscrafters.com) and Pearle Vision (www.pearlevision.com), replacement eyeglasses usually can be created in one hour. These companies have multiple stores in the Orlando area. Some Wal-Mart stores also offer inhouse vision centers capable of making prescription eyeglasses and replacing contact lenses quickly. The addresses and phone numbers of these companies are listed in Section X, "Personal Services."

In order to purchase replacement prescription eyeglasses, sunglasses, or contact lenses, you will need a copy of your current prescription from your eye doctor, or the eyeglass company will have to contact your eye doctor directly. If this isn't possible, you can pay for an on-site eye exam. (This is something your insurance may or may not cover. Speak with your hometown optometrist's office before proceeding with the exam.)

MEDICAL OR DENTAL EMERGENCIES

See Section X, "Personal Services," for contact and referral information for Orlando-area doctors, dentists, and hospitals. Many doctors and dentists offer immediate appointments on an emergency basis, if necessary. The emergency rooms at the area hospitals are open 24 hours per day.

- Florida Hospital (www.flhosp.org) operates several full-service hospitals in the Orlando area, including:

- Florida Hospital Orlando, 601 East Rollins Street, (407) 303-5600
- Florida Hospital Celebration Health, 400 Celebration Place, Celebration, (407) 764-4000. (This is the closest hospital to the Walt Disney World Resort.)
- Florida Hospital East Orlando, 7727 Lake Underhill Road, (407) 303-8110
- Florida Hospital Kissimmee, 2450 North Orange Blossom Trail, Kissimmee, (407) 846-4343
• Florida Hospital also operates 15 Centra Care walk-in medical facilities (407-200-2300, www.centracare.org) throughout the Orlando area. Hours of operation vary. Locations include:
- Orlando International Airport—(407) 207-0601
- Kissimmee—(407) 390-1888
- Lake Buena Vista (Disney area)—(407) 934-2273
• Doctors-on-Call (407-399-3627) is available 24 hours per day and will arrange to have a doctor visit you at your hotel room in Orlando (or the surrounding areas).
• To quickly obtain a dentist referral, call (800) DENTIST.

TIP
To obtain an outpatient doctor or medical specialist referral from Florida Hospital, visit www.flhosp.org, or call one of the hospitals directly.

If you experience a medical emergency while in the Orlando area, dial 9-1-1 from any telephone or call your hotel's front desk or operator (dial 0). For nonemergencies, your hotel's concierge can provide personalized referrals for a wide range of medical specialists in the area. Some hotels even have a nurse or doctor on call who will come to your guestroom. In some cases, you may have to pay for medical services upfront and later apply for reimbursement from your insurance company.

TIP
If you see a doctor, dentist, or eye doctor, for example, while in Orlando, be sure to obtain copies of all new medical records to provide to your primary doctor(s) when you return home.

CELLULAR PHONE-RELATED PROBLEMS

If your cell phone gets lost or stolen, call your service provider immediately to suspend your service. If you subscribe to a repair or replacement insurance plan through your service provider, you can arrange to have a new (refurbished) phone sent to you via overnight courier, typically within two business days.

If you lose or forget your charger or need a new accessory, there are Sprint/Nextel (866-438-1371), AT&T/Cingular (866-CINGULAR), T-Mobile (800-866-2453), Verizon (800-256-4646), and other cell phone stores located throughout the city. Many hotel and resort concierges also stock a selection of chargers for popular cell phone models or will send someone out on your behalf to purchase a replace charger for you.

LOST ITEMS

If you misplace something important or leave an item behind, the first thing to do is call the lost and found department of the hotel, resort, airline, airport, rental car company, theme park, or attraction where you think the item might have been lost or left.

Be prepared to give a detailed description of your item, your reservation number (if applicable), along with the time and date when you noticed the item went missing. If you left an item in your hotel room, for example, have your reservation number and check-in and checkout dates on hand. Also, be sure to give the lost and found office your contact information.

When contacting the lost and found department of an airline or rental car company, be sure to speak with someone in the Orlando office when you file your report. If the lost item has significant value, you'll also want to contact your insurance company.

The following are some useful lost and found phone numbers:

- *Orlando International Airport lost and found*: (407) 825-2111
- *Orange County Convention Center lost and found*: (407) 685-1202
- *Walt Disney World Resort lost and found*: (407) 824-4245
- *Universal Studios Orlando lost and found*: (407) 224-4244
- *Islands of Adventure lost and found*: (407) 224-4245
- *SeaWorld lost and found*: (407) 363-2400
- *Rental car company*: See your rental agreement and call the local Orlando phone number that's listed.
- *Airline*: Call the airline's main number and ask for the lost and found office in Orlando (or the city where your item

was lost). Have your flight number and travel dates on hand.
- *Hotel*: Call the hotel's front desk or concierge and ask for the lost and found department.

TRAVEL NOTES

APPENDIX

TRAVEL CHARTS AND
WORKSHEETS

The following charts and worksheets will help you keep track of your expenses and time. Feel free to reproduce them for each trip you take.

TIPPING RECOMMENDATIONS

SERVICE	RECOMMENDED TIPPING GUIDELINES
Bartender	Between 15 and 20 percent of bar tab or $1 to $2 per drink.
Bell captain (luggage attendant)	$2 per bag.
Concierge	$2 to $100 (depending on the service offered).
Curbside luggage check-in	You will typically pay a fee of $2 per bag for this service. Tip an additional $1 to $2 per bag.
Drink server	$1 to $2 per drink or 15 to 20 percent of the total bar tab.
Hotel housekeeper	$1 to $2 per night (leave the tip at the conclusion of your stay).
Limousine driver	15 percent of the total fare.
Personal shopper	15 to 20 percent of the total purchases made on your behalf.
Restaurant host/hostess	This is optional. Consider tipping $2 to $10 (depending on the quality of the restaurant, whether you've requested a specific table, or if the host/hostess reduced your wait time).
Room service	Virtually all hotels automatically add a 15 to 20 percent tip and delivery charge to the room service bill. It is optional whether you choose to give an additional tip.
Taxi driver	15 percent of the total fare.
Tour guide	10 to 20 percent of the total fee paid for the tour.
Valet parking attendant	$1 to $2 each time the car is parked or delivered.
Waiter/waitress (party of fewer than six people)	15 to 20 percent of the total bill.
Waiter/waitress (party of seven or more)	15 to 20 percent of the total bill (including alcohol). In many cases, the restaurant will automatically add a gratuity to the bill for large parties.

TIP CALCULATION CHART

AMOUNT	10%	15%	20%
$1.00	$ .10	$ .15	$ .20
$2.00	$ .20	$ .30	$ .40
$3.00	$ .30	$ .45	$ .60
$4.00	$ .40	$ .60	$ .80
$5.00	$ .50	$ .75	$1.00
$6.00	$ .60	$ .90	$1.20
$7.00	$ .70	$1.05	$1.40
$8.00	$.80	$1.20	$1.60
$9.00	$.90	$1.35	$1.80
$10.00	$1.00	$1.50	$2.00
$11.00	$1.10	$1.65	$2.20
$12.00	$1.20	$1.80	$2.40
$13.00	$1.30	$1.95	$2.60
$14.00	$1.40	$2.10	$2.80
$15.00	$1.50	$2.25	$3.00
$16.00	$1.60	$2.40	$3.20
$17.00	$1.70	$2.55	$3.40
$18.00	$1.80	$2.70	$3.60
$19.00	$1.90	$2.85	$3.80
$20.00	$2.00	$3.00	$4.00
$25.00	$2.50	$3.75	$5.00
$30.00	$3.00	$4.50	$6.00
$35.00	$3.50	$5.25	$7.00
$40.00	$4.00	$6.00	$8.00
$45.00	$4.50	$6.75	$9.00
$50.00	$5.00	$7.50	$10.00
$55.00	$5.50	$8.25	$11.00
$60.00	$6.00	$9.00	$12.00
$65.00	$6.50	$9.75	$13.00
$70.00	$7.00	$10.50	$14.00
$75.00	$7.50	$11.25	$15.00
$80.00	$8.00	$12.00	$16.00
$85.00	$8.50	$12.75	$17.00
$90.00	$9.00	$13.50	$18.00
$95.00	$9.50	$14.25	$19.00
$100.00	$10.00	$15.00	$20.00
$125.00	$12.50	$18.75	$25.00
$150.00	$15.00	$22.50	$30.00
$175.00	$17.50	$26.25	$35.00
$200.00	$20.00	$30.00	$40.00
$250.00	$25.00	$37.50	$50.00
$300.00	$30.00	$45.00	$60.00
$350.00	$35.00	$52.50	$70.00
$400.00	$40.00	$60.00	$80.00
$450.00	$45.00	$67.50	$90.00
$500.00	$50.00	$75.00	$100.00
$1,000.00	$100.00	$150.00	$200.00

TRAVEL ITINERARY WORKSHEET

Departure date: ___/___/___
Return date: ___/___/___
From: _____
To: _____

Hometown Ground Transportation to Airport

Service provider: _____
Phone number: _____
Reservation/confirmation number: _____
Pick-up location: _____
Pick-up time: _____ Drop-off time: _____

Airport Parking Information

Parking lot name/location: _____
Parking spot location/identifier: _____

Airline Information

Airline: _____
Phone number: _____
Airline frequent flier number: _____
Flight number: _____
Departure time: _____
Arrival time: _____

Connecting flight number: _____ Connecting flight city: _____
Connecting flight departure time: _____
Connecting arrival time: _____

Connecting flight number: _____ Connecting flight city: _____
Connecting flight departure time: _____
Connecting arrival time: _____

Rental Car Information

Rental car company: _____
Phone number: _____
Confirmation/reservation number: _____
Pick-up time/location: _____
Drop-off time/location: _____
Type of vehicle requested/reserved: _____

Orlando Ground Transportation from Airport

Service provider: _____
Phone number: _____

TRAVEL ITINERARY WORKSHEET, continued

Reservation/confirmation number: _____
Pick-up location: _____
Pick-up time: _____ Drop-off time: _____

Hotel/Resort Accommodations
Hotel/resort name: _____
Phone number: _____
Address: _____
Confirmation number: _____
Check-in date: _____
Check-out date: _____

Orlando Ground Transportation to Airport
Service provider: _____
Phone number: _____
Reservation/confirmation number: _____
Pick-up location: _____
Pick-up time: _____ Drop-off time: _____

Airline Information
Airline: _____
Phone number: _____
Airline frequent flier number: _____
Flight number: _____
Departure time: _____
Arrival time: _____

Connecting flight number: _____ Connecting flight city: _____
Connecting flight departure time: _____
Connecting arrival time: _____

Connecting flight number: _____ Connecting flight city: _____
Connecting flight departure time: _____
Connecting arrival time: _____

Hometown Ground Transportation from Airport
Service provider: _____
Phone number: _____
Reservation/confirmation number: _____
Pick-up time: _____ Drop-off time: _____

EXPENSE TRACKER WORKSHEET

Page #____ of ____

Expense Description	Date	Price	Payment Method* (circle one)	Receipt (circle one)	Expense Type** (circle one)
		$	$ CC TC	Yes / No	P B
		$	$ CC TC	Yes / No	P B
		$	$ CC TC	Yes / No	P B
		$	$ CC TC	Yes / No	P B
		$	$ CC TC	Yes / No	P B
		$	$ CC TC	Yes / No	P B
		$	$ CC TC	Yes / No	P B
		$	$ CC TC	Yes / No	P B
		$	$ CC TC	Yes / No	P B
		$	$ CC TC	Yes / No	P B
		$	$ CC TC	Yes / No	P B
		$	$ CC TC	Yes / No	P B
		$	$ CC TC	Yes / No	P B
	Total Expenses:	$			

*Note: Payment methods include: Cash ($), Credit Card (CC), or Traveler's Check (TC)

**Expense types include: Personal (P) or Business (B)

TRADE SHOW MEETING PLANNER

Date:

Time	Location (Booth or Meeting Room Number)	Company	Contact Person	Purpose of Meeting	Notes

FREQUENT TRAVELER PROGRAM WORKSHEET

Airline				
Program Name				
Account/Member Number				
Membership Status				
Phone Number				
Web Site Address				
Username and Password				

INDEX

A

Airlines
- clubs and lounges, 21, 23
- frequent flyer programs, 30–33
- servicing Orlando International (MCO), 3–6

Airport, Orlando International (MCO)
- airline clubs and lounges, 21, 23
- airlines servicing, 3–6
- curbside check-in, 15
- driving distances and directions to popular Orlando area destinations from, 99–101
- fast-food dining options, list of, 20–21
- ground transportation options, 25–28
- hotels located near the airport, 23–24
- map of, 17
- navigating your way through, 15–25
- rental cars, 27–28
- retail shops and services, 18–20
- security considerations and tips, 10–15
- shared-van, bus, car/limousine service, 25–26, 27
- shopping map, 22
- sit-down dining options and bars, 21
- store or service locations, list of, 18
- stuck at the airport?, 23–25
- taxi service, 26–27
- terminal layout and available services, 16–23

ticket counters (departures) and baggage claim (arrivals), 16–18
Alcoholics Anonymous, 246
Alternative accommodations for business travelers, 84–85
Amtrak service to and from Orlando, 28–29
Attending a business meeting or convention, 209–210. *See also* Orange County Convention Center (OCCC)
Audiovisual equipment rentals, photography, and production companies, 226–227

B

Balloon services, 227
Banking and financial services, 228–229
Boxes and shipping supplies, 229
Bus
　charter companies, 98, 229–230
　The Lynx, public bus transportation system throughout Orlando and surrounding areas, 30
　service to and from Orlando, 30
　shuttles, 98
Business services, 225–244
Business travel advice from top Orlando resort concierge, 75–78
Buying a new outfit fast or removing a stain, 271

C

Caterers, 230
Cell phone
　related problems, 274
　services and accessories, 230–232
Chauffeured limousines and town cars, 94–96
　companies servicing Orlando, 95–96
Chiropractors, 246
Computer rentals, repairs, sales, data recovery, and technical support, 232–233
Concierge
　advice, 75–78
　restaurant recommendations, 75, 104
　services, 86
Credit cards, 233–234

D

Day spas, 206–207, 253–255
Delays, dealing with travel and weather, 265–266
Dental emergencies, 272–273
Dentists, 246–247
Department stores, 247–248
Dinner shows, 112
Discount cards/multiday passes, 161–162, 163, 184–187
Doctors, 248
Driving around Orlando, 98–101
Dry cleaners, 248–249

E

Emergencies and travel-related problems, help for, 263–275
Entertainment in Orlando, 137–175
　Around the World at Epcot Segway Tour, 138–140
　Bob Carr Performing Arts Center, 140
　Boggy Creek Airboat and Wildlife Safari Rides, 141–142

Cirque de Soleil La Nouba, 142–143
Comedy Warehouse, 143–144
discount cards/multiday passes, 161–162, 163
Disney Fishing Excursions, 144
exclusive tours and activities for upscale business travelers, 162
golf courses, 166–169
helicopter tours, 144–145
Kennedy Space Center, 145–146
Orlando Hot Air Balloon Rides, 146–148
Orlando Museum of Art, 148
professional sporting events/venues, 163–165
Richard Petty Driving Experience, 149–150
Seaworld's Discovery Cove, 150–153
Skyventure Orlando Indoor Skydiving, 153–154
tickets to sold-out shows, concerts, sporting events, 165–166
Titanic: The Exhibition, 154–155
top 15 activities and attractions for business travelers, 138–163
Universal Orlando Theme Parks—Universal Studios, Islands of Adventure, and CityWalk, 155–161
Event listings, 138
Expense tracker worksheet, 282
Eye wear
replacing prescription, 272
stores and optometrists, 249–250

F

Faces Skin Care, 253–255
FedEx Kinko's locations, 234–235
Fitness centers and gyms, 250–251
Florida Mall, 170–171
Florists, 235–236
Foreign currency exchange services, 236
Frequent flyer/traveler programs, 30–33
Frequent traveler program worksheet, 284

G

Getting around town, 87–101
Getting to Orlando, 2
Golf courses, 166–169

H

Hair salons and barbers, 251
Hospitals and walk-in medical centers, 251–252
Hotels
business amenities checklist, 51
Celebration Hotel, 54–55
concierge services, 75–78, 86
Disney's Grand Floridian Resort and Spa, 55–57
Disney's Yacht and Beach Clubs, 57–58
Entrepreneur Magazine's Business Traveler Top 15 Business-Friendly Hotels in Orlando, 52–79
Gaylord Palms, 58–60
Ginn Reunion Resort, 60–62

Hard Rock Hotel at Universal Orlando (Loews), 62–63
help finding occupancy, 85
Hyatt Regency Grand Cypress Resort, 63–65
Hyatt Regency Orlando International Airport, 65–67
JW Marriot Orlando Grande Lakes, 67–68
list of major chains in Orlando area, 83–84
located near Orlando International Airport (MCO), 23–24
Peabody Hotel, 68–69
Portofino Bay Hotel at Universal Orlando (Loews), 70–71
Ritz Carlton Orlando Grande Lakes, 71
Rosen Plaza Hotel and Rosen Centre Hotel, 72–73
Rosen Shingle Creek, 73–74, 75–78
understanding the ratings, 53–54
Walt Disney World (WDW) resorts, summary of select, 79–82
Walt Disney World Swan and Dolphin, 74, 78–79
Hotels.com, 25, 85

I
I-Ride Trolley, the, 96–97
Internet access from anywhere, 52–53

J
Jet charters, 236–237
Jewelry stores, 252

L
Lake Buena Vista Factory Stores, 171
Laptop computer, lost, stolen or damaged, 270–271
Lawyers, 237
Locksmiths, 237
Lost items, 274–275
Lost or stolen credit card, driver's license, and/or passport, 269–270
Luggage
  and shoe repair services, 259
  lost, 266–269
  shopping for the perfect, 36–39
Lynx public bus system, 96

M
Mall at Millenia, 171–172
Maps
  Orange County Convention Center (OCCC) layout, 212
  Orange County Convention Center (OCCC) North/South Concourse, 216, 292
  Orange County Convention Center (OCCC), West Concourse, 217, 293
  Orlando area, 291
  Orlando International Airport (MCO), 17, 294
  Orlando International Airport (MCO) shopping map, 22
Media listings for Orlando, 173–175
Medical emergencies, 272–273
Meeting and banquet room rentals, 238

Messenger services, 238
Morse, Timothy Allen, 75–78

N

Nail salons, 255–256
Newspapers and regional magazines, 173–174

O

Office supply superstores, 239–240
Online travel services, 7–9
Orange County Convention Center (OCCC), 210–223
    dining options at and near, 215, 218
    directions to from downtown Orlando area, 213
    directions to from Orlando International Airport, 100, 213
    directions to from Walt Disney World Resort (Lake Buena Vista) area, 213
    exhibitor services, 221–223
    guest services, (407) 685-1202, 220
    layout, 212
    map of North/South Concourse, 216, 292
    map of West Concourse, 217, 293
    navigating around, 215
    parking, 214
    services and amenities, 218–220
    taxi service to and from, 214
    tips for attending a convention or trade show, 220–221
    trolley service to and from, 214–215

Orlando area map, 291
Orlando International Airport (MCO). *See* Airport, Orlando International (MCO)
Orlando Premium Outlets, 172

P

Packing for your business trip, 35–46
    before-leaving-home checklist, 46
    carry-on bag checklist, 44
    optional items, 45–46
    packing checklist, 41–44
    tips for business travelers, 39–40
    TSA restrictions, 39, 40, 45
    weather in Orlando, 40–41
Personal services, 245–261
Pharmacies, 256–258
Pointe Orlando, 172
Prescription refills, 272
Prime Outlets Orlando, 172–173
Public transportation, 96–98
The I-Ride Trolley, 96–97
The Lynx public bus system, 96
    Walt Disney World (WDW) transportation system, 97–98

R

Radio stations, 174–175
Rental cars, 27–28, 90–94
    companies servicing Orlando, 92–94, 258
Reservations, travel, 2–3
Restaurants
    Benihana, 114–115
    Brown Derby, 115–116
    Buca Di Beppo, 105–106
    Butcher Shop Steak House, 116

Cala Bella, 116–117
Capital Grille, 117–119
Del Frisco's Prime Steak and Lobster, 119–120
dinner shows, 112
Dux, 120–121
Emeril's Restaurant Orlando, 121–122
Entrepreneur Magazine Business Traveler Top 20 Fine-Dining, 113–134
ESPN Club, 106
Everglades Restaurant, 122–123
Forte Restaurant, 123–124
Grape Wine Bar, the, 107
Hard Rock Cafe, 106–107
Hooters, 107–108
Jack's Place, 124–126
Jimmy Buffet's Margaritaville, 108
LaCoquina's Chef Table, 126–127
Maggiano's Little Italy, 127–128
McCormick & Schmick's Seafood Restaurant, 128–129
Medieval Times Dinner and Tournament, 109
Melting Pot, the, 109
Morton's Steak House, 129–130
NASCAR Sports Grille, 109–110
NBA City, 110
Palm Restaurant, 130–131
Planet Hollywood, 110–111
Porterhouse Restaurant, 131–132
Portobello Yacht Club, 132
Rainforest Cafe, 111
Ran-Getsu of Tokyo, 132–133
Ruth's Cris Steak House, 133–134
theme and specialty, 105–113
tips for ordering fine wine with your meal, 134–136
Tommy Bahamas Tropical Cafe, 111–112
Tony and Tina's Wedding, 112
Wine Room, the, 112–113
Room service, ordering, 104–105

S

Secretarial and temporary employment services, 240
Security services, 241
Shipping and freight services, 240
Shopping opportunities for busy business travelers, 170–173
Souvenir shops, 173
Sporting events, professional, 163–165
Staffing services, 240

T

Tailors and clothing alterations, 259
Taxi service/rates, 26–27, 88–90
Television stations, 174
Theme parks, 155–161, 183–204
 phone numbers, 260
Tickets to sold-out shows, concerts, sporting events, 165–166
Tip calculation chart, 279
Tipping recommendations, 278

Trade show exhibit sales, installation, repair, and dismantling, 241
Trade show meeting planner, 283
Translation services, 242
Travel charts and worksheets, 277–284
Travel itinerary worksheet, 280–281
Travel itinerary, making last minute changes, 264–265
Travel notes, 34, 102, 176, 224, 262, 276
Traveler's checks, 242
Truck rentals, 230
Tuxedo rentals, 260–261

U

U.S. Post Office locations, 243–244
Universal Orlando Theme Parks
  directions from Orlando International Airport, 101
Universal Studios, Islands of Adventure, and CityWalk, 155–161
UPS shipping/store locations, 243

V

Visitors Bureau for Orlando/Orange County, 85, 138, 223

W

Walt Disney World (WDW) Resort
  budgeting your time when visiting the theme parks, 188–191
  day spas, 206–207
  dining information/reservations for over 100 restaurants (407) WDW-DINE, 104
  directions from Orlando International Airport, 100–101
  Disney Hollywood Studios, the, 198–201
  Disney Institute, 208
  Disney's Animal Kingdom, 201–204
  Disney's Boardwalk, 206
  Downtown Disney area and Pleasure Island, 170, 204–206
  Epcot, 195–198
  hosting private corporate events, 207–208
  Magic Kingdom, the, 191–195
  overview, 177–208
  perks for resort hotel guests, 79–82, 181–183
  summary of select resorts, 81–82
  theme parks, 183–204
  tickets/passes for theme parks, 184–187
  transportation/parking system, 97–98, 187–188
  understanding the guest information boards and Fastpass, 189–191
  web site and list of phone numbers for travel planning, www.disneyworld.com, 179–181
Weather in Orlando, 40–41
Welcome to Orlando, 1–34
Western Union electronic money-transfer services, 244

Wheelchair and scooter (ECV) rentals, 261
Where to dine in Orlando, 103–136. *See also* Restaurants
Where to stay while in Orlando, 47–86. *See also* Hotels
Wine, tips for ordering with your meal, 134–136

ORANGE COUNTY CONVENTION CENTER LAYOUT

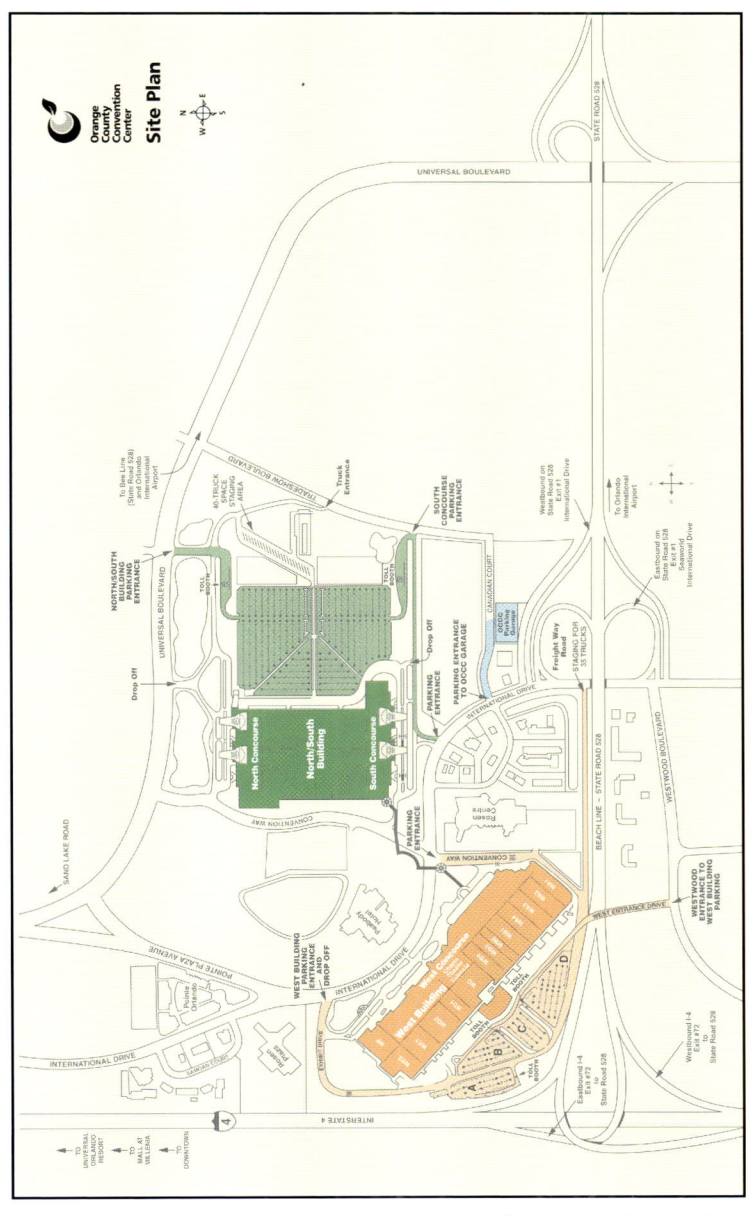

Map courtesy of Orange County Convention Center.

MAP OF ORLANDO AREA

Created by Daniel L. White.

MAP OF ORLANDO AREA

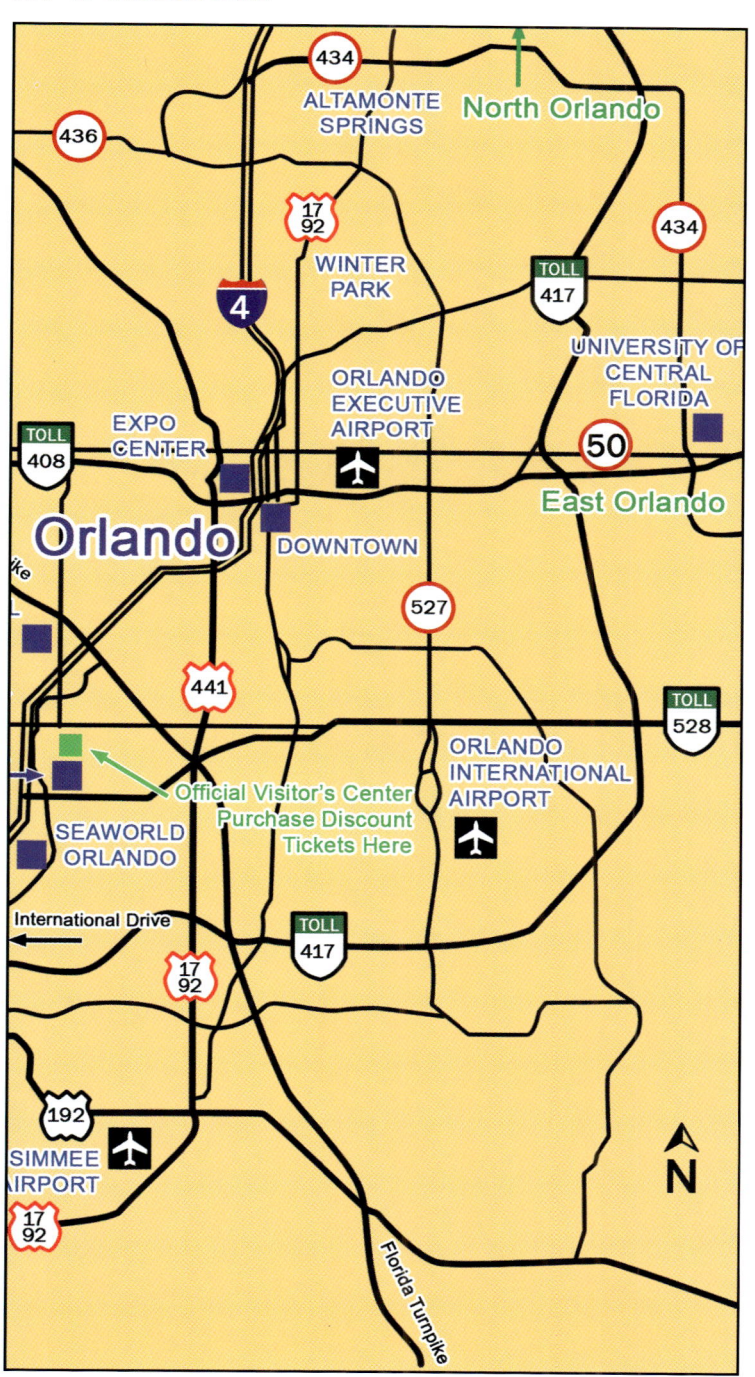

Created by Daniel L. White.

MAP OF ORLANDO INTERNATIONAL AIRPORT

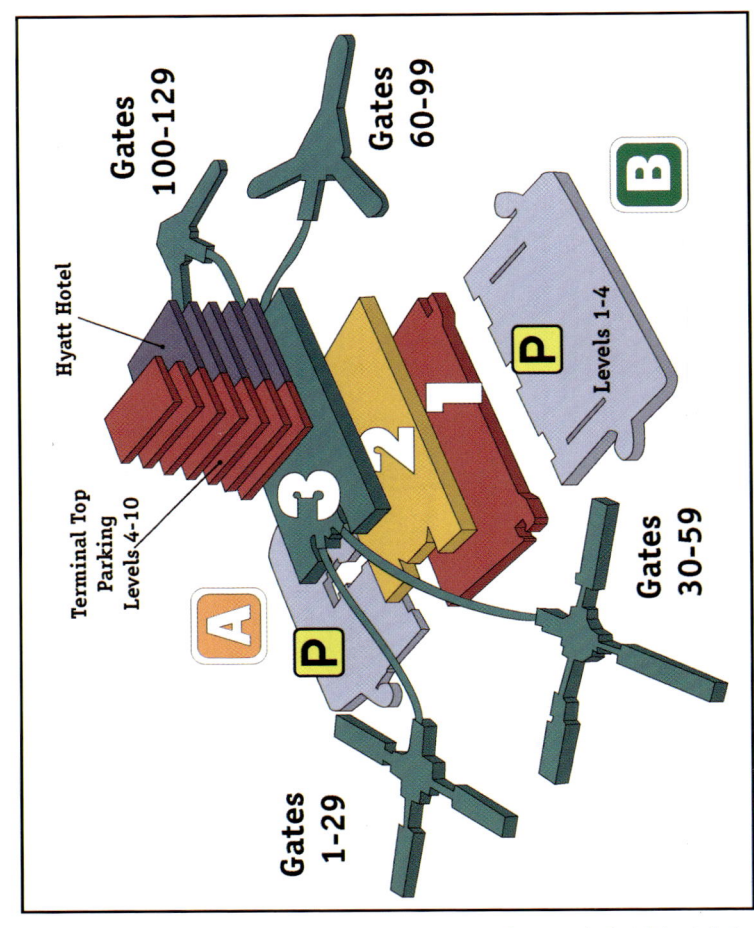

Map courtesy of Greater Orlando Aviation Authority.